Going by Contraries

Under the Sign of Nature

EXPLORATIONS IN ECOCRITICISM

Michael P. Branch
SueEllen Campbell
John Tallmadge
EDITORS

Robert Bernard Hass

Going by Contraries

ROBERT FROST'S
CONFLICT WITH
SCIENCE

UNIVERSITY PRESS OF VIRGINIA
CHARLOTTESVILLE AND LONDON

The University Press of Virginia
© 2002 by the Rector and Visitors of the University of Virginia
Printed in the United States of America on acid-free paper
First published 2002

9 8 7 6 5 4 3 2 1

Library of Congress Cataloging-in-Publication Data

Hass, Robert Bernard, 1962–
    Going by contraries : Robert Frost's conflict with science / Robert Bernard Hass.
        p. cm. — (Under the sign of nature)
    Includes bibliographical references and index.
        ISBN 0-8139-2111-2 (cloth : alk. paper) — ISBN 0-8139-2112-0 (pbk. : alk. paper)
    1. Frost, Robert, 1874–1963—Knowledge—Science. 2. Literature and science—United
States—History—20th century. 3. Darwin, Charles, 1809–1882—Influence. 4. Science in
literature. I. Title. II. Series.
    PS3511.R94 Z743 2002
    811'.52—dc21

                                                                        2001007450

For my parents

Contents

Acknowledgments

I would like to thank a number of people without whom this project would not have been possible. First, I would like to thank Christopher Clausen, my dissertation director, whose guidance, encouragement, critical acumen, and gentle wisdom helped make this project an enjoyable one from the beginning. I would also like to thank the other members of my doctoral committee at Penn State, who contributed their various talents in remarkable ways. Sanford Schwartz was particularly helpful in regard to Bergson and modern epistemology. Robin Schulze helped me ground my work more fully in the tradition of nineteenth-century nature writing and was especially helpful with the chapter on Darwin. Emily Grosholz made sure my math and physics were correct, while Jeffrey Walker helped me clarify my ideas and connect them to recent critical theory. William Pritchard, professor of English at Amherst College, graciously agreed to serve as an outside reader and offered me several valuable insights into Frost's life and work.

A number of other people were also instrumental in seeing this book through to publication. Michael Anesko read the entire revised manuscript and offered me several valuable criticisms, while Sean Grass tirelessly read through several drafts of my introduction and let me know when I finally got it right. I would also like to thank Don Sheehy, my first and best teacher of Frost's poetry, and Jack Peters, who encouraged me through every phase of the project. I would especially like to thank Bruce Weigl, my good friend and mentor, who not only read large portions of this manuscript but also guided me wisely through my years of graduate study and taught me what it means to be a writer. I am grateful to Boyd Zenner and Ellen Satrom, my editors at Virginia, and Joanne Allen, my copyeditor, whose sound advice and professionalism made the publication process a pleasurable experience; to Mimi Ross, of Henry Holt, and Peter Gilbert, executor of the Frost estate, for granting me permission to use Frost's texts without fee; to Phil Cronenwett, of Dartmouth College Library, and John Lancaster, of Amherst College Library, for allowing me to print archived material; and to my many fine colleagues and friends at Penn State who gave me advice and encouragement as I navigated my way through graduate school.

Finally, I would like to thank my family, particularly my father, Louis F. Hass, emeritus professor of biochemistry at Penn State, and my mother, Rosalyn G. Hass, a trained zoologist, for their encouragement and many pleasant discussions concerning my work. I reserve my deepest gratitude, however, for my wife, Suzi, and my son, Matthew, who continue to inspire me.

I am grateful to the following publishers and organizations for permission to reprint published material:

"Accidentally On Purpose," "All Revelation," "Any Size We Please," "At Woodward's Gardens," "The Bear," "Birches," "The Demiurge's Laugh," "Desert Places," "Design," "Directive," "The Egg And The Machine," "For Once, Then, Something," "Hyla Brook," "Kitty Hawk," "The Lesson For Today," "Mowing," "Neither Out Far, Nor In Deep," "New Hampshire," "The Onset," "Pan With Us," "The Pasture," "Pod of the Milkweed," "The Road Not Taken," "The Secret Sits," "The Self-Seeker," "The Silken Tent," "Skeptic," "Some Science Fiction," "Spring Pools," "There Are Roughly Zones," "To a Moth Seen In Winter," "West-Running Brook," "The White-Tailed Hornet," and "Why Wait For Science" from *The Poetry of Robert Frost*, edited by Edward Connery Lathem, © 1936, 1942, 1951, 1954, 1956, 1960, 1962 by Robert Frost, © 1964, 1970, 1975 by Leslie Frost Ballantine, © 1923, 1928, 1934, 1947, 1969 by Henry Holt and Company. Reprinted by permission of Henry Holt and Company.

From *Interviews with Robert Frost*, edited by Edward Connery Lathem, © 1966. Reprinted by permission of Henry Holt & Co., LLC.

From letters 42, 53, 64, 70, 73, 170, 255, 356, and 453 from *Selected Letters of Robert Frost*, edited by Lawrance Thompson, © 1964 by Lawrance Thompson and Henry Holt and Co. Reprinted by permission of Henry Holt & Co., LLC.

From *The Letters of Robert Frost to Louis Untermeyer*, edited by Louis Untermeyer, © 1963 by Louis Untermeyer, © 1991 by Laurence S. Untermeyer. Reprinted by permission of Henry Holt & Co., LLC.

From "Education by Poetry," "The Constant Symbol," and "The Figure a Poem Makes," from *Selected Prose of Robert Frost,* edited by Hyde Cox and Edward Connery Lathem, © 1956 by The Estate of Robert Frost, © 1946, 1959 by Robert Frost, © 1949, 1954, 1966 by Henry Holt and Co. Reprinted by permission of Henry Holt & Co., LLC.

"The Future of Man" was originally presented at "The Future of Man": A Symposium Sponsored by Joseph E. Seagram & Sons, Inc. on the Dedication of its Headquarters Building in New York at 375 Park Avenue, September 29, 1959. Reprinted by permission of the Estate of Robert Frost and Joseph E. Seagram & Sons, Inc. Unpublished version reprinted by permission of the Estate of Robert Frost and Dartmouth College Library.

Selections from Robert Frost's unpublished notebooks are reprinted by permission of the Estate of Robert Frost and Dartmouth College Library.

"Interview with Jonas Salk" originally appeared as a 1956 radio broadcast conducted by WQED, Pittsburgh. Reprinted by permission of WQED and the Robert Frost Collection, Amherst College Archives and Special Collections.

Going by Contraries

Introduction

If the time should ever come when what is now called science, thus familiarized to men, shall be ready to put on, as it were, a form of flesh and blood, the poet will lend his divine spirit to aid the transfiguration, and will welcome the being thus produced, as a dear and genuine inmate of the household of man.

William Wordsworth, preface to *Lyrical Ballads*

TO BEGIN A BOOK ON ROBERT FROST AND SCIENCE WITH A QUOTATION from Wordsworth may seem odd. Separated by an ocean and nearly a century of unprecedented cultural change, the two poets should have had incompatible artistic temperaments. Yet Frost shared several affinities with the romantic poet whom he early acknowledged as one of his favorites. One can only imagine a conversation the two might have had. Frost might have remarked how he, like Wordsworth, viewed nature and rural life as material resources for instruction; how he took pride in expressing his insights in a poetic vernacular that aspired to the rhythms of common speech; or how each of them might best cultivate the attention of a large and adoring public. Perhaps the most important question the young Frost might have asked, however, would have concerned the problem of science and what he should do about it. Occupying a historical position in the twentieth century similar to Wordsworth's in the nineteenth, Frost understood that as the soot from coal-fired factories descended upon the pastures north of Boston, and as newly forged railways linked New York City to Walden Pond and beyond, America was being defined increasingly by science and technology, which he perceived as threats to both religious consolation and the cultural prestige of poetry itself. If poets at the beginning of the nineteenth century really were the "unacknowledged legislators of the world," as Shelley claimed, then by the end of the century it was clear to Frost that scientists had replaced them as the arbiters of truth. Although Wordsworth early in his career welcomed scientists into "the household of man," it is not difficult to imagine that while conversing with Frost he might have faltered at the younger poet's difficult question and, avoiding an answer, diverted the conversation toward a discussion of his Lake District childhood.

Such a response would have been unacceptable to the maturing Frost. As the mantle of poetry, science, and industry fell upon Americans, Frost struggled to find an acceptable place for his poetry in a modern world that had all but discarded the poet as a relic from an unenlightened past. And, unfortunately, the romantic response to science—the intuitive worship of a transcendent being behind nature—no longer seemed an adequate answer to scientists' charges of poetry's antirationalism. Having read Darwin long before he ever read Plato,[1] Frost recognized that the several idealisms of Wordsworth, Shelley, and Emerson were at best spurious claims made on behalf of metaphysical and religious certainty. Although Frost admired each of these poets and wanted to believe in the spiritual consolations they could offer, Darwin had taught Frost that the poet could no longer believe in Plato's realm of fixed, ideal forms, as Shelley had done, or in the idea that nature had been purposefully designed for human contemplation, as Emerson had proclaimed nearly sixty years earlier.[2] By the time Frost came of age and began to write serious poetry, the Emersonian concept of nature as an analogue for a kind and benevolent deity had been replaced among the scientifically educated by the view that nature's mechanisms were based solely upon accident, competition, and survival. With both designer and telos absent from the post-Darwinian world, species suddenly became expendable, and the fate of humankind no longer mattered to an indifferent universe.

For many American poets writing at the turn of the century this view of nature translated into spiritual crisis. As the lessons from evolutionary biology and geology facilitated a new and widespread religious skepticism, American writers were left groping for spiritual certainties. The longstanding Protestant notion that it was courageous to accept spiritual knowledge based on faith alone came increasingly under attack as fossil remains disproved the Bible's claims about the age of the earth and Darwinian theory facilitated a popular, mistaken belief that humans had evolved from apes. As Roy Harvey Pearce accurately described the situation, the American poet "was in the position of the first Adam, cast out of his new world. But he had no Raphael to give him a vision of the ultimate rightness of his fall from a natural state."[3] Humans had been driven from their rightful position at the center of the natural order, and in the view of many serious American writers at the turn of the century it was scientists who waved the flaming swords.

Frost fully understood the consequences of a world dominated by science and chronicled his age's accompanying spiritual anxieties in one of his earliest poems, "The Demiurge's Laugh" (1913). Stating in his introductory gloss to *A Boy's Will* that "The Demiurge's Laugh" was "about science," Frost took his title from Plato's creative deity, who constructs the material universe according to immutable physical laws. Comparing the Demiurge to a "Demon," Frost's speaker recounts in a compelling narrative how his early belief in science as a guide to a better life has led to despair and a profound inability to find evidence of a divine spirit. Framing the narrative between the opening line, "It was far into the sameness of the wood," a line that recalls Dante's confusion in *The Inferno*, and "Thereafter I sat me against a tree," Emerson's symbol for organic unity and benevolence in nature, Frost subverts much of the Western literary tradition, rejecting all hope of either a forgiving Christian God or a benevolent romantic spirit. As the speaker ignorantly and blissfully follows the progressive and enthusiastic ideals of science (the Demiurge), the light of knowledge begins to fail, as it did not for Dante, and the situation reverses, so that the speaker, instead of pursuing the Demiurge, now finds himself pursued:

> The sound was behind me instead of before,
> A sleepy sound, but mocking half,
> As of one who utterly couldn't care.
> The Demon arose from his wallow to laugh,
> Brushing the dirt from his eye as he went;
> And well I knew what the Demon meant.[4]

Although the speaker never reveals what he "well knew," the parable's lessons are clear: science can never lead to utopia nor satisfy humans' spiritual needs. The material world that science explores is not just indifferent to the human condition in a post-Darwinian universe; in Frost's early poetic imagination it is a malevolent force that mocks and abandons human beings in their most dire circumstances. No Virgil or Beatrice appears to guide the poet through spiritual crisis; no glimpse of divine spirit shimmers in the leaves. Science has stunned humans into recognition that they are alone in a world of matter that offers neither purpose nor redemption. And as the poem implies, they can do nothing but attach themselves, as the speaker does, to a nostalgic symbol (Emerson's tree or the biblical tree of knowledge) and cling to it in the hope that somehow it can shelter them from the "demon" of uncontrollable scientific knowledge.

Clearly, the portrait of science that Frost painted as a young man is both terrifying and condemning. But if Frost believed early in his life that science was his great nemesis, confrontation was necessary only because he had not yet begun to question the philosophical assumptions underlying scientific materialism. From the time Bacon, Locke, and Newton ushered in the glories of the Enlightenment, British and American intellectuals had by and large viewed science as a rational discipline whose inquiry was detached from the subjectivity and imagination of the observer. Devoid of human emotion and armed with a powerful method, science, unlike art or religion, could be certain of its claims because its discoveries satisfied the experimental criteria and rigorous scrutiny of its practitioners. Objectivity, inductive observation, and strict adherence to the scientific method eventually proved their reliability by giving rise to myriad technological inventions that transformed an agrarian society into an industrial one within a few generations. The great technological success in harnessing power and controlling nature, in turn, tended to confirm the prevailing view that science was the best hope for alleviating social ills and for finding a clear window to truth.[5] With scientific materialism dominating British and American culture by the end of the nineteenth century, it is no wonder that Frost was nagged for much of his life by the haunting suspicion that a modern, practical society would always choose the scientist over the poet as a guide to a better life. To the young Frost, it seemed as if Thomas Love Peacock's remarkable prophecy in *The Four Ages of Poetry* (1820) was coming true. In a modern society, the "ornamental" was quickly being subordinated to the "useful," which continued to "draw attention from the frivolous and unconducive."[6]

However bleak the prospects for poetry may have looked to a young man who more than anything wanted to become an important poet, Frost had one advantage over Wordsworth that allowed him to find an acceptable resolution to the problem of science. Despite coming of age during the height of materialism and positivism, Frost lived and wrote long into a century that began to challenge the very epistemological foundations upon which these schools of inquiry rested.[7] In the period before Frost began to write his first poems for the Lawrence High School *Bulletin,* small pockets of scientists and philosophers were already beginning to doubt mid-nineteenth-century claims that science would one day exhaustively describe the mysteries and mechanisms of nature. Although natural philosophers (the term *scientist* was coined by William Whewell in 1840) as early as Newton had thought that they would one day discover the grand design of the universe, and thus the grand designer, new developments in mathematics, geology, and physics cast doubt upon the very principles that had given rise to belief in the so-called clockwork universe. Increasingly, physical reality failed to fit so easily into the immutable models the Enlightenment had constructed; and as scientists kept adding to their already long list of achievements, their very successes began to undermine the mechanistic certainties their predecessors had erected.[8]

In particular, the development of the first non-Euclidean geometry by Nikolai Lobachevski and Janos Bolyai in the 1830s commenced a debate on the way scientists and philosophers would eventually come to perceive science and nature.[9] As Lobachevski and Bolyai found a plausible alternative to Euclid's fifth postulate, they simultaneously demonstrated that absolute knowledge based upon a priori assumptions was fallacious. The truths of Euclidean geometry were only as good as the axioms upon which they were based, and as new models of geometry began to spread throughout scientific communities, several philosophers began to suspect that human efforts to explain nature were merely projections of mind that shed little light upon the ontological structures of the physical universe.[10] The correspondence between Euclidean geometry and the world of physical space proved to be severely limited (as Einstein would later demonstrate), and as new concepts in science and mathematics offered plausible alternative explanations of the universe, a new epistemological dilemma profoundly affected the way scientists and philosophers would debate the breadth, function, acquisition, and integrity of knowledge.

Instead of claiming, as Kant had, that man's organizational faculties of mind corresponded to the ideal forms of Euclidean space and time, a small group of philosophers and scientists claimed that humans' conceptual systems were limited, subjective constructs of mind that helped them negotiate a reality they could never know with rational certainty. Departing from French positivism, then the dominant intellectual tendency, leading thinkers like William James, Henri Poincaré, and Ernst Mach asserted that man could never escape his subjectivity as he acquired knowledge. Perhaps the clearest articulation of this new epistemology emanated from James,

Frost's first intellectual mentor, who claimed that scientific truths were not definitive accounts of nature but useful, limited guides through an experiential flux:

> Up to about 1850 almost everyone believed that science expressed truths that were exact copies of a definite code of non-human realities. But the enormously rapid multiplication of theories in these later days has well-nigh upset the notion of any one of them being a more literally objective kind of thing than another. There are so many geometries, so many logics, so many physical and chemical hypotheses, so many classifications, each one of them good for so much and yet not good for everything, that the notion that even the truest formula may be a human device and not a literal transcript has dawned upon us.[11]

According to James, minds and objects were implicated with each other, and because of this interdependency, science could only offer useful approximations that satisfied practical human needs. For James, people were still largely ignorant about the true nature of physical reality and their relationship to it; science, like poetry and myth, offered numerous varieties of interpretation, each beneficial as long as it provided useful and practical models to live by.

In addition to those who challenged Enlightenment assumptions by suggesting that scientific conventions served to organize rather than describe physical space, another school of philosophy challenged Enlightenment epistemology on different grounds, arguing that scientific concepts actually *denied* people access to reality. This movement, alternately called "spiritualism" or "voluntarism," emerged in France during the third quarter of the nineteenth century and sought to rescue "spiritual" reality from the scientific humanism of August Comte, whose positivist views of matter and nature were then dominating Continental philosophy. Ultimately seeking to restore the vitality of the Catholic church in France, this group of thinkers, spearheaded by Maine de Biran, Felix Ravaisson, Jules Lachelier, and Emile Boutroux, modified Cartesian dualism, extending even further the traditional split between spirit and matter. Suggesting that science excludes certain realities that do not conform to deterministic or mathematical quantities, the voluntarists emphasized that certain mental and physical processes could operate independently of rigid scientific laws.[12]

Such explanations of nature and consciousness, although initially not well received, eventually found popular expression in the work of Henri Bergson, another of Frost's most important intellectual mentors. In his first book, *Time and Free Will* (1889), Bergson argued that matter, language, quantity, and concept were inadequate representations of a "true" reality because they fixed in static form natural processes that were continually in flux. In later books, such as *Creative Evolution* (1911) and *Introduction to Metaphysics* (1913), Bergson defined "true reality" as a process of continual becoming in which each moment of creation was permeated by all other moments. Like James's "stream of consciousness," Bergson's creative reality, the *élan vital*, was an immanent force that operated beneath the surface of intellectual conventions. According to Bergson, because reality is fundamentally mobile rather than static, what the intellect creates by means of concepts is simply the appearance of the way the world actually exists. Thus, scientific knowledge is not an accurate representation of immutable physical law but rather a set of imposed constructs that quantify, categorize, and reduce matter to discrete units and deterministic progressions.

Although Bergson accepted the idea that the human intellect cannot avoid quantifying matter in the acquisition of knowledge, he intimated that it was possible to recover the *élan vital* through aesthetic rather than scientific processes. Whereas James suggested that the artist abstracts from the stream of consciousness the aesthetic forms that provide guides through experiential chaos, Bergson maintained that art gives us a truer account of reality because it frees consciousness from its tendencies to quantify material processes. Instead of representing a fixed, stable reality, art reveals the flux of all experience:

> [W]e shall perceive that the object of art is to put to sleep the active
> or rather resistant powers of our personality, and thus to bring us into
> a state of perfect responsiveness, in which we realize the idea that is
> suggested to us and sympathize with the feeling that is expressed. In the
> processes of art we shall find, in a weakened form, a refined and in
> some measure spiritualized version of the processes commonly used to
> induce the state of hypnosis. Thus, in music, the rhythm and measure
> suspend the normal flow of our sensations and ideas by causing our
> attention to swing to and fro between fixed points, and they take hold
> of us with such force that even the faintest imitation of a groan will
> suffice to fill us with the utmost sadness.[13]

Although no definitive evidence exists that Frost ever read *Time and Free Will*, it is reasonable to speculate that he learned about Bergson's theories of art from T. E. Hulme, who translated Bergson's *Introduction to Metaphysics* in 1912.[14] We do know that Frost read extensively in *Creative Evolu-*

tion, particularly those passages that explain how an intuitive consciousness can direct the ego toward the creative life force.[15] According to the Bergson of *Creative Evolution,* the intuitive vision, although constantly engaged in the present moment, has the capacity to recall the past. Acting in accordance with its own needs, our intuitive "sympathy" seeks to escape from convention, immerse itself in the creative flux, comprehend the world as continually "being made" (rather than having "been made"), and liberate human action from deterministic physical laws:

> Our own consciousness is the consciousness of a certain living being, placed in a certain point in space; and though it does indeed move in the same direction as its principle, it is continually drawn the opposite way, obliged, though it goes forward, to look behind. This retrospective vision is . . . the natural function of the intellect and consequently of distinct consciousness. In order that our consciousness shall coincide with something of its principle, it must detach itself from the already-made and attach itself to the being-made. It needs that, turning back on itself and twisting on itself, the faculty of seeing should be made to be one with the act of willing.[16]

As is evident from these two passages, Bergson countered the legacy of positivism, as did the romantics, by privileging intuition over reason, impression over concept, and art over science. Bergson differed from many of the romantics, however, in his insistence upon an immanent and dynamic rather than static and transcendent supernaturalism. The modern artist, like the romantic, provided the medium through which one gained knowledge of the world beyond matter. For Bergson, however, that knowledge could never rest in a static ideal or be expressed in conceptual terms. Rhythm, music, and metaphor thus became for Bergson the most important means of recovering the *élan vital,* as these processes provided the intellect with the tools for a more comprehensive account of reality.

That Bergson often practiced what he preached is especially evident in the graceful prose of his texts. Although denounced by Bertrand Russell, who called the French thinker "common," Bergson continued to write philosophy with a poetic grace and flair that eventually led to a tremendous vogue among both the French and the American intelligentsia. Having earned the nickname "the liberator," Bergson cultivated a reputation in America as one of the few intellectuals who could respond rationally to the deterministic philosophy of Herbert Spencer. Urging his followers to "take life by storm," Bergson facilitated, in the decade prior to World War I, a surprising optimism that became the hallmark of an entire generation of American writers, including such important figures as Willa Cather and Thornton Wilder.[17] William James also applauded Bergson, suggesting that "new horizons loom on every page you read." His graceful prose was "like the breath of the morning and the song of birds."[18] What impressed James most about Bergson was his attempt to "spiritualize" Darwin and "naturalize" Christianity without subscribing to the dogmatic claims of either system.[19] Bergson occupied a middle ground between idealism and materialism, the dominant philosophical traditions of the nineteenth century. He posited an invigorating view of the universe that saw endless possibilities for renewal and discovery, and his legacy inspired a growing wave of industrialists, who saw his philosophy as a symbol of progressivism and an emerging American capitalist ethos.

Frost himself was not immune to such sweeping intellectual influences, and as much of his mature verse indicates, James's and Bergson's conceptions of science would hybridize as he developed his ideas about poetry. Had Frost arrived on the poetry scene only thirty years earlier, he might have answered charges of poetry's antirationalism by agreeing with his aesthete forerunners, Poe and Wilde, that poetry was nothing but ornament, whose value lay primarily in the creation of aesthetic satisfaction and pleasure. Although Frost's earliest ruminations on poetry did concern aesthetics, primarily the justification for his verse forms, he ultimately quarreled with Poe's ideas that poetry had "no concern whatever either with duty or truth" and that its chief attribute was the "rhythmical creation of beauty."[20] Such an aesthetic removed poets from their central position as interpreters of culture and assigned them instead to the unflattering, subordinate role of popular entertainer.[21]

Frost, however, following the example of Sidney, demanded more than entertainment from poetry and urged poets to cultivate greater intellectual rigor. In his most important defenses of modern poetry, "Education by Poetry" (1930), "The Figure a Poem Makes" (1939), and "The Constant Symbol" (1946), Frost argued that poetry should be more than mere ornament or beauty; it should also engender "delight" and "wisdom" or, if unable to deliver on that scale, represent a "clarification" of life.[22] Like his younger contemporaries Eliot and Pound, Frost recognized that most late-nineteenth-century poetry had deteriorated into either effete mannerism or escapist verse that bore little relevance to the problems associated with modern life. To them, the fantastical realms of "The Raven" seemed trite and childish when compared with the discoveries of the electron and the X ray, and as popular poetry deteriorated more and more into the trivial or sentimental, they felt obligated to restore greater rationality to poetry if for no other reason than to establish a moral foundation from which they could begin to challenge science. Or as Frost suggested in "On Extravagance: A Talk" (1962), poets had to wrestle with what he called the "poetry nuisance" and explain to a scientific and technologically driven culture why poetry still mattered.[23]

But Frost, in his own efforts to subvert Poe's art-for-art's-sake aesthetic, refused to subscribe to the revolutionary, experimental poetics of his American modernist contemporaries Ezra Pound, T. S. Eliot, William Carlos Williams, and Marianne Moore. In their concerted efforts to make poetry "new," as Pound had exhorted his peers to do at the beginning of the century, each at various times adopted the language and methods of science in an attempt to make poetry more authoritative. Excessive emphasis upon the image, objectivity, and impersonality tended to reduce poetry's epistemological capabilities by restricting it to a nonargumentative presentation of "data." These practices in turn gave rise to the New Criticism, whose proponents scrutinized the inseparable structure and content of a poem while divorcing it from social, political, or philosophical content. In fact, a brief glance at early modernist defenses of poetry reveals a critical language steeped in scientific metaphor. Pound claimed that poems were the "mathematical equations for the human emotions." Eliot asserted that the poem was not an "expression of emotion, but an escape from emotion" and that the chief goal of the poet was to find the "objective correlative," an architectural structure that might be isomorphous with the poet's interior psychological mood. Marianne Moore, one of the most deeply religious of the modernists, seemed torn between her loyalties to the aesthetics of T. S. Eliot and those of Wallace Stevens and offered the rather confusing statement that poets were "literalists of / the imagination" who searched for "imaginary gardens with real toads in them."[24] William Carlos Williams, the most scientifically trained poet of his generation, often concentrated his poetic gaze upon mundane sensory data and made famous the phrase, "no ideas but in things."[25]

With so much emphasis placed upon objectivity and experimentation, poetic texts, so the thinking went, were artifacts or "works" that reflected the complexities of a modern psyche that had been irrevocably severed from the perceived glories of the remote past. Modernist poems were not so much imaginative constructs as they were reports of empirical observation. The major difference between science and the "science" of poetry, however, was

that the poet examined not the nature of the physical world, as did the physicist, but rather the countless mutations of the human psyche, which, when
objectified, could reveal the mind's adaptations to the immense complexities of modern life. Although Frost may have tacitly admired Pound's and
Eliot's marriage of content and form as well as their emotional restraint,
their attempts to objectify the inner world by reducing it to the material of
the outer world meant that instead of restoring poetry's epistemological
capabilities, Pound and Eliot actually conceded the cultural authority of
science. They saw endless experimentation with form and persona as the
poetic counterpart to new and improved scientific experimentation and
carried out these practices with the idea that greater difficulty in technique
might yield truths that could then compete with or complement those of
science. So disturbed was Frost by the modernist revolution that in 1916 he
denounced it as an overreaction to sentimentality: "[T]here is a crowd of
'emotionalists' who throw all to the winds except emotion," he noted. "I
think they're perhaps worse than the 'intellectualists,' who are the other
extreme. But a happy mixture, that's it."[26]

Of course, the kind of emotional and intellectual balance that Frost
eagerly sought in twentieth-century poetry was exactly the balance that
every major English poet up to Keats had taken for granted. But how was
Frost to restore a convincing rational authority to a cultural medium whose
authority had been usurped by a scientific world-view?

To answer this challenge, Frost had to depart radically from his poetic
contemporaries and develop a theory of verse that challenged the authority of conceptual knowledge itself. Instead of advocating an aesthetic that
conformed to the "truth" standards of science, Frost, following James and
Bergson, attempted to minimize the truths of science so that they would be
more compatible with the humble claims he made for poetry.[27] Although
Frost always maintained a respect for scientific discoveries that could be
empirically verified, he remained skeptical about discoveries that worked
only under a contrived set of conditions or those, such as the theory of evolution, whose certainties he thought acquired their prestige largely because
of their accompanying theoretical conjecture. (Watson and Crick did not
formulate the molecular structure of DNA until 1953.) Unlike the early
Eliot and Pound, Frost observed that many "scientific truths" often resided
in the realm of contingent knowledge and therefore could be criticized
along the same lines as poetry and rhetoric.

As Frost immersed himself more and more deeply in the scientific
polemics of his day, particularly those in physics and astronomy, he came

to realize, along with James and Bergson, that scientists and poets alike were limited by the very nature of their inquiry and depended upon metaphorical expression to reveal the full implications of the truths they sought to convey. Both sets of practitioners used language or equations to bridge the gap between the known and the unknown: the scientist designed experiments to test an imagined model of physical nature, and the poet manipulated language to explore an imagined phenomenon of human experience. As always for Frost, the danger arose when the poet or scientist allowed conceptual or theoretical models to ossify into claims of immutable truth. Frost's engagement with science in the 1920s and '30s had taught him that conceptual models of the physical universe could be just as mutable as models for human behavior, especially when scientists attempted to explore matters of spirit and value. As Bergson had suggested, science could never adequately quantify human nature, and any attempt by scientists to do so was a breach of the legitimate boundaries of their discipline. Frost publicly advanced this belief in "Education by Poetry" (1930), suggesting that the roots of a scientific "hubris" extended far beyond the nineteenth century, all the way back to ancient Greece: "Once on a time all the Greeks were busy telling each other what the All was. But best and most fruitful was Pythagoras' comparison of the universe with number, Number of what? Number of feet, pounds, and seconds was the answer, and we had science and all that has followed in science. The metaphor has held and held, breaking down only when it came to the spiritual and psychological or out of the way places of the physical."[28]

The longstanding conflicts between matters of fact and matters of spirit, between the concept of the poem as willed form (the classical idea of maker) and the concept of the poem as bestowed revelation (the romantic idea of *vates*), shaped Frost's developing aesthetic, which synthesized James and Bergson. Frost learned from the "radical empiricist" James that it was possible to achieve a degree of truth in poetry, the "momentary stay against confusion" that could blaze new trails through a chaotic and sometimes threatening flux of experience.[29] He learned from Bergson, however, that if one were to participate in a vital creative spirit, one would have to probe beneath the surface of intellectual conventions to recover the creative forces that impell nature forward in a process of continual becoming. Indeed, many of Frost's best-known poems offer not only a "clarification" that helps shape the poet's environment but many clarifications, often contradictory, that sustain their claims within the dynamic field of the poem itself. As Richard Poirier has suggested, Frost, "while creating poetic structures we can believe in," simultaneously and beneficially exploited "the deconstructive tendencies of his own structures."[30] Indeed, any careful reading of Frost's poems in the mature work from *North of Boston* on reveals that he composed poems such as "Mending Wall," "The Road Not Taken," "Design," and "The Onset" with an eye toward double entendre, in which thesis and antithesis contradict and merge with each other within the dramatic field of the poem.

In Frost's hands, ostensibly simple phrases such as "good fences make good neighbors" mean both one thing and its opposite. Not only do fences protect and isolate the self from others but fences also necessitate a saving communion and shared purpose among the very people the enclosures are supposed to keep out. Such vague diction in Frost is not just a clever manipulation of linguistic possibilities but also the very heart of a metaphysics that limits the power of rationality and concept. For Frost, the cognitive process that erects such antithetical structures cannot logically resolve them. To reconcile thesis and antithesis, to find a unity in multiplicity, one must employ a different cognitive process based upon intuition. Frost's pairing of opposites, many of which end in an irresolvable aporia, thus becomes a poetic demonstration of how conceptual thinking falsifies a continuous reality by improperly dividing it.

Perhaps the most poignant demonstration of Frost's reluctance to make sweeping claims in his poetry can be found in "The Road Not Taken," one of Frost's most popular poems and one so widely misunderstood that its title has permeated popular culture in the form of a cliché. Although the poem is well known, I quote it in its entirety as a point of departure:

> Two roads diverged in a yellow wood,
> And sorry I could not travel both
> And be one traveler, long I stood
> And looked down one as far as I could
> To where it bent in the undergrowth;
>
> Then took the other, as just as fair,
> And having perhaps the better claim,
> Because it was grassy and wanted wear;
> Though as for that the passing there
> Had worn them really about the same,
>
> And both that morning equally lay
> In leaves no step had trodden black.
> Oh, I kept the first for another day!

> Yet knowing how way leads on to way,
> I doubted if I should ever come back.
>
> I shall be telling this with a sigh
> Somewhere ages and ages hence:
> Two roads diverged in a wood, and I—
> I took the one less traveled by,
> And that has made all the difference.
>
> (*CPP&P* 103)

As many critics have noted, Frost's subject descends from Emerson's "Self-Reliance" and its idea that "whoso would be a man, must be a non-conformist." Forced to confront a choice between two available options in life, the speaker claims he has chosen the alternative that others have refused. He elects to take the "one less traveled by" and acknowledges that such a decision will have large consequences: he regrets that he will never again return to the moment of decision that might have influenced the course of his life. One way of reading "The Road Not Taken," then, is to see it as Frost's poetic declaration of independence from a society that values utility more than it does aesthetics. By becoming a poet, by defying the status quo, and by being "misunderstood," Frost answered Emerson's exhortation to discover life on one's own terms.

While this altogether common reading seems plausible, the text complicates such an easy reading as it deconstructs itself and subverts any attempt at mastery. The second stanza, for example, insists that the two roads the speaker encounters have been worn equally. Although the speaker presumes to choose between the two paths, his observation that "the passing there / Had worn them really about the same" suggests that real choice may be nothing but an illusion. Natural or social forces, by which "way leads on to way," may have chosen for him. Perceived in this manner, the poem thus becomes a dramatic stage upon which the age-old debate over free will and determinism plays itself out, with the poet never coming to a definitive conclusion about either position. Clearly, the empirical evidence is sufficient to validate either view, yet Frost's speaker, who is sorry he cannot "travel both / And be one traveler," regrets that he cannot resolve his intellectual dilemma. In the last stanza, as the perceiving "I" makes the choice, Frost divides the speaker's yearning ego into two distinct parts. The "I" at the end of the line and the "I" at the beginning of the next line represent the two conceptual options that the poet longs to unify. And the "difference" that Frost speaks of is not just the Emersonian notion that one should distinguish oneself from others but also a mathematical quantity that has divided reality into two extremes that are mutually exclusive. A consistent world-view, it appears, cannot be based upon definitive truths but merely upon a collection of individual choices.

"Life," wrote Frost, "sways perilously at the confluence of opposing forces. Poetry in general plays perilously in the same wild place. In particular it plays perilously between truth and make-believe."[31] A justification of Frost's familiar method of sustaining opposites, this statement bears a striking resemblance to passages in Bergson's *Introduction to Metaphysics,* in which the French philosopher, following Hegel, posits that knowledge is a dialectic of irreconcilable contraries that can be perceived only by intuition:

> Concepts . . . generally go together in couples and represent two contraries. There is hardly any concrete reality that cannot be observed from two opposing standpoints, which cannot consequently be subsumed under two antagonistic concepts. Hence a thesis and an antithesis which we endeavor in vain to reconcile logically, for the very simple reason that it is impossible, with concepts and observations taken from outside points of view, to make a thing. But from the object, seized by intuition, we pass easily in many cases to the two contrary concepts; and as in that way thesis and antithesis can be seen to spring from reality, we grasp at the same time how it is that the two are opposed and how they are reconciled.[32]

In what is perhaps his most deeply Bergsonian poem, "West-Running Brook," Frost asks us not only to "go by contraries" but also to abort the impulse toward easy generalizations that obscure a creative life force. In asking us to adopt the philosophical manner of the two participants in "West-Running Brook," Frost seeks to preserve the tough-minded realism of James and the more tender-minded idealism of Bergson. The very act of the creative consciousness presupposes that the mind can, and should, shape meaningful forms out of the objects in nature. Yet the creative consciousness should also intuitively direct itself toward an unknown source from which those objects and forms in nature emerge. By recognizing how the mind can continually exhaust itself in the formation of antithetical concepts, we can begin to understand how the *élan vital* continually exhausts itself through matter. "It is this backward motion toward the source, against the stream, that we most see ourselves in" (*CPP&P,* 238). For Frost, the poetic imagination mirrors the *élan vital* and so reveals to us alternative realities that lie beyond concept and matter.

Frost's lifelong technique of metaphorical construction and deconstruction, his refusal to perpetuate didactic certainties, and his willingness to suspend contradictions all emanate from his strong desire to attack the kind of conceptual knowledge that was then being advocated by scientific materialists. As Frost continued to immerse himself in the intellectual and scientific debates of his day, the ideas he culled from Bergson and James eventually coalesced into a poetic vision that made it possible for him to reinterpret the two major problems that nineteenth-century science had forced him to confront. The Jamesian pragmatist in Frost allowed him to propose valuable though limited truths that could help restore poetry's cultural value, while the Bergsonian vitalist in him allowed him to forge a clear distinction between physics and metaphysics, thus preserving the spiritual reality he yearned for. This aesthetic positioning between instrumentalism and vitalism, at once the source of both his dualism and his spiritual drifting, remained with Frost for the rest of his life and helped him to negotiate a tentative truce with science.

That Frost did eventually reinterpret his quarrel with science is evident in one of his last and most important essays, "The Future of Man," in which he suggests that science is more like poetry and religion than might otherwise have been thought. Although Frost modified the original version of his essay and did not actually deliver the following lines (to a symposium sponsored by Joseph P. Seagram in 1959), the prose nevertheless illustrates Frost's change of heart toward the end of his life. As one might expect, the Bergsonian notion of the *élan vital* is central to Frost's argument. "I am in danger of making all this sound as if science were all," wrote Frost. "It is not all. But it is much. It comes into our lives as domestic science for our hold on the planet, into our deaths with its deadly weapons, bombs and airplanes, for war, and into our souls as pure science for nothing but glory; in which last respect it may be likened unto pure poetry and mysticism. It is man's greatest enterprise. It is the charge of the ethereal into the material. It is our substantiation of our meaning. It can't go too far or deep for me."[33]

This view of science is obviously quite different from the view espoused in "The Demiurge's Laugh" and reflects both the maturation of Frost's thought and the changes in science that allowed such a reconciliation to occur. Although Frost's progress toward this rapprochement was by no means continuous, it is possible to see that as a materialist version of science began to break down under the weight of new scientific discovery, he recognized the limitations of science and ultimately viewed it as a system of historically embedded metaphorical paradigms that were epistemologically suspect and therefore susceptible to revision. Regarding science in this manner, Frost reasoned that the real creative force behind science was the same as the creative force behind poetry: our unique capacity to project an imaginative spirit into and beyond the coherent, fragile, perceptible forms that we have constructed.

As Frost grew more and more confident that nineteenth-century claims made on behalf of science and certainty were excessive, he felt better able to dismiss disagreeable scientific conclusions not only because he was afraid that they might eventually eradicate religious faith but also because they were epistemologically equivalent to those of poetry. Science, like poetry, depended upon well-crafted metaphors that could never fully approach, explore, or explain the full complexity of nature or the human spirit. Having demonstrated (to his mind) that the truths of poetry could be just as valuable as those of science, Frost could then confidently resurrect some of the arguments behind Sidney's defense of poetry. For Sidney, the purposes of poetry were to "delight and to instruct";[34] for Frost, the poem began in "delight" and ended in "wisdom." For both Frost and Sidney, poetry served as a midwife between philosophy and entertainment and was important because it contained insight into human nature in forms that made the reader's discovery of that knowledge pleasurable. "Science," wrote Frost, "can't describe us. . . . The wonderful description of us is in the humanities, the book of the worthies and unworthies through the ages, and anything you talk about in the future must be a projection from that."[35]

Whether one can accept Frost's argument is another story. Although poetry lately seems to be recovering some of the audience it lost in the early part of the century, and although recent philosophers of science such as Hans-Georg Gadamer and Thomas Kuhn would probably have been receptive to many of Frost's ideas,[36] people today rarely turn to poets for the kind of knowledge they need to negotiate life's difficulties. Part of the reason for this reluctance is that science, despite the postmodern effort to portray it simply as another version of socially constructed discourse, has proven remarkably effective at conveying reality accurately. Although contemporary theorists have been right to point out that science has often discarded its false starts and mistaken concepts, the idea that the discipline can only offer useful approximations of reality disregards the power of the scientific method to correct experimental error. Postmodern historians have been quick to point out that one-time credible concepts such as the geocentric universe, phlogiston, and the luminiferous ether proved false and unduly influential, but they have also tended to be very selective in their evidence, often ignoring more rigid fundamentals such as the laws of thermodynamics and gravitation, which have proven remarkably stable and immune to scientific revision. Frost himself often harbored fears that science was indeed "right," that its mechanistic certainties might eventually prove the nonexistence of a higher being, and that its technological advances might one day destroy not only traditional Judeo-Christian values but civilization itself. He also understood that scientific truths did not collapse easily and did so only when succeeding laws represented an improved interpretation of reality. It is therefore not uncommon to find throughout his work strong contradictions, recantations of previous statements, or poems side by side that alternately praise the scientific spirit and condemn it as a "complacent ministry of fear."[37]

Despite such contradictions, however, I believe that it is possible to demonstrate that Frost's thinking about science generally evolved over the course of his career in the following manner: First, because Frost had a healthy respect for empirical evidence, and because American culture valued science over other forms of knowing, Frost continued to immerse himself in the biological and astronomical arguments of the day so that science's "truthful" knowledge might confirm for him the existence of "divine design." Second, the concepts Frost learned from his early scientific inquiries disappointed his need for cosmic purpose, as most nineteenth-century scientific conclusions proved that natural phenomena operated without divine intervention, and this disappointment manifested itself in his poetry of existential despair and loneliness. Third, following James and Bergson, Frost reinterpreted his conflict between science and religion and decided that science, like poetry, was a limited mode of metaphorical or instrumental perception that helped us shape reality. Fourth, as new developments in science overturned a belief in mechanistic determinism, Frost learned that the materialists' claims to certainty were excessive, and he subsequently developed a hermeneutics of natural science, portraying it as a historically embedded and linguistically mediated activity. Fifth, toward the end of his career, Frost equated science with poetry, ultimately applauding the Promethean spirit of science in his last important poem, "Kitty Hawk."

Reducing a complex poet's career to a set of simple steps is a dangerous proposition, especially when the poet is one who warned readers all of his life against the kind of stultifying reductions for which literary critics are notorious. Nevertheless, this study explores the peaks and troughs of Frost's career as it developed against the backdrop of twentieth-century science.

By examining in a chronological manner the historical, scientific, and biographical circumstances that led to the writing of many of Frost's most important poems, I aim to show how Frost's art developed in response to the problems science posed for him. Most critics have either failed to consider Frost's poems about science or subordinated them to other themes, such as Frost's treatment of pastoral, his defense of formal prosody, or his attacks on socialism. What I intend to show is that many of these themes are largely indebted to the larger scientific and intellectual ferment out of which they emerged. No poet, for example, could have written "Design" had not the material and scientific circumstances of his or her era paved the way for such a poem.

The few critics who have noticed Frost's important ties to science have tended to distort the poet's views in favor of either a sentimental theosophy or an austere naturalism. Lawrance Thompson, for example, claims that Frost saw science as the "enemy of religion" and therefore "dismissed" it, particularly its "evolutionary concepts."[38] John Hiers extends Thompson's distortion, suggesting that Frost, "as the artist in search of form, viewed science and technology as the eroding agents of traditional systems of ethical values which provide meaningful form amidst the chaotic flux of relativism."[39] While Frost was certainly concerned with rescuing religious belief from science, he was neither as orthodox in his religious practice nor as fanatically opposed to science as Thompson and Hiers imply. Instead, Frost preferred a Jamesian approach to religious experience, one in which an individualized religious eclecticism might supplant the timeworn dogmas of organized religion. Like James, Frost thought it possible to distinguish between religion and ecclesiastical institutions, and he therefore developed an idiosyncratic faith that culled its consolations from a variety of sources— from Emerson, from Swedenborg, and from diverse writers of the Old Testament. Thus, science was not the enemy; indeed, Frost admired the discipline's great achievements. Science became a problem only when it degenerated into a rigid system of polemical orthodoxies that threatened the individual's power to interpret reality or the existence of God on his or her own terms.

In contrast, Robert Faggen's groundbreaking *Robert Frost and the Challenge of Darwin* views Frost from the opposite perspective. Seeing Lucretius and Darwin as the guiding forces behind Frost's material awareness and eco-precociousness, Faggen argues that Frost's engagement with these figures grounded him more fully in a scientific and empirical tradition, ultimately leading to a repudiation of his religious belief. For Faggen, Frost's religious gestures, in the aftermath of his engagement with Darwin, evolved into the hollow "forms of religious expression." He concludes his book by suggesting that Frost became "more skeptical of religious experience, caught between viewing God as either nonexistent or powerless before cruel sublunary powers."[40]

In my reading of Frost's career, I see the opposite development as being more plausible. Although Frost certainly became more and more skeptical about the veracity of both religious and scientific orthodoxies, it was, paradoxically, his growing skepticism that helped him overcome materialism and restore his religious faith. Because science, in Frost's maturing view, could no longer prove nor disprove the existence of God, he, like James, saw religious faith as a rational and psychologically beneficial response to life's problems. As James made clear in *The Will to Believe,* when no clear method exists to settle the question of religious belief, individuals must ultimately decide for themselves, and they must often base those decisions upon intuition and emotion rather than upon factual evidence. Despite moments of perception, Faggen misinterprets the larger development of Frost's career, which was not the long and difficult waning of belief, as Faggen would have it, but rather an arduous struggle to move through materialism and toward a more confident faith, what Frost would call later in his career "a wisdom beyond wisdom."[41] In the final analysis, Faggen thus tends to treat Frost as a philosophical monist while ignoring the poet's deepening mysticism and his rejection of those who imposed monistic systems upon reality. Although Faggen's emphasis on the "empirical" Frost aptly corrects the sentimental views of Frost's early apologists, such a synchronic account of Frost's life and work overlooks the poet's reinterpretation of science, his positive use of scientific discoveries in his poetry and prose, his belief that the creative spirit of science was natural to human existence, and perhaps most important, his own denial of extreme views. "People misunderstand me sometimes," wrote Frost, "they think I'm antiscientist."[42]

I propose to offer a more balanced account of Frost's relationship with science and reveal how a self-conscious dialectic between matter and spirit undergirded Frost's career. In reading Frost as a philosophical dualist, I extend the work of Guy Rotella, Darrel Abel, and Ronald Martin, all of whom argue convincingly that modern science, rather than leading Frost toward a positivist epistemology, reinforced his growing skepticism by showing him how "the primacy of experience" affects our interpretation of reality and reveals "the indeterminacy of any ultimate structure beneath it."[43]

In demonstrating how and why Frost overcame his fear of materialism,

I adopt the method he would have preferred and travel by contraries back to his most important sources in Bergson, James, Darwin, Eddington, Einstein, and Bohr. Where historical and textual evidence is unavailable, I employ N. Katherine Hayles's field model of cultural history and demonstrate how one's intellectual cultural matrix—what Hayles terms a "climate of opinion"—can stimulate parallel developments in philosophy, literature, and science.[44] Such a method not only illustrates how various disciplines can cross-fertilize one another but also dispels the notion that cultural change occurs only as a consequence of one-way causal influences. Finally, because Frost was largely self-educated, some of the evidence for his knowledge of scientific concepts must come from the poems themselves. Chapter 1 explores the scientific and intellectual context that Frost inherited as he began to think about poetry and explains the reasons behind his refusal to sanction either naturalism or romanticism, a feature of his work that prompted Yvor Winters to label Frost a "spiritual drifter." Chapter 2 focuses primarily on Frost's response to Darwinian evolution and how he enlisted the thought of William James and Henri Bergson to find a viable intellectual response to natural selection. Chapter 3 examines Frost's lifelong love of astronomy and shows how new developments in physics overturned materialism and restored his belief in divine purpose and design. Chapter 4 repudiates the longstanding idea that Frost wrote about the same themes for the duration of his career and argues that Frost's aesthetic evolved through three distinct phases—vitalist, metaphorical, and organicist—which correspond to his shifting attitudes toward materialism. The final chapter explores Frost's maturing response to technology and discusses how its Promethean spirit assured Frost that humans do not live in a world of dead matter but in a world where imagination penetrates the spiritual foundations of reality.

Perhaps the best illustration of how an intellectual matrix helps stimulate parallel developments in divergent disciplines can be found by comparing the writings of Jacob Bronowski, a mid-century physicist, with those of Frost. Although the two never met, it seems obvious that a new "climate of opinion" led them to similar conclusions about the nature of scientific inquiry. "The discoveries of science, the works of art," wrote Bronowski, "are explorations—more, are explosions, of a hidden likeness. The discoverer or the artist presents in them two aspects of nature and fuses them into one. This is the act of creation, in which an original thought is born, and it is the same act in original science and original art."[45] This convergence should strike readers with a sense of wonder: How was it possible for two individuals from such different disciplines and backgrounds to concur on the nature of creativity? Such obvious similarities suggest that Frost and Bronowski were the products of a shift in perception, one that not only began to question the intellectual foundations of nineteenth-century science but also recognized that science can be understood only in relation to the linguistic and practical context in which it functions. Indeed, as new developments in physics and mathematics undermined the doctrines of materialism and positivism, both Frost and Bronowski recognized that the perceived hostility between science and art was tenuous and that a rapprochement between the two disciplines was once again possible.[46] This book is the story of those changes in perception and how Frost's recognition of them allowed him to reinvest nature with spirit and find an acceptable place for his art.

1. A Narrow Choice the Age Insisted On

I'm what is called a sensibilitist,
Or otherwise an environmentalist.
I refuse to adapt myself a mite
To any change from hot to cold, from wet
To dry, from poor to rich, or back again.

It seems a narrow choice the age insists on.

"New Hampshire" (1923)

ONE OF THE MOST IMPORTANT DRIVING FORCES BEHIND ALL OF FROST'S poetry was his strong desire to preserve a teleology that could justify human hopes and achievements so they might not be buried, as Bertrand Russell once claimed, "beneath the debris of a universe in ruins."[1] One need only experience the loneliness and despair in poems such as "Desert Places," "Once by the Pacific," or "The Most of It" to know that Frost was, despite his frequent bravado and claims to the contrary, profoundly afraid of the "empty spaces between stars," of the possibility that no rational force existed to direct the universe and its myriad inhabitants. Frost's acute fear of a universe that had been stripped by Darwin of its teleological and progressive features often was a source of debilitating disillusionment. Unlike writers who rejoiced in the freedom that a godless universe afforded, Frost tended to agree with William James that a purely material universe devoid of divine spirit and purpose would inevitably undergo a "final wreck and tragedy."[2] Indeed, some of Frost's greatest fears may have been exacerbated by his reading of James's *Pragmatism* (1907), specifically James's inclusion of Lord Balfour's jeremiad against a dominating materialist world-view:

The energies of our system will decay, the glory of the sun will be
dimmed, and the earth, tideless and inert, will no longer tolerate
the race which has for a moment disturbed its solitude. Man will go
down into the pit, and all his thoughts will perish. The uneasy consciousness which in this obscure corner has for a brief space broken
the contented silence of the universe, will be at rest. Matter will know
itself no longer. "Imperishable monuments" and "immortal deeds,"
death itself, and love stronger than death, will be as if they had not been.[3]

For Frost, who was perhaps more tender-minded than most in his generation, such brutal conclusions were to be resisted with the utmost energy.
As Norman Holland suggests in his incisive psychoanalytic study, *The
Brain of Robert Frost,* one of the principal inspirations for Frost's poetry
was his debilitating fear of "abandonment," which he alleviated, as Holland
suggests, first by conjuring up the "image of the world threateningly focused on himself" and then by "using words to control and manage and
finally to end that frightening prospect."[4] While contemporary readers may
be rightly skeptical of those who reduce a complex poet's psyche to a few
Freudian motifs, Holland nevertheless extracted an important theme in
Frost's life that can be extended, without extrapolation, to a fear of what I
would like to call "cosmic abandonment."[5]

What Frost desired most from the cosmos was not his "own love back in
copy speech," as he wrote in "The Most of It," but the meaningful and consoling "counter love, original response" (*CPP&P,* 307), which eluded his
most heartfelt entreaties. In Frost's imagination, the universe never responded in typical Emersonian or Wordsworthian fashion; when it did
respond, it did so with a perceived malevolence that often shook the poet
to the core. An excerpt from one of Frost's unpublished notebooks confirms
this notion. Written around 1927, the passage reveals Frost's tendencies
toward paranoia and projection, two qualities that would eventually find
their most poignant expression in "Once by the Pacific": "I seek others—
they never seek me. And most of those I seek turn their backs and flee from
me. All but the waves. I don't go to the waves. I can stand on the beach and
the waves come to me. They never turn their backs on me and run away.
They come and come as if they wanted me."[6]

Fear such as this was for Frost an altogether too frequent malady. As Holland and others have noted, his penchant for such overwhelming fears was
not so much a daily state of mind as it was a condition induced by personal
tragedies. His severe and recurrent losses, usually carefully buried behind a

carefully cultivated public persona, often induced long periods of spiritual crisis. The early death of a stern and demanding father; the loss of his beloved mother to cancer; the death of his infant son Elliott; the institutionalization of his sister, Jeanie, and his daughter Irma; the fatal postpartum infection of Marjorie, his favorite daughter; the death by suicide of his son Carol; and his complicated relationship with his wife, Elinor—these calamities accumulated over time, intensifying the abstract injustice of the universe and plunging him into long bouts of spiritual despair. Unfortunately, most of Frost's biographers have failed to notice the sheer courage with which he confronted the frequent assaults on his mental stability and attempted to right himself. Frost understood that to maintain his delicate psychic balance, to justify his own existence, he first had to alleviate his fear of divine abandonment, of a world without purpose, and he did this by continually searching—in poetry, in history, in philosophy, and especially in science—for any kind of evidence that might satisfy his religious appetites without also denying his rational sense. Like a good Puritan, Frost wanted to find in the natural world and its accompanying signs evidence for the existence of a caring God. Like a good scientist, however, he doubted religious dogma and struggled to base his belief in God upon the principles of reason rather than upon the fallacies of faith.

A rational quest for God was a difficult endeavor for Frost because advances in nineteenth-century science had spoiled traditional approaches to religion. As physicists, biologists, and geologists began to disprove many of the premises upon which orthodox religious systems rested, scientists and other "enlightened" members of society began to disclaim not only the truths of biblical events but the whole concept of spiritual reality itself. In the nineteenth century, reason and faith diverged for the first time in modern history, and the ensuing split compelled many thinking persons at the turn of the century to choose one over the other as the proper guide to life. As Frost suggests in "New Hampshire" (1923), the age demanded a narrow choice between the naturalistic despair of the scientific rationalists and the transcendent ecstasies of the romantic pulpit, a choice between being a "puke" and being a "prude," as Frost so memorably phrased the dilemma in "New Hampshire" (CPP&P, 160).

Many of Frost's contemporaries did make a choice, but as T. S. Eliot resurrected the old assurances of the Anglican Church in Four Quartets, and as Wallace Stevens celebrated a vision of life that descended "downward into darkness, on extended wings,"[7] Frost wavered between these two approaches to life and simply refused to align himself wholeheartedly with either one. Although Frost might have preferred the religious consolations of *Four Quartets,* the great problem for him, as it was for any poet who had been deeply immersed in the legacy of American romanticism, was that his pursuit of a meaningful religious experience was ultimately censored by a scientifically informed imagination that could not accept the validity of the religious consolations he had stumbled upon. All of the scientific evidence he absorbed tended to support conclusions that either confounded his spiritual longings or ran counter to the popular theological consolations he had heard about as a boy. As Thompson asserts, Frost "wanted to be pluralistic in the sense that he could combine naturalism and mysticism, physics and metaphysics, skepticism and mysticism." Thompson also argues that Frost's "fluctuations between these extremes produced some inconsistencies which puzzled him almost as much as they puzzled the intimate members of his family and, eventually, some of his readers."[8] Given the times, however, such confusion in Frost is understandable. As Frost well knew, the intellectual climate was not receptive to such an outdated approach to either science or God, and by the turn of the century it seemed to him that scientists and sociologists had deemed science and religion such irreconcilable adversaries that anyone who attempted to force a reconciliation between the two was to be dismissed as either naive, anti-intellectual, or quixotic.

Frost's reluctance to accept the narrow choices that the age insisted on, however, was neither an eccentric idiosyncrasy nor a deliberate posture but rather a well-informed, consistent, and calculated response to a dominating scientific ethos that had arisen during the third quarter of the nineteenth century. In particular, three distinct nineteenth-century discoveries, about all of which Frost had an adequate layman's knowledge, combined to provide the scientific basis for the "irreconcilable" split between scientific and religious explanations of nature. These discoveries—Dalton's atomic theory, the law of the conservation of energy, and the theory of evolution—informed and at length supported a pervasive cosmology that interpreted all natural and social phenomena in terms of matter, motion, and force.[9]

Reviving the atomism of Epicurus, Democritus, and Lucretius, Dalton demonstrated mathematically that all things in nature were made of small, indestructible particles that oscillated in perpetual motion, attracting and combining with one another to form the various molecules that composed the physical world.[10] While atomic theory was not really new or, in itself, exceptionally interesting, it did acquire greater significance when viewed in association with the newly established law of the conservation of energy.

Derived on the Continent independently by Hermann von Helmholtz and Rudolf Clausius about 1850, this mathematical principle showed how quantities of energy within a closed mechanical system remained constant despite the manifold changes in physical reality.[11] Refined by engineers who desired to increase the mechanical efficiency of practical machines, force (or energy, as Lord Kelvin later termed it) was thought to be an animating, unrestricted quality that could never be created or destroyed since it directed physical processes in a continual and uniform distribution and redistribution of atoms and energy. John Tyndall, then the leading physicist at the Royal Institution, described the law in *Fragments of Science* (1861): "The Proteus changes, but he is ever the same; and his changes in nature, supposing no miracle to supervene, are the expression, not of spontaneity, but of physical necessity. A perpetual motion, then, is deemed impossible, because it demands the creation of energy, whereas the principle of Conservation is no creation but infinite conversion."[12]

Although atomic theory and the law of the conservation of energy provided a convincing explanation for inorganic change, organic matter posed an altogether different problem. If energy conservation bound matter to universal physical laws, then what additional principle might account for the differences between living and nonliving things? Up until the 1850s, American and European romantics, especially Emerson and Swedenborg, had rationalized this problem by insisting that organic beings were not simply complex combinations of material units but living "vessels" filled with a mysterious, transcendent, and life-giving force. According to Emerson, the material world served as a symbol for a divine, unifying spirit that was ultimately indivisible by scientific explanation. I "nod" to the "fields and woods," wrote Emerson in *Nature,* "and they nod to me."[13] The proof, of course, depended upon a "proper" interpretation of nature. As long as one could resist the urge to "murder to dissect"[14] and channel perception toward the sacred, one might agree with Swedenborg that "astonishing things . . . correspond so entirely to supreme and spiritual things, that one would swear the physical world was purely symbolical of the spiritual world."[15]

The appearance in 1859 of Darwin's *On the Origin of Species* suddenly contested the romantic idea of a transcendent reality, as it provided scientists with a hypothesis that could reconcile organic and inorganic processes. Although evolution and selective breeding had been discussed before Darwin and Wallace, what was different in their work was the theory of natural selection, which claimed that the organic function of living beings could be explained as a response to changing environmental conditions.[16] According to Darwin, some groups of individuals were better suited than others to survive disruptive environmental changes. By fortuitous variation, species survived, thrived, reproduced, and evolved at apparently random and unequal rates in response to ever-changing environments with limited food sources. Considered in association with Laplace's nebular hypothesis (which in its simplest form explained the evolution of the universe as a contracting and cooling cloud of incandescent gas), the principle of natural selection linked in a vast cause-and-effect determinism all organic and physical processes. Even the human mind, at one time thought to be the special product and proof of divine love, was now nothing but a highly developed by-product of matter and energy, a complex system of atoms and molecules with a peculiar chemical capacity to contemplate itself. Herbert Spencer, the chief proponent of the new "synthetic philosophy" in England, summarized naturalism in several popular science books that sold more than 370,000 copies in America between 1862 and 1903.[17] Perhaps more optimistic in his assessments of progressive change than either Darwin or Huxley, Spencer modified the theory of natural selection, arguing that all beings moved from lower to higher states of evolutionary development. In *First Principles* he defined the new scientific world-view in a manner similar to Tyndall. The law of evolution, he wrote, was "an integration of matter and concomitant dissipation of motion; during which the matter passes from an indefinite, incoherent homogeneity to a definite, coherent heterogeneity; and during which the retained motion undergoes a parallel transformation."[18]

Although few people found Spencer's definition helpful, by 1865 the laws of evolutionary mechanics had become virtually universally accepted. The reasons for this sudden prestige are not altogether clear, but several changes in the nineteenth century seem to have contributed enormously to materialism's growing vogue. First, the ever-increasing professionalization of science allowed well-trained men to disseminate and test ideas against growing international standards. Chaucer's medieval portrayal of scientists as eccentric alchemists bent upon turning lead into gold had long been overturned by the astounding achievements of Galileo, Newton, and Descartes, whose international reputations helped to establish science as an esteemed vocation. In addition to the continually growing number of scientists around the world, the expanding production of machines, a phenomenon which ushered in the Industrial Revolution and helped to create the almost unspeakable horrors of British and American industrial labor, provided concrete evidence that the law of the conservation of energy (later called the first law of thermodynamics) was indeed true. For the first time in history, matter and energy could be described and calculated in terms of mechanical work and efficiency. While an intelligent scientist could still remain skeptical about some of the unknown forces controlling the machine-like regularity of the world, only a fool could dismiss the validating evidence provided by the steam engine or the loom. With more and more well-trained minds available to solve the problems of work and energy, society could rest assured knowing that the future lay in good, practical hands—or so it seemed.

Finally, no one, not even those scientists inclined toward religious belief, had ever found any convincing evidence to suggest that physical processes could be attributed to miracles, spirits, ghosts, God, or any other supernatural beings. The available evidence supported a view that saw the universe as a system of perpetual, progressive change that worked independently of supernatural intervention. Natural phenomena could be attributed to universal forces, or "laws," that operated upon matter in a vast chain of cause-and-effect determinism. Nineteenth-century science made possible, for the first time in nearly two thousand years, a wholly secular explanation of the cosmos. Huxley, who was perhaps the most vocal supporter of the new cosmology, was so enthusiastic about recent scientific developments that he predicted, albeit prematurely, that a scientific ethos would ultimately extend its benefits to all disciplines if only a rational society would exhibit a mature willingness to accept scientists as the bearers of truth. Speaking in 1866 to an audience of laborers, Huxley suggested:

> If these ideas [recent scientific discoveries] be destined, as I believe they are, to be more and more firmly established as the world grows older: if that spirit be fated, as I believe it is, to extend itself into all departments of human thought, and to become co-extensive with the range of knowledge; if, as our race approaches its maturity, it discovers, as I believe it will, that there is but one kind of knowledge and but one method of acquiring it; then we who are still children, may justly feel it our highest duty to recognize the advisableness of improving natural knowledge, and so to aid ourselves and our successors in our course toward the noble goal which lies before mankind.[19]

In the emerging age of science and sociology, theologians, poets, and humanists were burdens to an enlightened society and were to be replaced in the Academy, as Plato had once suggested, by those who honestly and without fear sought to unveil the truth. To Huxley, conventional Christianity was equivalent to the primitive and, as such, had only limited value in a practical, mature, and civilized modern society.

That Frost tried stubbornly to reconcile science and religion throughout his career not only is a testament to his strong independence of mind but also helps explain the persistent metaphysical drifting that Yvor Winters found so disturbing about his poetry.[20] In many respects, Frost's confusing theodicy is a consequence of his unique moment in American history. A society in transition toward the secular made it nearly impossible for him to reconcile the two competing versions of the world that had dominated his youth: one ruled by the benevolent God of Emerson and Swedenborg, whose ideas he inherited from his pious mother; the other, the mechanistic universe of Darwin, whose ideas he inherited from his agnostic father and the popularizers of nineteenth-century materialism. What was a sensitive young man with a penchant for phobias, depression, and rage to believe?

If Frost's struggle over the existence of God sounds vaguely reminiscent of Tennyson and typically like a nineteenth- rather than a twentieth-century problem, it is necessary to remember that Frost *was* a product of the nineteenth century. Because Frost seems so much a part of the twentieth century, it is sometimes hard for casual readers to remember that when he was born, in 1874, San Francisco was still largely a frontier gambling town that would not hear about the defeat of Custer by Sitting Bull and Crazy Horse until two years later. It is perhaps even harder to believe, primarily because he got such a late start on his literary career, that by the turn of the century Frost was already twenty-six years old, a father of two, a cultivator of "fancy white wyandotts" on his Derry, New Hampshire, farm, and as yet unacquainted with his nearest important literary contemporaries, Willa Cather and Wallace Stevens. Curiously, each of these writers would certainly have been old enough to have heard not only about the deaths of the popular Emerson and Whittier but also about the closing of the American frontier and the final displacement of the American Indian onto the reservation. Perhaps more important, each would also have been old enough to have heard about the discovery of the X ray, radioactivity, and the electron and to marvel at the unimaginable successes of the light bulb, powered flight, and the automobile. By contrast, most of the writers whom we usually associate with "high" modernism were still children. At the turn of the century, Ezra Pound and T. S. Eliot were only fifteen and twelve years old, respectively, while F. Scott Fitzgerald, William Faulkner, and Ernest Hemingway were all infants under the age of four and by age twenty-six would have considered electric lighting, automobile transportation, and powered flight normal rather than exceptional.

What I mean to suggest by this brief chronological comparison is that cultural change and conflict occurred so rapidly between the time of Frost's birth and the start of World War I that it is possible to distinguish profound differences in modernist writers separated by only one decade. While one could easily set up several particular categories of difference, such as the older generation's ambivalence toward myth, Freud, expatriation, and symbolist "collage" techniques, the single most important general difference is that the older generation, which grew up with deeply religious parents or grandparents, was affected primarily by the jarring shift from a predominantly religious culture to a scientific culture, whereas the younger generation, which grew up with parents whose confidence in God had largely waned, was affected more by the ensuing moral bankruptcy of Western civilization and by the devastating consequences and horrors of World War I. The available historical memories of the older modernists were quite different from those of the younger modernists; consequently, their intellectual and literary concerns were qualitatively different.

The case becomes much clearer when we compare the literary subjects of Frost, Cather, and Stevens (and to some extent Marianne Moore) with the most prevalent literary concerns of the younger modernists. Instead of joining Pound, Eliot, and Hemingway in their condemnation of a decaying civilization—the "old bitch, gone in the teeth," as Pound phrased it[21]—first-generation modernists such as Cather, Stevens, and Frost concentrated less upon the actual tragedies of war than they did upon the nineteenth-century epistemological dilemmas that in part conceived of war as a tragic though inevitable outcome of radically new ways of perceiving the world. Although each of the older modernists detested war, and some, including Frost, lost close friends in the trenches of France, war and its destruction seldom permeate their work as dominating subjects. Although the earlier group certainly felt guilty for writing beautiful poetry while the towns and cathedrals of Europe burned, they nevertheless refused to satirize early-twentieth-century culture and overtly rejected the impulse to erect political utopias; rather the task at hand was "what to make of a diminished thing," as Frost put it (*CPP&P*, 116), or, as Stevens put it, how to engage the "poem of the mind in the act of finding what will suffice."[22] If American romanticism sought to find in the phenomenal world an irradiant spiritual energy that could lead a writer or reader to a transcendent state of being, then the task for the early modernists, the first children of Darwin and materialism, was to figure out what to do once the correspondence between nature and spirit had been severed.

In response to this problem, Frost and Cather gravitated toward the ideas of optimists such as James and Bergson, leading thinkers who resisted the basic tenets of materialism, reconfirmed the imagination's pivotal role in the shaping of reality, restored belief in some kind of divine, directing power, and validated a spiritual life as an acceptable variety of experience. A heightened response to any ideas that could restore spirituality, defeat nihilism, and recover what had been lost was especially characteristic of Frost, who incorporated many of their new ideas into his poetry. In contrast, though one could certainly make an exception for the Marianne Moore of "The Pangolin" and the Eliot of *Four Quartets*, later modernists such as Pound and Williams consciously rejected most philosophical ideas that displayed any affinity with the recent religious or romantic past. As their poems veered more and more away from a mystical tradition, becoming more and more experimental and more overtly political, it became clear to them, especially Pound, that their attempts to make their poetry more scientific neither alleviated the problem of poetry's cultural displacement nor solved the nightmare of spiritual poverty. Indeed, the seeds of many modernist literary failures—Williams's *Kora in Hell*, H.D.'s *Hermetic Definition*, and a significant portion of Pound's *Cantos*—were sown in the late-nineteenth-century debates over what kind of knowledge was most appropriate in the formation of truth: should one adhere primarily to Emersonian "reason" or Lockean "understanding," intuitive judgment or rational sense, imagination or science?

Clearly, there was a divergence of opinion between the two generations. While Pound and Williams promoted "imagism," Frost and Stevens continued to write in the lyric tradition of their immediate predecessors. While Frost immersed himself in T. E. Hulme's metaphysical theories, many of which Hulme derived from Bergson, the young Pound attached himself to Hulme's poetic theories, most of which, in direct conflict with Bergson, predicted a period of "dry, hard, classical verse" whose aim was "accurate, precise, and definite description."[23] The most startling divergence, however, lay in the methods by which each generation responded to literary tradition. While the older generation seemed content to operate in the dialectical tension between dissent and respect for romantic writers such as Wordsworth and Emerson, the younger modernists sought to overthrow any ideas that smacked of sentimental religion. Overt poetic revolution was especially characteristic of Pound, who once wrote that "philosophy since Leibnitz has been a weak trailer after material science, engaging men of tertiary importance."[24] It is reasonable to infer from this statement that he meant Kant, Hegel, Emerson, and any writer whose ideas displayed any similarity to the "crap like Bergson."[25]

Of course literary differences existed within and among the older generation too, and it would be folly to suggest that the ideas each writer appropriated from James and Bergson could ever have produced any uniform solutions to the problem of religious belief in the post-Darwinian age. Wallace Stevens, for example, a poet who espoused a belief that the modern mind was no longer able to believe in God as its greatest imaginary construct, explored how the poet's imagination might create a "supreme fiction" to take the place of God. Contrary to Frost, who affirmed that it was reasonable to believe in something one never knew to be true (but which might be true), Stevens, following Santayana, affirmed the idea that it was not only reasonable but entirely proper to believe in something that one could most assuredly assume to be false.[26] Conversely, Willa Cather established in *O Pioneers!* a heroine who intuitively recognized the mysterious, creative laws of nature, threw herself into the life of the soil, and stoically accepted and participated in her own purposeful destiny. As I suggest in my introduction, Frost not only saw the power of the imagination to transform and ameliorate both external and internal threats but also sought to challenge the audacity of dominating scientific conclusions whose claims exceeded the available empirical evidence or failed to acknowledge the limitations of human perception.

Despite these large and important differences, what groups Frost, Cather, and Stevens onto the same branch of the literary family tree is their recognition that human subjectivity does not merely derive from matter or mechanics. To them, the imagination was an indispensable, immaterial reality that invented order, beauty, moral judgment, and truth. For each of these writers, the simple rendering of an image or scene was unequivocally a failure of the mind to remain flexible in the face of the physical world—a failure to create, as Stevens suggested, "meaning in design / Wrenched out of chaos."[27] However much these poets differed in temperament and in their solutions to the problems of the modern world, each vocally acknowledged the constructivism and relativism that the nineteenth century inherited from Kant. To deny or acknowledge the mind's pivotal and independent role in the shaping of reality was to deny the very process of creation, to ignore the modern poet's responsibility to invent a meaningful self, to thwart the mind's ability to adapt to the overwhelming stimuli of the modern world, and to succumb to the forces of mechanistic determinism. The brute facts of the material world—Frost's hissing snow or Stevens's "junipers shagged with ice"[28]—provide boundaries to projected realities, but in Frost and Stevens there is always an imaginative reality beyond matter that enables the poet to forge from material resources a meaningful design. Matter is both the stimulus and the product of creation, yet creativity exists as a separate, autonomous activity in which matter serves as evidence and resource, not as explanation.

In many respects, then, the early modernists' belief in the instrumental capacities of the mind anticipated salient developments in the philosophy of science, particularly in regard to contemporary hermeneutics. Although Frost, Stevens, and Cather never formalized their responses to scientific naturalism, their belief that one's immediate environment, personal experiences, and cultural traditions influenced and constrained interpretation called into question the very notion of objectivity. The idea that one's historical context and personal needs helped to determine both the subject and the method of scientific investigation suggested to them that the data one perceived were theory-dependent rather than independent of the systems of thought in which they were embedded. Not only were they skeptical of scientific conclusions purported to be objective but they developed, in consequence, a critical self-consciousness that challenged the results of perception by acknowledging how one's subjective prejudices might distort them.

Frost demonstrates the difficulty of achieving objectivity in one of his finest lyrics, "For Once, Then, Something" (1920). One of the rare hendecasyllabic poems in Frost's repertoire, this lyric, along with related poems such as "All Revelation," "Fragmentary Blue," "New Hampshire," and "A Star in a Stone Boat," established Frost's belief that the imagination engaged, transformed, and created the physical world of the mind's desires. While some critics have suggested that Frost's work from the early '20s is too self-consciously smug or clever, one cannot help but notice the aptness of the shaping metaphor, which shows us how perception and material forces act upon one another in the creation, interpretation, and distortion of truth:

> Others taunt me with having knelt at well-curbs
> Always wrong to the light, so never seeing
> Deeper down in the well than where the water
> Gives me back in a shining surface picture
> Me myself in the summer heaven godlike

Looking out of a wreath of fern and cloud puffs.
Once, when trying with chin against a well-curb,
I discerned as I thought beyond the picture,
Through the picture, a something white, uncertain,
Something more of the depths—and then I lost it.
Water came to rebuke the too clear water.
One drop fell from a fern, and lo, a ripple
Shook whatever it was lay there at bottom,
Blurred it, blotted it out. What was that whiteness?
Truth? A pebble of quartz? For once, then, something.

(*CPP&P,* 208)

Like the disturbing and oft-anthologized poem "Design," "For Once, Then, Something" ends its venture into the nature of truth with a question the speaker refuses to answer. Structurally divided into two equal halves, the poem sustains an extraordinary tension as it yokes the affective and self-canceling strengths of the spiritual and the material worlds. In the first half, the nonchalant speaker emphasizes his inability to escape the influencing power of subjectivity as it transforms and shapes the world according to human needs. "Always wrong to the light," the speaker, despite his efforts to gain a proper perspective, sees only his own godlike image (wreathed like Apollo) staring back at him, coloring and thus limiting his ability to penetrate beyond surface appearances. No matter how hard he tries, the speaker cannot fully recover a definitive reality, as consciousness acknowledges its own participation in the formation of knowledge.

Had Frost ended the poem there, contemporary readers might be tempted to equate this theory of knowledge with a more extreme version of postmodern solipsism, in which nature itself is considered a "text" whose existence is bound by the prison houses of subjectivity, ideology, and language. As several readers have noticed, however, Frost, while certainly approaching this position, never concedes that material processes are only mental constructs.[29] As the next six lines indicate, the tangible world and its forces— the fern, the drop of water, and the energizing ripple—interrupt and limit the subjective creations of the projecting self. The poet, the maker and shaper of his reality, finds himself framed by the manufactured stones of the well, which in turn are framed by the mysterious and wilder elements of the natural world. Composing in such a self-negating, deconstructing manner, Frost thus playfully confirms Democritus's adage "Of truth we know nothing, for truth lies at the bottom of the well." Is the deepest reality purely material—the "pebble of quartz"—as nineteenth-century scientists would claim? Or is it something spiritual—a transcendent truth—as the romantic poets would claim? There is only an intuited "something," a whiteness, that, like Melville's "great white whale," never fully discloses its meaning.

The struggle to find secure knowledge and the reluctance of the natural world to provide it is one of the most important and pervasive themes in Frost's poetry. Yet despite the theme's ubiquity, the struggle is one that Frost seems content *not* to resolve. Though others may have "taunted" Frost for his teleological drifting, one would certainly be hard-pressed to find in all of his poetry any departure from this position. Consider, for example, "The Secret Sits," a whimsical, minor poem from *A Witness Tree* (1942): "We dance round in a ring and suppose, / But the secret sits in the middle and knows" (*CPP&P*, 329). Even the later "Masques," two long poems that some see as evidence of the poet's conversion to a more conventional form of Christianity, display a round measure of witty skepticism, particularly when Job demands answers from a God who has long refused to reveal himself. In fact, revelation, certainty, and truth, as Frost's well-known poem "Neither Out Far Nor In Deep" establishes, remain inaccessible to the mind that desires them. What strikes one so forcefully about this poem, however, is that Frost applauds the majestic vigils people construct in an effort to satisfy their endless curiosity for ultimate truths that cannot be comprehended:

> They cannot look out far,
> They cannot look in deep.
> But when was that ever a bar
> To any watch they keep?
>
> (*CPP&P*, 274)

Perhaps the best critical description of Frost's deepening skepticism and his belief in the ephemerality of all knowledge, including scientific knowledge, was given in 1963 by Irving Howe, who, while eulogizing Frost, offered some shrewd and favorable opinions about the poetry. While perhaps overemphasizing the naturalistic tendencies in Frost's work, Howe nevertheless astutely attributes to Frost a Blakean awareness that any understanding of nature begins with the projections of an individual consciousness:

> The best of his [Frost's] poems are neither indulgences in homely
> philosophy nor wanderings in Romanticism. If anything they are anti-

pathetic to the notion that the universe is inherently good or delightful or hospitable to our needs. The symbols they establish in relation to the natural world are not, as in Transcendentalist poetry, tokens of benevolence. These lyrics speak of the hardness and recalcitrance of the natural world; of its absolute indifference to our needs and its refusal to lend itself to an allegory of affection; of the certainty of physical dissolution; but also of the refreshment that can be found through a brief submission to the alienness of nature, always provided one recognizes the need to move on, not stopping for rest, but remaining locked alone in consciousness.[30]

Poetic playfulness, uncertainty, contradiction, and paradox permeate Frost's work to such an extent that one might even suppose that many of his poems were merely elaborate pranks or linguistic tectonics designed solely to challenge those who would thwart the creative capacities of mind with firm answers. Writing in 1926, Frost reiterated this idea, suggesting that the intellect functions best when debating two opposing ideas that are somehow mystically united. In a letter to Sidney Cox, an old teaching colleague from his Plymouth Normal School days, Frost suggests that easy, spoon-fed answers should be omitted from the classroom in favor of a more rigorous dialectical method:

> Clash is all very well for coming lawyers, politicians, and theologians. But I should think there must be a whole realm or plane above that— all sight and insight, perception, intuition, rapture. Narrative is a fearfully safe place to spend your time. Having ideas that are neither pro nor con is the happy thing. Get up there high enough and the differences that make controversy become only the two legs of a body the weight of which is on one in one period, on the other in the next. Democracy Monarchy; Puritanism paganism; form content; conservatism radicalism; systole diastole; rustic urbane; literary colloquial; work play. I should think too much of myself to let any teacher fool me into taking sides on any one of these oppositions.[31]

This is fairly lofty advice, especially from a poet well known to have perpetuated his own brand of established prejudices. Yet the skepticism Frost espouses here, however prejudiced it, too, may be, remained throughout his career such a consistent and compelling feature that it calls for explanation. Why would Frost advocate such willful uncertainty when much of the intellectual world, particularly in positivist and analytic circles, was busy trying to escape from the Kantian paradigm in an effort to reaffirm the possibility of a secure, objective reality? This ambivalent stance, so often termed the "Frostian posture," appears often in Frost's poetry, leading one to wonder why he would sanction such incertitude and its implications of terror, relativism, and absurdity. Several distinct advantages must have presented themselves for him to sustain such a puzzling position in a literary milieu that demanded definitive answers.

While there are no easy solutions to this problem, the most obvious answer is that uncertainty was a much less terrifying experience than was a blind acceptance of nineteenth-century deterministic "certainties," which had succeeded in banishing God from the universe. Although Frost knew well that skepticism could in itself become a debilitating source of anxiety (especially since relativism threatened traditional institutions that codified moral behavior), the effect of such anxiety paled in comparison with the fear that scientific naturalism elicited from him. Doubt about God was not the same as an absence of God, and while this position was in itself no guarantee of the soul's salvation (doubt was not confirmation of God either), it offered Frost a consoling compromise between naturalism and idealism. Skepticism protected him from both atheistic denial and blind faith. Like the Drumlin Woodchuck's carefully crafted back entrance, Frost's skepticism yielded several plausible escape routes that could lead him away from the dangers and nightmares of mechanistic determinism.

Frost's growing skepticism also helped him to reaffirm the autonomy of the imagination and, by extension, the whole notion of free will, which, as James and Schiller had recognized, was a necessary component in any variety of religious belief. James had observed in *The Will to Believe* that one's rational belief was dependent upon prior emotional predispositions that revealed themselves once a legitimate choice was made. Belief in God was dependent upon will, volition, hope, and firm commitment to a courage strong enough to will the future into a coherent reality.[32] In order for the mind to shape meaningful order out of chaos, free will had to exist and exert itself as the imagination's directing force. Volitional will liberated one from the shackles of determinism. As Schiller had put it nearly one hundred years earlier:

> As long as man derives sensations from a contact with nature, he is her slave; but as soon as he begins to reflect upon her objects and laws he becomes her lawgiver. Nature, which previously ruled him as a power, now expands before him as an object. What is objective to him can

have no power over him, for in order to become objective it has to experience his own power. As far and as long as he impresses a form upon matter, he cannot be injured by its effect; for a spirit can only be injured by that which deprives it of its freedom.[33]

To Frost, the best evidence for the existence of free will was creativity itself. As Frost reiterated in talks, essays, and letters, an established freedom in one's material enabled the poet to transform the phenomenal world and ameliorate its harmful effects. Artistic freedom also forced the poet to acknowledge the power of that world to resist transformation. The poem, Frost once wrote, "is like a current carrying the eel grass with it, combing it like hair in different directions without uprooting it from its initial clarity, its fixed meaning."[34] Of course the "fixed meaning" Frost refers to here is the tangible, material world that the poet shapes into meaningful form by exploiting the possibilities of language. The poet, however, does not sculpt nature into a static symbol in the manner of Swedenborg or Emerson; rather, the poet shapes and reshapes the available material into a dynamic text that invites many (though not unlimited) interpretations, advocates play and flexibility, and, above all, resists closure despite its efforts to remain "rooted" to the page. The material world and the spiritual world exist in separate realms, yet each acts upon the other. Matter both resists the current and succumbs to it; spirit both shapes matter and is constrained by it. And central to this metaphor is the notion of drifting, of continual flexibility, which is both the source and the object of the poem's joyful attraction. For Frost, conceptual and teleological drifting, far from something to be resisted, is in fact the saving act of redemption toward which every poet should strive.

In addition to providing the poet with a solution to the problems of materialism, Frost's skepticism laid the foundation for a poetics that emphasized human values. Recognizing that doubt rather than certainty was perhaps more characteristic of actual experience, Frost devoted himself to an aesthetic that would enable others to recognize the power of the imagination's redemptive capacities. Anticipating many of the techniques of contemporary "language poetry," Frost stressed the idea that a poet should regard his activity as a performance. "I look at the poet as a man of prowess, just like an athlete," wrote Frost. "He's a performer. And the things you can do in a poem are various. . . . Somebody has said that poetry among other things is the very marrow of wit."[35]

Frost also demanded equal athletic "prowess" and wit in readers, who, by the very act of reading, collaborated with the poet to form meaning. The very openness of many of Frost's texts and the stern demands he places upon his readers' imaginations underscores his firm belief that meaning should never be parceled out in ready-made packages. Scholarly annotations and footnotes were to him especially damaging to free poetic play, as fixed meanings and definitions restricted his readers' abilities to discover "delight and wisdom" for themselves. In fact, Frost welcomed critical disagreement over his poems. "There can be no sweeter music to my ears," Frost once wrote, "than the clash of arms over my dead body."[36] Poetry should be the evidence of the poet's "will braving alien entanglements" (*CPP&P,* 787). As the poet negotiates the physical world, and as the reader engages the poem, each participates in the construction of meaning. The absence of "definitive" conclusions about the natural or supernatural world consistently attracts and entangles readers, as each contributes to any interpretation individual desires, experiences, and continually shifting contexts. The text is thus the site of communication, and the poem a reflection of human sympathies, the very figure and extension of love itself.

The last benefit Frost secured from his antifoundationalism was a developing belief that all forms of knowledge were epistemologically equivalent. That Frost was thinking along these lines is evident from several passages in the notebooks. Writing in one of his later notebooks (probably about 1950), Frost drew the figure of a square, which he entitled "The Great Square of Pegasus (The Winged)," and labeled the points "Art," "Philosophy," "Religion," and "Science."[37] What is so striking about this simple figure, aside from the fact that Frost embeds it between pages that discuss the role of science in society, is that he accords each discipline an equivalent status, an equal illuminating magnitude. Although it is impossible to know for certain what compelled him to jot down such a figure, the context suggests that he accepted the Kantian notion that all representative forms of knowledge—the religious, the artistic, the philosophic, and the scientific—are vital to a fully meaningful life and should be preserved.[38]

Frost ultimately departed from Kant, however, in his disagreement with Kant's view that rational or scientific explanations of the universe displayed greater cognitive value than art and were therefore to be given privileged status. If all disciplines depended equally upon a limited consciousness, one that required an analytical vocabulary and method to see what it wanted to see rather than what was actually there, then how was it possible for the scientist to assert with calm certainty the truth of a hidden law that lay beyond a material awareness of it? Frost did not seriously question the existence of verifiable physical objects like rocks or trees. But, following Nietzsche, he challenged science, arguing that we cannot be sure about what is true because we have no transcendent framework outside of consciousness to ground that decision. Our conceptions of the invisible world—a world of theory, laws, and forces—inevitably remain incoherent because perception depends upon hypothetical speculation. This is what Frost means when he says that scientists get lost in their material. Science breaks down because metaphorical constructions cannot possibly accommodate all of the mysteries and shaping forces of the cosmos. In "Education by Poetry," Frost writes,

> Greatest of all attempts to say one thing in terms of another is the philosophical attempt to say matter in terms of spirit, or spirit in terms of matter, to make the final unity. That is the greatest attempt that ever failed. We stop just short there. But it is the height of poetry, the height of all thinking, the height of all poetic thinking, that attempt to say matter in terms of spirit and spirit in terms of matter. It is wrong to call anybody a materialist simply because he tries to say spirit in terms of matter, as if that were a sin. Materialism is not the attempt to say all in terms of matter. The only materialist—be he poet, teacher, scientist, politician, or statesman—is the man who gets lost in his material without a gathering metaphor to throw it into shape and order. He is the lost soul.[39]

By extension, even when scientists can gather a metaphor to throw the real world into shape, they cannot be sure whether those created forms constitute truth. Though constructed forms may comfort us, it is clear to Frost that form alone cannot make the universe a less mysterious place. Like a "piece of ice on a hot stove," even a scientific metaphor "must ride on its own melting."[40]

Surprisingly, it was scientists, and not poets, who became Frost's allies in support of this idea since it was they who first recognized the philosophical problems associated with classical physics and scientific verification. Even though many advocates of nineteenth-century materialism were still convinced at the beginning of the twentieth century that the "anthropomorphic notion of a deliberate architect and ruler of the world was gone forever,"[41] the scientific foundations that made such sweeping judgments possible were beginning to collapse.

The first crack to appear was one that many believers in evolution had largely ignored. The second law of thermodynamics, discovered by Rudolf

Clausius in 1865, stipulated that energy dissipated in every conversion process until it became unusable. According to this law, matter did not evolve toward higher states of being, as Spencerian progressivism argued, but rather toward greater inefficiency and disorder.[42] Similarly, Max Planck's newly developed quantum mechanics claimed that energy existed in discrete units that could occupy intermediate states not, as classical mechanics claimed, during a gain or loss of energy, but only when energy absorption or emission was sufficient enough for quanta to "jump" levels. While these two laws combined to challenge the scientific foundations of determinism, perhaps the greatest usurper of scientific authority was Einstein. In a single bold idea—that there is no absolute motion in the universe, only relative motion—Einstein dismantled classical mechanics and demonstrated that they were valuable only in a limited domain of phenomena.[43] As these developments flourished, scientific theories whose truths depended upon mathematical proofs were suddenly susceptible to revision, which led many to believe that a new interpretation of nature was not only possible but also necessary. As revolutionary discoveries in physics ushered in a new century, determinism as it was earlier understood was on the verge of becoming an anachronism.

That the breakdown of determinism was the subject of much inquiry at the turn of the century is evident in the philosophical debates that took place in the first two decades. In particular, the Fourth International Congress of Philosophy, held in Bologna in 1911, focused upon the philosophical problems that modern physics generated. The event, covered by T. E. Hulme, who was then working as a correspondent for the British scientific journal *Nature,* attracted more than five hundred people, whose main interests lay in discerning more accurately the relationship between science and philosophy. In this forum alone, several philosophers began to discuss the implications of the new physics and how these discoveries suddenly called into question the very possibility of scientific certitude.

Jules Henri Poincaré, the French mathematician whose reputation rested upon his theory of functions, examined the question whether the laws of nature might evolve with the physical changes of the universe. The physicist Paul Langevin's paper, "L'évolution de l'espace et du temps," argued that the "laws of mechanics, once considered absolute, are not so." Even Bergson, whose lecture was the one most anticipated, argued that intuition and not scientific analysis should become the dominant method of philosophy. While these lectures represent only a portion of those given at the Congress, they represent a general tendency among the participants to reject the system-building philosophies of the previous century. "Philosophy," wrote Hulme, "does seem to be steering away from its traditional form. It is beginning to form a more fluent and a less rigid and systematic conception of truth."[44] In several respects, these arguments echo the sentiments of William James. Poking fun at Spencer's synthetic philosophy, James had parodied the theory of evolution as a "change from a know-howish untalkaboutable all-alikeness to a somehowish and in general talkaboutable not-all-alikeness by continuous sticktogetherations and something-elseifications."[45]

The cumulative effect of this kind of talk upon Frost can hardly be overestimated. As Frost immersed himself more deeply in the new physics, gleaning information from Hulme and other outlets, such as the *Scientific American* and Arthur Eddington's *Nature of the Physical World*,[46] he began to understand that one's historical moment helps to determine not only the course of scientific investigation but also the validity of scientific truth. Truth was not derived merely by incremental discovery or greater and greater experimental precision. Truth was also dependent upon metaphorical models whose imaginative assumptions constantly shifted. To Frost, this idea also seemed to be true for the science of the nineteenth century. As the idea of a machinelike universe faded from his imagination, Frost could confidently welcome the challenge science presented to religion:

> Let religion enter into combination with the science of its time: for it will whether we like it or not. It did anciently with such science as there was in the beginning. It does today in the mind of the modernist. The science it takes up is always the falsest part of religion, however, and the part that is most subject to change. The science of religion in Genesis seems ridiculous now—and the science of religion in early Christian times. The science that religion takes over today religion will sooner or later drop. The science changes. The religion persists. The religious part of religion has been nearly the same 5,000 years at least.[47]

Frost's growing awareness that nineteenth-century determinism had been dismantled by a cosmology that was at once more mysterious, more poetic, and more congenial to his personal needs ultimately allowed him to accept the possibility that God might exist. If science could not unlock the deepest truths of existence, then scientists also could not be certain that God was dead. Although this belief was small consolation for a man who desperately sought divine purpose in the universe, Frost nevertheless clung to this shard of hope in an effort to stabilize his life. At stake, of course, was the preservation of the human soul: "Just when belated outsiders have got it in their heads that as part of a machine universe they are in danger of having to regard themselves as machines[,] Just when they are on the point of giving up the fight for their souls[,] science calmly announces that the universe is not a machine[,] whatever people may be."[48]

Although his movement toward belief in God was never as dramatic as Eliot's, as Frost reached middle age he slowly began to reaffirm the religious beliefs of his childhood.[49] To the end of his life, however, the skeptically minded Frost maintained an ambivalent attitude toward all organized religions, preferring to confront the mysteries of the universe on his own terms. "I don't go to church," Frost once wrote, "but I look in the window."[50] Such a position was necessary if he was to be philosophically consistent. If skepticism led him to repudiate the system-building philosophies of an earlier century, then that position necessarily demanded an equivalent repudiation of religious orthodoxy. Like Job, who endured the trials and misfortunes of existence, Frost patiently waited for a God who had not yet come.

2. Darwin

The matter with the Mid-Victorians
Seems to have been a man named John L. Darwin.

"New Hampshire" (1923)

LIKE MANY YOUNG MEN IN THE LATE NINETEENTH CENTURY, ROBERT
Frost first learned about Charles Darwin from an older brother. Nearly ten
years older and already an experienced botanist, farmer, and jack-of-all-
trades, Carl Burell, though not related to Frost by blood, nevertheless exerted upon his younger friend an influence usually reserved for an intimate
family member.[1] Although Frost's attraction to Burell fell well short of idol-
atry, the twenty-five-year-old must have at least seemed to him remarkably
up-to-date and sophisticated. It was Burell who first introduced Frost to
Tom Sawyer and *Huckleberry Finn,* Burell who stimulated his early interest
in botany, and Burell who taught him the rudiments of farming and how
to breed "fancy white wyandotts" on the poet's New Hampshire farm. By
the time the two had met in the halls of Lawrence High School, this awk-
ward, stuttering misfit (as Thompson describes Burell) had already assembled a considerable scientific library. He had stocked his bookshelves with
the controversial works by Darwin, Huxley, and Spencer, which he gener-
ously shared with the eager fifteen-year-old Frost, who had been warned by
his devout mother not to believe the "blasphemous and shocking claims of
the evolutionists." Like most rebellious teenagers, who find the forbidden
seductive, Frost responded to Burell's generosity almost immediately, and
in what is perhaps one of the stranger twists of fate, he yielded to an even
more significant temptation: Burell, the man who first introduced Frost to
natural selection, also first urged him to write poetry.

Little evidence exists to illuminate how Frost first reacted to Darwin's ideas. Nothing suggests that he reacted with the despair of Tennyson, whose own struggles with evolution led to the midlife melancholia that Eliot so astutely observed about him, nor did he react with the anger and shock of W. H. Hudson, who, after first hearing about Darwin, refused to speak to the older brother who had loaned him a copy of *On the Origin of Species*.[2] What little evidence does exist might lead one to suppose that Frost's initial response to natural selection was based largely upon a misinterpretation of Darwin's key points. Addressing a group of students at the University of Detroit in 1962, for example, Frost, speaking on metaphor, recalled how he had calmed his mother's fears about Darwin by suggesting that God, instead of making "man out of mud," had made man "out of prepared mud."[3] Although Frost often repeated this anecdote to evoke humor during his lectures, such tongue-in-cheek evidence belies an early essay he wrote for the Lawrence High School *Bulletin* in 1892. There, in what was already emerging as a distinctive prose style, Frost addressed the question of religious belief in a post-Darwinian era: "A custom has its unquestioning followers, its radical enemies, and a class who have generally gone through both these to return to the first in a limited sense,—to follow custom,—not without question, but where it does not conflict with the broader habits of life gained by wanderers among ideas. The second class makes one of the first and third. This is best exemplified in religious thought and controversy. It is the second class that would have an inquisition to compel liberality."[4]

To those who would situate the development of Frost's poetic idiosyncrasies in his post-Harvard years, this passage should come as a surprise, for here the high-school senior already displays several intellectual attitudes that would eventually become enduring features of his literary career. His stern repudiation of intellectual extremism and determinism, his advocacy of conservatism in politics (notice the comparison of "radical enemy" to the Inquisition), and his insistence upon a freely chosen will that could enable one to "wander among ideas" should strike a familiar note to those acquainted with Frost's later essays and letters. More relevant to this discussion, however, is the fact that each of these attributes arises primarily out of Frost's desire to resolve a family conflict—to find a reasonable compromise that could allay both his mother's religiosity and Burell's growing atheism. Although these two positions may have seemed at one time irreconcilable, Frost convinced himself that he could meet the challenge of Darwin with only a slight remodeling of his inherited religious beliefs. The construction of a different kind of God, one partially reconfigured against

Christian orthodoxy by the trial of evolution, seemed to him a likely solution to his problem. He only had to go by contraries, suspend thesis and antithesis, extract the most congenial elements of each system, and acknowledge the limited validity of both poles without wholly sanctioning either. To Frost, Darwin had not yet dissolved the familiar comforts of organized religion, and for the moment it seemed to him that a wholly satisfactory synthesis was still possible.

That Frost would devote the next sixty years of his life to trying to reconcile evolution and religion he could not have predicted. Yet Frost's lifelong struggle with Darwinian concepts, particularly those ideas that emphasized determinism, reflects a much broader American tendency to preserve the nineteenth century's hard-won belief in the power of individuals to shape their own future. As Frost suggests in "New Hampshire" (1923), a humorous poem that burlesques much nineteenth-century thought, "John L. Darwin," like John L. Sullivan, the last of the great bare-knuckles heavyweight champions, had tried to pummel "Mid-Victorians" into a cowering acceptance of scientism. In general, however, most nineteenth-century Americans had simply refused to accept Darwinism, partly because the Civil War impeded the critical reception of *On the Origin of Species* but more because Darwinism, in its purest form, challenged the rugged individualism that had precipitated the formation of America itself.[5] To both cultured and noncultured Americans, the British exportation of Darwinian ideas threatened to undermine not only the religious freedoms that had so distinguished America from its European ancestors but also the very philosophical principles that had made the experiment in democracy feasible in the first place. If, for example, one could no longer believe in purposeful design, as Darwin contended, then, by extension, one could also no longer believe in the concept of natural law, which, based upon Locke's *ex nihilo nihil fit* maxim, had laid the foundations for American belief in reason, liberty, human dignity, and natural rights.[6] Several national predispositions militated against Darwin's acceptance in America and influenced even the brightest and most "objective" American thinkers. At stake, or so it seemed to many at the time, was the very survival of the new nation, whose political foundations had been laid by philosophical propositions rather than by collective ethnic traditions and whose manifest destiny was thought to guarantee the preservation of human dignity and happiness.

The first of these predispositions, as Henry May has astutely observed, was a deeply felt belief in the eternal reality of moral ideals.[7] Justice, liberty, industry, frugality, piety, mercy, and prudence, the stern moral standards

that had informed Puritan behavior, continued to flourish as largely unquestioned ideals well into the early twentieth century. Sanctioned in the
seventeenth century by scripture and in the eighteenth century by Jeffersonian deism, a belief in the immutability of ideals found expression during Frost's childhood most notably in Emerson's essays and in the philosophical lectures of the Harvard idealist Josiah Royce. Although the Puritan
doctrines of depravity and predestination had by this time become quaint
relics from the past, the Puritan impulse to discern providence in the facts
and signs of nature persisted in the eighteenth and nineteenth centuries,
first in the Enlightenment's assumption that God was most visible in the
intricate perfection of the natural world and later in the romantic insistence that all of the elements in nature, including humankind, were bathed
in a benevolent, transcendent deity. Even though it was clear to many that
social behavior had changed and would continue to change, most European Americans had never doubted the innate goodness of America. Proof
for such belief lay in America's sublime and enduring landscape. Expansive
prairies, lofty mountains, and teeming forests served as an apology for the
moral superiority of the nation and provoked such a strong emblematic
connection between Americans and God that even a powerful dissenter
such as Darwin could not easily sever it. As late as 1913, George Santayana,
at the time the dean of American materialists, commented upon the persistence of Puritan-based Christian morality, which, though weakening,
still mounted a formidable challenge to the Darwinian hypothesis. "The
present age," he wrote, "is a critical one and interesting to live in. The civilization characteristic of Christendom has not yet disappeared, yet another
civilization has begun to take its place."[8]

As Santayana knew, however, the transition in America to a "post-Chris-
tian" culture had not been as abrupt as the one that had occurred only
twenty-five years earlier in Britain. That the battle lines between Christianity and science had never clearly formed in America (as they had in Britain
for such adversaries as Thomas Huxley and Archbishop Samuel Wilber-
force) was in large part due to a continuing belief in social and moral progress.[9] Ever since John Winthrop had proclaimed, in 1630, that his Massachusetts Bay Colony would become a beacon of moral hope and progress,
a "city upon a hill," as he termed it, white Americans had always displayed
a profound faith in the regenerative capacities of the New World. Whether
one sought moral perfection in the reformed Protestantism of Massachusetts or liberation from oppressive indentured servitude in a Virginia
homestead, most colonists, given the immense opportunities of the New

World, could live out their lives knowing that they were taking part in the beneficence of what John O'Sullivan would later term "Manifest Destiny."

Surprisingly, rather than dissolving this enduring faith in upward progress, competing versions of evolution, most notably neo-Lamarckism, reaffirmed the idea that people could hasten the evolutionary process toward perfection.[10] Just as the giraffe had willingly stretched its neck to reach fruit on the highest branches and then passed that specialized ability on to succeeding generations, most Americans believed they had played their own special part in speeding up the progressive movement toward moral, physical, economic, and political perfection. It was this kind of thinking that helped the aging Walt Whitman ameliorate his despair over the Civil War. If, as he rationalized, young men accurately perceived their moral imperatives and were willing to sacrifice themselves in the name of abolition and the Union, then the war could be justified as a necessary purifying stage in the nation's progress toward a higher moral plane. In addition to sanctioning a "moral" war, such progressivism also contributed enormously to Spencer's enduring popularity in America. Spencer's altered version of evolution, one that argued for the inevitability of coherence and design, fired the imaginations of many liberal theologians, who suddenly began to conceive of God not as a transcendent creator of matter and giver of moral law but rather as an immanent universal force that propelled creation forward toward higher and higher states of perfection. As May accurately observed, not only did evolution seem compatible with God but "evolution had become God," and the mainstay rather than the enemy of moral progress.[11]

The last national predisposition to facilitate the American resistance to Darwinism was a widely shared academic belief in the necessity of an autonomous American culture.[12] Motivated by nationalistic ardor, many nineteenth-century academicians sought to emancipate American art and literature from British authority by calling for nonderivative works that would be commensurate with the spirit and grandeur of the new land. This early American romantic impulse inevitably expanded into the realm of science and inspired the work of early American naturalists such as Audubon, Bartram, and Wilson. So ubiquitous was the call for a national culture that Americans began to donate funds to scientific and artistic institutions. As museums for the visual arts opened in mid-century, American scientists, for the first time, began to house natural-history collections of indigenous species in American rather than British museums.[13] One proponent of this endeavor, Dr. James McKey, even went so far as to exhort his peers to "study and examine for themselves, instead of blindly using the eyes of foreign naturalists, or bowing implicitly to a foreign bar of criticism."[14] To establish international prestige, so the argument went, American scientists had to reject British influence and observe nature through a distinctly American national subjectivity. Only then could they explore the wonderful intricacies of the new land, measure and record in America's diverse flora and fauna the evidence for God's existence, and establish once and for all complete intellectual and cultural independence.

Given that such longstanding national predispositions were already in place, it is not surprising that many American scientists resented being upstaged by yet another internationally prominent Englishman. Louis Agassiz, for example, easily the most famous American scientist of the day (though a Swiss immigrant), rejected Darwin on the grounds that the time span necessary for natural selection to occur could not possibly have elapsed.[15] Stubbornly clinging to his belief that the Creator designed and then extinguished individual species as he thought or did not think of them, Agassiz, relying heavily upon theories of glacial catastrophe, contended that the appearance and disappearance of species reflected God's powerful, fickle, and well-ordered mind. In a similar repudiation of Darwin, Joseph Le Conte, a prominent geologist and evolutionist, defended Lamarck's insistence upon acquired characteristics and suggested in the face of mounting evidence that "useful changes, determined by education in each generation, are to some extent inherited and accumulated through the race."[16] Even the Harvard scientist Asa Gray, the first and most vociferous champion of Darwin in America, tried relentlessly to justify his Quaker beliefs even as he admitted that Darwin's argument was a "legitimate attempt to extend the domain of natural or physical science."[17] Indeed, many respected American scientists who should have been receptive to Darwin clung to familiar comforts and extracted from evolutionary thought only those ideas that were most congenial to their fundamental religious or political beliefs.

The persistence of these beliefs, coupled with the fact that no one had yet found an adequate biological mechanism to explain how genetic variations were transmitted from one generation to another, facilitated in most American scientific circles a widespread skepticism about the viability of Darwin's theory. Not until the 1930s, when the science of genetics and heredity combined with the Darwinian framework to complete the "modern synthesis," would evolution by natural selection be fully accepted in America as the basic theory of biology.[18] Because of this delay, Darwin's theory hybridized into several modified varieties that no longer resembled his original intention, and as these corrupted versions became more widely known to an educated public, many Americans tended to latch on to the "optimistic" features of each, believing what they wanted to believe despite the charges of sentimentality and ignorance that issued from British intellectuals.

In spite of the persistence of these colonial and nationalistic impulses, isolated pockets of unconditional acceptance continued to grow in number, and for those who swore fealty to the purest form of Darwinism the cultural implications were devastating. As any careful reader of *On the Origin of Species* well knew, Darwin had claimed two goals: to show, first, that species had not been separately created and, second, that natural selection had been the chief agent of change. Although evidence to support organic evolution had been available to Darwin for years, what distinguished him from his contemporaries was his firm conviction that evolution could only be attributed to a process he called "Natural Selection" (Darwin always capitalized the term), a random and, what is more significant, *directionless* agent for variation and biological change. According to Darwin, no matter how hard one tried, one simply could not locate the activity of God in any evolutionary process. This radically new concept not only destroyed the old, Platonic notion that individual species were merely imperfect copies of preexisting abstract forms (the creationist argument), it also challenged the Aristotelian concept of entelechy and teleological perfection (the progressivist argument), an idea that had allowed the Catholic Church and evolutionists such as Lamarck and Spencer to justify God's extinction of individual species. As these two philosophical pillars of religious faith began to crumble beneath the weight of the Darwinian model, it became increasingly apparent to those who fully understood it that the most cherished ideals of American culture were in danger of rapidly becoming obsolete. Arguments for God from design and upward progress no longer obtained, and to those who were frightened by such devastating losses few convincing alternatives made themselves available in the battle against late-nineteenth-century despair.

Alternatives did exist, however, many of which were still being hotly debated at Harvard College, where Frost had enrolled as a special student in the fall of 1897. Although Frost's stay there lasted for only two years, he "caught on" and "toned up" enough, as he put it, to absorb and understand most of the prevailing attitudes toward Darwin, several of which were still contending for prominence during the last years of the nineteenth century.[19] In general, three possibilities presented themselves: one could accept the Darwinian model and revel in the liberating freedom of a completely material universe; contest the model because it lacked validating empirical evidence; or question the veracity of the model in terms of the Kantian proposition that humans can never know the noumenal world because their knowledge is limited by the categories and forms of sensibility.

The first of these alternatives, and the one most disconcerting to Frost, found its most ardent champion in George Santayana, the youngest member of the Harvard philosophy department, with whom Frost had taken a survey course in the history of Western philosophy during his freshman year. Though Santayana had generally displayed little interest in science, he believed, along with most materialists, that all phenomena could be attributed to the spatial and temporal processes of physical nature—to the "chaos of sensations" (Nietzsche's term). Santayana claimed that in contrast to the chaotic, sensational forces of physical reality, intellectual conventions, human values, and particularly the idea of God were merely imaginative constructs that "rendered fit" an idealized version of human experience. As Santayana made clear in *Interpretations of Poetry and Religion* (1900), a book he was writing while Frost attended Harvard, "faith and the higher reason of the metaphysicians" were "forms of imagination believed to be avenues to truth . . . not because their necessary correspondence to truth can be demonstrated . . . but because a man dwelling on those intuitions is conscious of a certain moral transformation, of a certain warmth and energy of life."[20]

On the surface, Santayana's clear distinction between material and mental forces bears a remarkable affinity to some of James's most important ideas. Both, for example, embrace instrumentalist versions of cognitive awareness and emphasize the positive psychological benefits that emanate from humans' constructive faculties of mind. What differentiates the two, however, is the stark contrast in metaphysical temperament. Whereas James believed that mental constructs could neither prove nor disprove the existence of God and so advocated religious belief, Santayana sought to purge his readers of the "metaphysical illusions" that religion had encouraged throughout history. Having dismissed altogether the possibility of some preexisting divinity, Santayana declared that the highest form of intellectual freedom occurred only when an individual constructed radically new conventions that conformed to a perception of an ideal existence. Poetry, Santayana thought, was by far the best medium for awakening man's dormant creative potential. When directed toward proper ends, poetry liberated the mind from its enfeebling habit of subordinating the imagination to transcendent sources of truth. The "great function of poetry," he claimed, was to

> repair to the material of experience, seizing hold of the reality of sensa-
> tion and fancy beneath the surface of conventional ideas, and then
> out of that living but indefinite material to build new structures, richer,
> finer, fitter to the primary tendencies of our nature, truer to the ulti-
> mate possibilities of the soul. Our descent into the elements of our
> being is then justified by our subsequent freer ascent toward its goal:
> we revert to sense only to find food for reason; we destroy conven-
> tions only to construct ideals.[21]

In a post-Darwinian universe devoid of any transcendent source of value, humans alone are the sole authors of truth, beauty, and goodness and there-fore must assume responsibility for their own actions. The existence of God and the intrinsic value of the universe are merely special types of illusions perpetuated by those whose own value-laden constructs have hardened into a repressive dogma. For Santayana, sustained belief in these conventions paralyzed humans' unique capacity to forge self-protective enclosures to shield them from the brute forces of an inherently meaningless cosmos.

While Santayana's solution to nineteenth-century materialism was at-tractive to a poet such as Wallace Stevens, whose own "blessed rage for or-der" became the core of his aesthetic, such a position ultimately disagreed with Frost's need to find greater solace and meaning in the world.[22] Like William James, who had once denounced Santayana's thought as the "per-fection of rottenness,"[23] Frost could not stomach the ease with which this eloquent fallen Catholic had dispatched the supernatural. Although he readily applauded Santayana's claim that poets were among the most free to break down stultifying conventions and boldly affirm a self-authenti-cated existence, he, along with James, could not abandon belief in an exter-nal source of truth that might serve as a bulwark for traditional moral value and religious belief. If free will, divine agency, and traditional moral values were all illusions, as Santayana professed, and if reality consisted of noth-ing but brute deterministic forces whose meaningless outcomes could be predicted, then life exhibited no real purpose and the poetic imagination was worthless. Much of Frost's psychological and physical well-being de-pended upon his own or others' assurances that morality was an integral part of the universe. In a stable universe, God could never be regarded as the author of evil; evil could be attributed only to those who had freely made a wrong choice between two available actions.

In addition to this personal quandary, Frost found Santayana's emphasis on illusory ideals socially destructive as well. With the ship of traditional ethics now set free to drift randomly upon meaningless cosmic tides, Frost feared that social customs and manners might eventually degenerate into extreme relativism.[24] Such radical revisions of proven ethical systems mounted a serious threat to civic order and necessitated not only philosophical resistance to Santayana but also political resistance to left-wing "utopians," who had culled their ideas from system-building thinkers such as Marx and Freud. To Frost, unquestioned devotion to religious, scientific, or political dogma could be just as dangerous to the free play of the imagination as radical dissent. Since Frost perceived Santayana as an adherent to the latter view, he rejected him on the grounds that he had not qualified his philosophy, as James had, with even the slightest allowance for the possibility of a god external to the material world.

To offset Santayana's solution to the problems Darwin posed, Frost immersed himself in the compensating ideas of gifted Harvard figures who did not share Santayana's proclivity for reducing the world to a network of cognitive illusions. On the empirical side of the Darwinian debate was Nathaniel Southgate Shaler, a former student of Agassiz's and a zoologist with whom Frost completed three rigorous semesters of evolutionary geology.[25] Although Shaler was careful to include in his course syllabus *On the Origin of Species* and *The Descent of Man,* he disputed Darwin's claim that structural adaptations always facilitated distinct evolutionary advantages. Basing his argument on an early study of brachiopods, Shaler contended that adaptational structures, while at times benefiting individuals, sometimes evolved at great organic cost to the species. Some structures, he declared, had no apparent utilitarian function and often appeared to be disadvantageous or even potentially antagonistic to an organism's survival. According to Shaler, the fossil and paleontological records could not explain the overall development of either phylum or group, nor could they account for the complexities of the human mind and its great capacities for language. Although it was clear that he did not object to all of the implications of natural selection (a position that greatly displeased Agassiz), as a trained scientist who believed in his own experimental methods, Shaler could not subscribe wholly to the Darwinian hypothesis. Instead, he believed in the possibility of a god who could generate species spontaneously. In his view, the geological and fossil record could not corroborate the Darwinian model, thus making the "general value of the hypothesis uncertain."[26]

While Shaler contested Darwin on scientific grounds, Josiah Royce, who had team-taught Frost's introductory philosophy class with Santayana, challenged Darwin on purely idealistic grounds.[27] Highly indebted to the German romantic tradition, Royce asserted that God was not only an omniscient entity but also the source of all cosmic purpose, a being whom we could know, oddly enough, by recognizing that scientific error actually exists as an integral part of experience. Outlining this theory in *The Religious Aspect of Philosophy* (1885), Royce claimed that one's recognition of scientific error implied the existence of a corresponding truth.[28] In Royce's view, science could disclose the world's secrets because its practitioners submitted their findings to a skeptical community of scientists who then tested those discoveries by subjecting them to rigorous standards of verification. Sustained inquiry that admitted to the possibility of error thus constituted for Royce the best proof for the existence of the "Absolute." Although one could never supply the corrective to all error, for the ability to do so would imply omniscience, one could, by directing one's collective reason away from error and toward truth, believe in an omniscient mind wherein ultimate truth must actually reside.

Accordingly, within this pragmatic framework, Royce invested scientists with a high degree of religious and spiritual significance. The very enterprise of science confirmed his notion that the universe was endlessly engaged in "the spiritual task of interpreting its own life."[29] Far from being mere observers and recorders of physical nature, scientists, like poets, took an active, imaginative role in structuring their modes of interpretation. According to Royce, scientists had the remarkable ability to "invent" the structural models that they then used to contemplate the objects of physical nature:

> A highly significant scientific hypothesis must not only be a sort of poetic creation. There is another consideration to be borne in mind. The number of possible new hypotheses, in any large field of scientific inquiry, is, like the number of possible new poems, often very great. The labor of testing each one of a number of such hypotheses, sufficiently to know whether the hypothesis tested is or is not probably true, is frequently long. And the poetic skill with which the hypotheses are invented, as well as their intrinsic beauty, gives, in advance of the test, no assurance that they will succeed in agreeing with experience. The makers of great scientific hypotheses,—the Galileos, the Darwins,—are so to speak, poets whose inventions must be submitted

to a very stern critic, namely, to the sort of experience which their sciences use. And no one can know in advance what this critic's verdict will be.[30]

As Royce would later make clear in "The Problem of Christianity," inductive observation and common sense suggested to him that the verdict with regard to Darwinism was not yet in. To him, the interpretive gifts that scientists possessed appeared to be preconditioned by a divine agent who had "tuned man's creative powers to the whole nature of the physical universe." Natural selection, he contended, "could never, by itself, have produced, through merely favoring the survival skills of skillful warriors or of industrious artisans, the genius which was so attuned to the whole nature of things as to invent the atomic hypothesis, or to discover spectrum-analysis, or to create electrical science."[31] For Royce, the mind's ability to contemplate its own existence and to locate its place in the physical universe served as the greatest proof that forces other than natural selection were responsible for designing the human mind. The slow process of adaptation could not possibly have accounted for the rich variety of invented hypotheses that scientists used to understand and explore nature. God, so it seemed to him at the time, had selected humans, above all other creatures, for this special purpose.

While it is impossible to tell just how much influence Royce had on Frost (Frost rarely mentions him in the context of Harvard), what needs stressing here is that the intellectual atmosphere of turn-of-the-century Harvard was filled with ideas that countered the scientism that had so dominated Western thought only two decades earlier. All of the intellectuals whom Frost had taken seriously—James, Royce, Santayana, and, later, Bergson—shared a resemblance in that they agreed that concepts were not true representations of eternal forms or essences but practical constructs that helped to order the sensory, chaotic flux of experience.[32] Although they differed in their metaphysical alignment and in the epistemological status they granted to concepts, each nevertheless believed that there was a distinct difference between the world that one shaped and knew and the elusive world that preceded one's cognitive shaping.[33] Accordingly, scientific hypotheses, perhaps the most sophisticated of all human constructs, were often just as vulnerable to rebuttal and revision as were rhetorical arguments that resided in the realm of contingent knowledge.

Darwinism, in particular, could perhaps be construed as just another special case of hypothetical deduction. Small fissures in the evolutionary model seemed to indicate as much. Although the Darwinian model appeared valid at the microevolutionary level, when, for example, one compared and contrasted finch beaks, it tended to break down into vague speculation, as Darwin himself admitted, at the macroevolutionary level as soon as one considered both the time constraints necessary for evolution to occur and the dearth of supporting evidence in the fossil record. In short, Darwinism, like the theories of ether and the geocentric universe, might be just another instance of error, and it espoused the truths that it did only because nobody had yet provided a more reasonable or comprehensive alternative to the mysteries of organic life.[34]

When one considers all the intellectual influences that helped mold Frost's early philosophical temperament, it is not difficult to discern how his thinking about Darwin developed during his post-Harvard years. From Shaler he had learned that Darwinism could be contested by inductive observation and by the painstaking gathering and collation of empirical evidence. From James and Royce he had learned that the bleak metaphysical implications of natural selection could be assuaged on the grounds that human perception was simply not sufficient to gain access to the deepest mysteries of the universe. And in Bergson, whom he would read enthusiastically only a few years later, he found compelling new arguments to rehabilitate belief in a spiritual reality. As these advocates of instrumentalism slowly began to challenge the materialist belief in scientific omniscience, their ideas coalesced in Frost and helped him come to terms with the consequences of natural selection.

Constructing his own arguments against the Darwinian hypothesis along similar lines, Frost concluded, sometime between 1912 and 1925, that natural selection was not impregnable law but rather a brilliant metaphor, a wonderful example of how one's synthetic imagination could construct explanatory models that could not be proven by empirical observation. In Frost view, Darwin's model had unfortunately hardened into the bedrock of a stultifying scientific imperialism:

> Another metaphor that has interested us in our time and has done
> all our thinking for us is the metaphor of evolution. Never mind going
> into the Latin word. The metaphor is simply the metaphor of the
> growing plant or of the growing thing. And somebody very brilliantly,
> quite a while ago, said that the whole universe, the whole of every-
> thing, was like unto a growing thing. . . . It is a very brilliant metaphor,
> I acknowledge, though I myself get too tired of the kind of essay that

talks about the evolution of candy, we will say, or the evolution of elevators—the evolution of this, that, and the other. Everything is evolution.[35]

Clearly, what Frost resented about the theory of evolution was not the quality of Darwin's original thinking—to do so would be to reject the habits of mind that formed the metaphorical basis of poetry itself—but the way Darwin's successors had applied the theory overwhelmingly to realms of knowledge that could not be explained by evolutionary paradigms.[36] Frost thought that Darwinism, although brilliant, had outgrown its metaphorical boundaries. It had combined with other fashionable currents of thought to form a law-bound deterministic "system" that not only dominated intellectual inquiry but also contributed to the age's growing anxiety over the existence of human initiative and free will.

Since it was these dimensions of experience, above all others, that Frost most desperately wanted to preserve, he dedicated much of his artistic energy to disclosing what he considered the fallacious nineteenth-century assumptions about scientific "truth." The "fact" had to be exposed as the "sweetest dream that labor knows," as Frost declares in "Mowing," and scientists, particularly those who swore fealty to Darwin, had to be purged of their delusions of epistemological supremacy. To achieve this end, Frost argued in his prose and poetry after 1925 that all cognitive perception was dependent upon a universal metaphoric habit of mind. Even scientific truths, he claimed, depended upon "metaphor" to throw matter "into shape and order." The great problem with metaphor, however, was that it always "[broke] down somewhere," and unless people had a "proper poetical education" and acknowledged metaphor's limitations—its "touch and go" beauty, as Frost phrased it—they could not know how far they might "expect to ride it."[37] In Frost's view, the intellectual custodians of the latter part of the nineteenth century had simply ridden Darwin's metaphor too far. Scientists had made the mistake of equating conceptual model with universal truth, and the consequences of this unfounded authority had been devastating to traditional ethics, individual genius, and metaphysical security.

Thus, Frost's appraisal of Darwin was not one of overt hostility, as Thompson has suggested, but instead a highly informed response rife with both admiration and resistance. Certainly Frost delighted in the ease with which Darwin had "thrown matter into shape and order," by the way he had metaphorically yoked organic and inorganic matter and adorned his theory in rich, poetic language. As a constructed concept, Darwin's model was a beautiful and simple example of man's freely willed creative capacities and a clear demonstration of how one man's reluctance to accept the standard metaphors of the day could effectively change the world. On the other hand, Darwin remained a threat because the evolutionary model had become a rigid paradigm that suppressed future creative potential and limited the possibilities for belief in God. Left unchecked, a literal acceptance of natural selection might not only dissolve what was left of the most cherished ideals of American culture but also destroy humans' ability to break down conventional modes of perception in order to see the world afresh.[38]

That this ambivalent response to Darwin was one of the most conspicuous features of Frost's life is evident in a wide range of poems that first surfaced in *Mountain Interval* (1916) and appear most conspicuously in *West-Running Brook* (1928) and *A Further Range* (1936). Being faithful to the first article of belief, the ability of metaphorical models to blaze new trails through the sensory flux of experience, Frost wrote several important poems that acknowledge the stark realities of a natural world shaped by evolutionary forces. Replete with images of warfare, waste, competition, and struggle, poems such as "Blue-Butterfly Day," "Pod of the Milkweed," and "Design" demonstrate how inaccessible the idyllic romantic past for which Frost often yearned was. In these poems of dramatic conflict the natural world seems so indifferent to human concerns and so brutal in its treatment of all living things that it often becomes difficult for him to find the escape hatch that frequently characterizes his solution to the terrors he faces. Such terrifying poetic moments, when his observations of nature most clearly reveal to him that his own extinction is immanent, require him to find new means of psychological protection. But how can the poet, a vulnerable individual in a world apparently indifferent to individuals, alleviate the threat of natural forces conspiring against him? How can Frost ameliorate his fear that he has been abandoned by a protective divinity? Even more to the point, how can he be sure that the threat of the natural world is not merely a projection from a dangerously fertile imagination?[39]

Typically, Frost finds redemption in one of two ways. Most often, he projects his deepest fears into his poems and then imaginatively transforms those fears by manipulating them in tangible, poetic language. When Frost scholars such as William Pritchard and Norman Holland speak of the "Frostian turn," they generally mean the manner by which he recreates the external world by shaping it imaginatively in accordance with his most heartfelt desires. While this solution is often sufficient ("The Onset" is a fine example of this technique), at other times the natural world is so over-whelming that it suppresses this redemptive act. During these times, when his imagination seems ineffective, Frost usually resorts to the second means of redemption, which is to attack the external threat by exposing the limi-tations and boundaries of the threat's operating metaphors.

In his Darwinian poems Frost frequently employs the second method when imagination alone seems insufficient. To compensate for these mo-ments of psychological paralysis, Frost exposes the boundaries of the Dar-winian metaphor, chipping away at natural selection while simultaneously taking care not to dissolve the idea of evolutionary change. Often, he fol-lows Shaler's example and challenges Darwin from an empirical perspec-tive. Poems such as "At Woodward's Gardens," "The White-Tailed Hornet," and "On a Bird Singing in its Sleep" read almost like scientific experiments, brief lessons in inductive observation whose conclusions typically differ from those in *On the Origin of Species* and *The Descent of Man.* Other poems chip away at Darwin's metaphor from a more metaphysical perspective. "West-Running Brook," "Directive," and "The Master Speed" demonstrate the human potential for discovering a supernatural reality by showing us how we might dissolve the concrete particulars that falsely partition what James and Bergson refer to as the "underlying" unity of experience. To-gether, these two salient features, imaginative transformation and concep-tual attack, form the general pattern of Frost's response to Darwin. Frost's objective is not to ridicule evolution but to contain it; not to deny the power and beauty of Darwin's original theories but to limit their effects upon cul-ture. Behind this pattern, and serving as its impelling force, is Frost's desire to rescue a small measure of hope that might save him from the emptiness of determinism.

Perhaps the most poignant demonstration of this pattern appears in "De-sign" (1922), Frost's best-known sonnet and the poem Lionel Trilling once cited as evidence of the oft-ignored darker elements that pervade Frost's work.[40] At first glance, the poem seems a synecdoche that suggests behind the intricate, delicate designs in nature lies a malevolent "designer." Here, as in many of his other poems that appropriate Darwinian motifs of com-petition and struggle, Frost ironically juxtaposes the poem's seemingly macabre events against symbolically "innocent" images so as to make the apparent designer of the universe appear even more diabolical than one might initially suppose:

> I found a dimpled spider, fat and white,
> On a white heal-all, holding up a moth
> Like a white piece of rigid satin cloth—
> Assorted characters of death and blight
> Mixed ready to begin the morning right,
> Like the ingredients of a witches' broth—
> A snow-drop spider, a flower like a froth,
> And dead wings carried like a paper kite.

(CPP&P, 275)

As Poirier, Brower, and Jarrell have astutely observed, the description of the spider, the wedding-dress satin of the moth, the glib reference to breakfast cereal advertising ("Mixed ready to begin the morning right"), the comparison of the dead wings to a child's toy, and the later comparison of the spider to a piece of candy (the snow-drop) combine with the light tone of the octet to reinforce the speaker's crescendoing fear that apparently random events may not be so random after all but predestined by a malevolent external force.[41] The small scene is a gross disruption of a harmonious cosmic order. The white elements of the poem (even the blue heal-all is an unnatural shade of white) emerge in the speaker's imagination as symbolic of something far more sinister than their innocent appearance initially signifies. Perhaps a directing deity has woven in violence as an integral part of the cosmos. Even more "appalling" to Frost is the starker possibility that no designer exists at all. Far from being preordained by divine providence, the relationship between the poem's organic creatures and their environment may have been determined only by the outcome of mindless, random processes in which the weakest organic beings (in this case the moth) fall prey to those better equipped by nature to survive in their environment.

Frost further heightens the poem's ironic tone by sustaining in the sestet the octet's stumbling meter, which corresponds to the speaker's confusion over what he has seen. Like a good nineteenth-century scientist, the speaker attempts to form conclusions based upon his observations. Unfortunately, he finds that answers will not easily formulate. He is left only with a series of questions, implicit in which are several disturbing assumptions about the deterministic character of the cosmos:

> What had the flower to do with being white,
> The wayside blue and innocent heal-all?
> What brought the kindred spider to that height,

Then steered the white moth thither in the night?
What but design of darkness to appall?—
If design govern in a thing so small.

(CPP&P, 275)

Unlike the scientist, the speaker refuses to infer from the given evidence any conclusions about the innate workings of natural forces he cannot see. The scene's effects, no matter how disturbing, cannot guarantee the validity of what he imagines to be their causes. Although some critics, Trilling included, have read the thirteenth line as a rhetorical question that affirms the presence of a dark designer, Frost renders such an easy reading improbable by an overt qualification in the final line of the poem. In this typical Frostian turn, signified by the last dash and by the accentual stress on "govern," Frost undercuts any assertions in the previous line and questions his ability to infer from design any definitive conclusions about the hidden structures of the universe. Frost will not commit the mistake of Ahab, whose ascription of evil to the white whale leads to his own destruction, nor will he corroborate the excesses of Emerson, who claimed to be delighted by the "choral harmony" of nature's designs. As the last line suggests, such excesses either way are merely anthropomorphic gestures that may or may not have any basis in reality. Darwin himself may have simply substituted one design for another. Lack of design, Frost suggests, is still a human construct that overturns a traditional belief that God intended the eyes for seeing, the heal-all for healing, and spiders for killing.

That Frost questions the relationship between mind and reality, and by implication the entire Darwinian metaphor, is further substantiated by his inversion of the internal structure of the sonnet. As anyone who has read an Elizabethan sonnet knows, one of the main features of the form is that it generally facilitates quick resolution. Most sonnet writers begin with an initial problem, usually some form of paradox, and then complicate it in the succeeding sections of the poem. Not until the volta—the sestet (or, in the case of the Elizabethan sonnet, the couplet)—does the writer resolve the problem. Rebuking tradition, Frost ends the poem with a clear statement of the problem itself. One wonders whether this lack of resolution is the flaw of a poet who has failed to come to grips with his subject, another example of what Yvor Winters called Frost's "teleological drifting," or the failure of the evidence at hand to provide the poet with definitive answers.

Given the immense difficulties of the problem, the latter interpretation seems more appropriate. To understand why Frost concluded his poem in this manner, we need to remember that before Darwin it had been almost inconceivable for anyone to attribute design to anything but an intelligent artificer presiding over the artifacts of his creation. Although John Locke and David Hume had been skeptical that designs in nature served as proof for God, nevertheless, finding no other alternative, they fell back upon the idea that all ordered matter was "designed" by a divine mind for a specific purpose.

In contrast, what Darwin offered the world was an argument for organic complexity without the aid of any preexisting mind.[42] Although patterned order existed as a real phenomenon in the natural world, Darwin suggested that all order, by way of natural selection, was essentially purposeless order. Clearly, Frost understood that it was this idea that provoked the most resistance and stirred the greatest emotions: if the intricate designs of biological organisms were merely the result of the mindless evolutionary forces, then how was it possible to exempt the products of mind from similar evolutionary explanations? Could it be that humans' own rationality, once thought to be a reflection of the divine mind, was merely an illusion? For many late-nineteenth-century intellectuals, this disturbing consequence was clearly what Darwin implied. Just as it had previously been inconceivable for anyone to attribute natural order to anything but God, in the late nineteenth century it became inconceivable for most materialists to attribute natural order to anything but mindless evolutionary forces. In T. H. Huxley's view, for example, the argument for God from design had "received its deathblow at Mr. Darwin's hands."[43]

In many ways Frost was inclined to agree with Huxley that the argument from design was dead, but he did so for philosophical rather than scientific reasons. As a budding skeptic, Frost began to question any theological conclusions based upon what he considered tenuous empirical evidence. Perhaps the genius behind "Design" lies in Frost's demonstration of how a creative psyche, freed from exterior deterministic constraints, can mold tradition to serve its own needs. Just as Emerson had once wholeheartedly believed that he could perceive in nature evidence of a benevolent designer, Frost suggests through his innovative form that it is also possible to believe in the inverse of that proposition. By flipping the internal "design" of the sonnet, Frost poetically mirrors a common cultural phenomenon: scientific forms, like poetic forms, change over time and emphasize different ideas. As Frost constructs his own version of the sonnet, he refuses to answer the question he asks at the end. He knows that "dark" design, benevolent design, and randomness may be derived only in relation to how well they satisfy one's individual need. William James, Frost's most important intellectual mentor, makes the same point in "The Sentiment of Rationality":

> [T]he essence, the ground of conception, varies with the end in view. A substance like oil has as many different essences as it has uses to different individuals. One man conceives it as combustible, another as a lubricator, another as food; the chemist thinks of it as hydro-carbon; the furniture-maker as a darkener of wood, the speculator as a commodity whose market price to-day is this and to-morrow that. The soap-boiler, the physicist, the clothes scourer severally ascribe to it other essences in relation to their needs.[44]

One might also suggest that for the transcendentalist nature is proof of God; for the scientist, proof of mindless forces; and for a poet who understands how knowledge is created, the occasion for metaphorical activity. As "Design" demonstrates, the wish influences the quality of the fact. Observation and interpretation, because of their constraining value-laden contexts, are not isomorphous with the structures of the physical world. The argument from design remains a blank cartridge, not because Darwin has said so but because cognitive experience, by its very nature, is prejudiced by a priori assumptions that impede our ability to interpret the natural world.

While many poems in the Frost canon attack science by challenging materialist epistemologies, others offer no redemption from the stark realities of Darwinian competition and waste. Minor poems such as "One Favored Acorn," "Blue-Butterfly Day," and "The Last Mowing" lament the transience of all living creatures and record life's fragility in scenes that often border on melodrama and sentimentality. In other poems, however, Frost's deft handling of evolution masks darker Darwinian implications in such a subtle manner that it is easy for inattentive readers to miss the point entirely. A good example of such deeply embedded meaning occurs in "The Pasture," a poem originally paired with "Good Hours" as a bookend in *North of Boston* and one of Frost's most frequently anthologized poems. Like *North of Boston*'s other well-known lyrics ("Mending Wall," "The Wood-Pile" and "Good Hours"), "The Pasture" masks several formidable Darwinian elements as it deceives us in its treatment of the natural world:

> I'm going out to clear the pasture spring;
> I'll only stop to rake the leaves away

(And wait to watch the water clear, I may):
I sha'n't be gone long.—You come too.

I'm going out to fetch the little calf
That's standing by the mother. It's so young,
It totters when she licks it with her tongue.
I sha'n't be gone long.—You come too.

(CPP&P, 3)

As Reuben Brower has noted, the tone of "The Pasture," "half-taunting and teasing," hints at "multiple intentions" and masks an underlying "serious-ness," which he also maintains keeps the tone from being "coy."[45] What informs that "seriousness," however, Brower never suggests. One possible explanation can be inferred by entertaining the reasons why the speaker and his companion need to venture into the pasture. Thompson, for example, has suggested that "The Pasture" is directed toward Elinor, Frost's wife, as an invitation to a sexual encounter. Still others see this lyric as a fine example of the caring, benevolent poet who seeks to protect his livestock from the bitterly cold nights of a harsh New England spring. Such optimistic interpretations, however, belie Frost's usual treatment of the natural world and do not consider the stuttering spondees at the end of each stanza, the underlying tone of seriousness that Brower noted, or the fact that Frost chose this poem, above all others, to begin his Pulitzer prize–winning Collected Poems. Surely the poem's sentimental invitation is not a sufficient reason to justify the poem's prominent position in such an important volume.

What, then, is Frost's rationale for placing the poem as the introduction to a body of work that so often centers on themes of isolation, fear, confusion, and apocalyptic extinction? One plausible explanation is that "The Pasture" perfectly announces that its author is aware of being caught in the transition between romantic and postromantic visions of the world, between the transcendental optimism of one and the post-Darwinian realism of the other. On the surface, the poem intends to entice a reluctant companion (as well as the reader) to join the speaker in what promises to be an enjoyable experience. That the work will take only a moment or two further suggests that the two participants will have time to enjoy each other's company and delight in the regenerative bounty of the natural world.

The lyric acquires more ominous significance, however, as soon as one considers the subtly disguised Darwinian elements that subvert the traditional pastoral motifs. The poem is not simply an invitation to communion and leisure; it is about a farmer who must complete the necessary and sometimes unpleasant annual rituals that will ensure his future survival. Anyone acquainted with the harsher realities of well-run farms will immediately recognize that one reason for the speaker's "going out to fetch the little calf" is not to protect the vulnerable offspring—that duty is amply fulfilled by the mother herself—but to separate the calf from its mother because it has not met the farmer's staunch criteria for successful husbandry. That the calf is so young further underscores the farmer's reluctance to intervene between mother and offspring. So young that it "totters" off balance beneath the mother, the calf is more fully vulnerable to the human threat. Rather than being naturally selected, it will be artificially selected by one who has no other alternative.

"The Pasture," then, is not so much a sentimental invitation to an audience schooled on the Fireside Poets as it is a brilliant example of how Frost rides the pastoral tradition into the twentieth century. Behind the poem's simple invitation lies a poem that yokes together images of renewal and decay (notice that the farmer, like the classical poets who cleansed Helicon, must clear away the rotten leaves from the spring), work and leisure, isolation and communion, invitation and reluctance, and, ultimately, romanticism and naturalism. By sustaining conflicting pastoral modes in an ongoing dialectic, Frost not only records his passage from the pre-Darwinian to the post-Darwinian world but also reveals himself as a mediator between the tender-minded nostalgia of the one and the tough-minded reality of the other. By placing this poem at the beginning of *Collected Poems*, Frost closes the gap between romantic and naturalistic excesses, which he perceives as a false dichotomy. Both tender-minded and tough-minded perceptions, he suggests, are simultaneously present in any moment of lived experience.

"To a Moth Seen in Winter" and "Pod of the Milkweed," written nearly forty years apart, extend the Darwinian "theme of wanton waste in peace and war" ("Pod in the Milkweed," *CPP&P*, 425) and speak to the severe lessons nature teaches us: the vulnerability of all living things, the transience of life, and the indifference of nature toward all individuals. Here, as in "Range-Finding," "Blue-Butterfly Day," "Unharvested," and "There Are Roughly Zones," the threat to Frost issues from "outer" weather, from the uncontrollable forces of nature, rather than from the "inner" weather of internal experiences, which the poet knows are potentially just as damaging.

"To a Moth Seen in Winter," written about 1900 but not published until 1942, exhibits threats also prevalent in "Once by the Pacific" and "The Demiurge's Laugh." Here, as in "Design," the supposed natural order of the cosmos is suddenly disrupted by the appearance of a white moth that has emerged far too late in the season to initiate a sexual union. In a gesture of sympathy, the speaker, recognizing in the moth's situation the inevitable destruction that he knows will follow, extends a "warm gloveless hand" as a resting place, a brief respite from the cold "wood" of other perches. He imagines that the moth has the capacity to respond, and when it does not, he attributes its refusal to its instinct-directed impulse to reproduce itself:

> And now pray tell what lured you with false hope
> To make the venture of eternity
> And seek the love of kind in wintertime?
> But stay and hear me out. I surely think
> You make a labor of flight for one so airy,
> Spending yourself too much in self-support.
>
> (*CPP&P*, 323)

Frost's stern attention to the detailed markings of the moth—"Bright-black-eyed, silvery creature, brushed with brown, / The wings not folded in repose, but spread"—further suggests that the moth's entire physical appearance has been modified by natural selection for the sole purpose of finding an appropriate mate.[46] Ironically, the "eternity" the moth seeks, whether in progeny or in something far greater, remains unattainable. The natural environment that produced this creature through natural selection now proves antagonistic and prevents the moth from attaining its biological goals. The speaker notices that something has gone terribly wrong. Even though there is no chance for successful reproduction, the moth's sexual instinct remains so powerful that it dictates all behavior and exhausts the moth's dedication to "self-support."

As the poem continues, the speaker personifies the moth more fully as the scene slowly reveals its meaning. He correctly notices the huge evolutionary distance between the moth's primitive reproductive drives and his own search for love, yet he begins to equate the two, linking himself closely to the moth's unfortunate fate. In pitying the moth, the poet actually begins to pity himself as he makes explicit the profound lesson he has learned:

> And what I pity in you is something human,
> The old incurable untimeliness,

Only begetter of all ills that are.
But go. You are right. My pity cannot help.
Go till you wet your pinions and are quenched.
You must be made more simply wise than I
To know the hand I stretch impulsively
Across the gulf of well nigh everything
May reach to you, but cannot touch your fate.
I cannot touch your life, much less can save
Who am tasked to save my own a little while.

(*CPP&P*, 323)

Despite the emotional address to a doomed creature, a tough-minded conclusion prevents the poem from descending into sentimentality. The physical and intellectual barriers that deny the speaker access to the moth are not unlike the barriers that thwart our efforts to save dying people. No matter how much one may yearn to save another in distress, or how much one would try to delay the inevitable outcome of life, the "gulf of well nigh everything" encloses the speaker in the reality that sympathy is no remedy for the "incurable untimeliness" of fate. As the speaker admits, he has learned from the moth that all life is unified by evolution, that nature is randomly wasteful and proliferate, and that its laws must be obeyed even though they threaten an individual existence.

While "To a Moth Seen in Winter" displays a Darwinian emphasis upon sexual selection that ultimately fails, "Pod of the Milkweed" (1954) explores the fate of individuals in an equally ironic setting in which sexual activity comes to fruition. Like other Frost poems that announce the infancy of decay at the height of spring or midsummer ("The Oven Bird," "Hyla Brook," "Nothing Gold Can Stay"), this poem juxtaposes vitality and waste in a reciprocal arrangement that suggests that both are necessary for life to continue. Fruition and regeneration, Frost observes, can occur only at great organic expense to those who struggle combatively for the limited resources available. Even though it lacks the butterflies' brightly colored regalia, the drably colored milkweed succeeds in attracting pollinators. In order to compensate for its dull appearance, the milkweed, as the narrator notices, has relied upon another adaptation, its sweet nectar, to attract hundreds of swarming butterflies. As Robert Faggen has aptly demonstrated, the milkweed flower, instead of promising a land of "milk and honey," lures the butterflies for its own reproductive purposes.[47]

The countless wings that from the infinite
Make such a noiseless tumult over it
Do no doubt with their color compensate
For what the drab weed lacks of the ornate.
For drab its fondest must admit.
And yes, although it is a flower that flows
With milk and honey, it is bitter milk,
As anyone who ever broke its stem
And dared to taste the wound a little knows.

(CPP&P, 425)

The "wound" the speaker feels so acutely derives from his recognition that nature has not equipped the butterflies with enough safeguards to protect them from the harsh environment. Unlike the bees, the butterflies "have no hives." His retreat feels like an insufficient response and cannot repel the "theme of waste" that reaches right to his "doorstep." The speaker knows that the butterflies, and perhaps even he, will exist only as long as it takes to reproduce another generation.

Frost further discloses his indebtedness to Darwin by transforming these delicate, ephemeral creatures into fierce, combative enemies. As Darwin makes abundantly clear in *On the Origin of Species,* the quest for food, like the instinctive drive to reproduce, guarantees survival only to those individuals adaptively equipped for such difficult conflict. Darwin reinforces this idea in *The Descent of Man,* where he records others' observations of how even the butterfly, traditionally a symbol for frailty, has an innate capacity for struggle and competition: "Although butterflies are such weak and fragile creatures, they are pugnacious, and an Emperor butterfly has been captured with the tips of its wings broken off from a conflict with another male. Mr. Collingwood in speaking of the frequent battles between the butterflies of Borneo says, 'They whirl round each other with the greatest rapidity, and appear to be incited by the greatest ferocity.'"[48] The battle motif is extended even further as equally matched combatants lengthen the struggle's duration:

Its flowers' distilled honey is so sweet
It makes the butterflies intemperate.
There is no slumber in its juice for them.
One knocks another off from where he clings.
They knock the dyestuff off each others' wings—

> With thirst on hunger to the point of lust.
> They raise in their intemperance a cloud
> Of mingled butterfly and flower dust
> That hangs perceptibly above the scene.
>
> (*CPP&P*, 425)

Clearly, Frost has read his Darwin well. Anthropomorphized to epic proportions, these individuals fight for no altruistic purpose; they lock themselves in an enduring struggle only to ensure the transmission of their own genetic material. Unlike human soldiers, they lose all of their identifying regalia to the point of an absurd equivalence. Only the milkweed takes on an air of superior adaptive ability. In being "sweet to ephemerals," it has unconsciously managed "to contrive" one day "too sweet for beings to survive." The flower's opulent bounty, while providing sustenance for the many, also increases its destructive capability.

In the poem's final section, the speaker attempts to rationalize the outcome of such wanton waste. Like the speaker of "Design" and "For Once, Then, Something," he refuses to form a definitive conclusion about what purposes may lie behind such violence. Waste remains the "essence of the scheme," since, after the destruction of so many struggling individuals, the outcome is a single instance of reproductive success:

> But waste was of the essence of the scheme.
> And all the good they did for man or god
> To all those flowers they passionately trod
> Was leave as their posterity one pod
> With an inheritance of restless dream.
>
> (*CPP&P*, 426)

The ambiguity of the word "pod," signifying either a chrysalis or a seed pod, further emphasizes how only one of the species involved in this drama has managed to reproduce. Although the milkweed appears to have had the evolutionary advantage up to this point, Frost suggests through the deliberate ambiguity of the word "pod" that superior adaptation is no guarantee for reproductive success.

What disturbs the speaker most, however, is the message that the single pod, fully poised with the potential for new life, reveals to him: "He seems to say the reason why so much / should come to nothing must be fairly faced." Perhaps more esoteric than they should be, these final lines, along with the coda, "And shall be in due course," fuse potential life and impending death into a larger cyclical process. Together the lines signify not only the absurd "waste" that will perpetuate itself with each ensuing life but also the speaker's hope that he will find some answers to the purpose of such competition. Neither conclusion, however, is wholly acceptable. As the somber tone of the ending announces, sustained mystery and stoic acceptance of wasteful evolutionary competition hardly seem satisfying solutions to the dilemma he has confronted. He yearns for more knowledge and can only hope that eventually his questions will be answered by someone—perhaps a scientist, poet, or god—who can justify the waste he has witnessed.

The delicate and complicated "Spring Pools" (1927), the opening poem in *West-Running Brook,* also reveals how Frost is sometimes helpless to offset the powerful spell of Darwin's metaphor. One of Frost's finest marriages of content and form, "Spring Pools," like the much-celebrated "Nothing Gold Can Stay," is a lamentation for all living things that inevitably succumb to seasonal process. It is also a historical chronicle that records the collapse of Platonic idealism, for whose stable certainties and enduring beauty the poet nostalgically yearns:

> These pools that, though in forests, still reflect
> The total sky almost without defect,
> And like the flowers beside them, chill and shiver,
> Will like the flowers beside them soon be gone,
> And yet not out by any brook or river,
> But up by roots to bring dark foliage on.
>
> (*CPP&P,* 224)

These delicate flowers and pools reveal not only a change in the speaker's mood but also changes in the larger intellectual currents of history that have given rise to modern consciousness. This poem also employs several different aesthetic principles, reflecting the various innovations of different schools of art, which, as Frost clearly demonstrates, have also responded to the same shifts in philosophical paradigms.

The first two lines locate consciousness in the realm of Platonic idealism. Each particular in the pool imperfectly copies a "sky almost without defect." In the subsequent lines, however, Frost transforms the glassy surface of the pool, which emphasizes classicism's strict demarcation between color and form, into an image infused with energy, motion, and instability. Anthropomorphized to the point that they fearfully "chill and shiver," the pools portend the stark Darwinian realities of events to come even as they embody the nineteenth century's romantic predisposition to view nature as directed process and continual flux. That the flowers and pools eventually merge into one another in a gesture reminiscent of a French impressionist painting—"flowery waters and . . . watery flowers"—further suggests just how far human consciousness has distanced itself from belief in the eternal reality of immutable abstract structures as well as in the artist's ability to capture "essences" precisely.

In the closing lines of the first sestet, the speaker suddenly realizes that these beautiful spring pools in perpetual flux have not been directed toward any purpose. They are swept away by neither "brook or river," but by the menacing trees, whose "pent-up" buds absorb the flowers' life-giving water. More powerfully enduring and better suited to their immediate environment, the foliating trees "darken" nature:

> The trees that have it in their pent-up buds
> To darken nature and be summer woods—
> Let them think twice before they use their powers
> To blot out and drink up and sweep away
> These flowery waters and these watery flowers
> From snow that melted only yesterday.

(*CPP&P*, 224)

As the loss of beauty mirrors the profound loss of the speaker's psychological security, his only recourse in such a desolate moment is to implore the trees to "think twice" and "reflect" upon their "powers" even though he knows they are incapable of any saving consciousness. Like the Oven Bird, to whom midsummer foretells inevitable waste and decay instead of fecundity, the speaker asks himself "what to make of a diminished thing" and, finding no available answer, can only yearn for a renewed promise of potential in "snow that melted only yesterday." In his dialogue with nature the speaker understands that nature simply cannot answer.

Together, "To a Moth Seen in Winter" and "Pod of the Milkweed" display how often Frost is paralyzed by an imagination copiously informed by Darwin. Neither poem reflects the poet's usual resolve to overcome his fear of annihilation by seeking out the loving support of community and family. Instead the poems' pervasive loneliness and violence cripple his ability to defeat external threats by transforming them through the saving acts of imagination. When Lionel Trilling labeled Frost one of the "darkest" American poets, he could have easily validated his assessment by citing any one of these "Darwinian" poems, as well as others such as "Bereft" and "Desert Places," which do not allude to Darwin at all.

Yet if Frost was one of our "darkest" poets, he was also a restless artist who never remained content to wallow in despair. Like Dante, when Frost found himself "astray" and "alone in a dark wood," he searched for a beacon to guide him toward more hopeful prospects. One of the poet's most resourceful means of finding a way out of this dark Darwinian wood was to challenge the theory of evolution with poems that argued conclusions very different from those in any of Darwin's major books. Nowhere is this challenge more evident than in *A Further Range* (1936), a collection teeming with anti-Darwinian poems and, as Poirier and Pritchard have noticed, the volume that occasioned the sharpest attacks from the political left of the 1930s.[49] Given Frost's proclivity to reject any system that suppressed autonomous creative activity, it is not surprising that he included in this volume both antisocialist and antiscientific poems as a demonstration of how the imagination can be thwarted by intellectual systems of several kinds. The titles of the individual poems immediately suggest that Frost had established a kinship between Roosevelt's New Deal politics and Darwinian evolution, finding in the former an ascending cultural metaphor that might dominate political thought as the latter had previously dominated scientific thought. By exposing the controversies associated with some of Darwin's more questionable ideas, Frost could also reveal the political flaws he perceived, sometimes naively, in contemporary socialist manifestos.

One of the subtitles for the volume, "Taken Doubly," intends to show how each poem in the volume might be "doubly" applicable to scientific and political systems. Both disciplines, Frost suggests, have conspired to thwart native intelligence and creative genius. One does not have to look hard to notice that poems such as "Design," "The White-Tailed Hornet," "A Blue Ribbon at Amesbury," "A Drumlin Woodchuck," and "There Are Roughly Zones" complement political poems such as "The Lone Striker," "Departmental," "Provide, Provide," "Not Quite Social," and "Build Soil." While Poirier has suggested that Frost's greatest intellectual weakness was his lack of historical awareness and his "insensitivity to the way social systems . . . can take on the appearance and force of nature,"[50] it seems to me that Frost's historical awareness was far keener than Poirier concedes. By placing political and Darwinian poems side by side, Frost suggests that Marxism and socialism, like natural selection, derive from an outdated form of nineteenth-century materialism and, as such, stand on tenuous philosophical ground. The book also suggests that adherence to dominating systems of thought during a period of rapid intellectual change can be a dangerous enterprise. All systems of thought, Frost suggests, be they political, scientific, or economic, can be revised by anyone who has enough historical perspective and imaginative courage to dispute culturally dominating ideas. "We are all toadies to the fashionable metaphor of the hour," Frost wrote in 1936. "Great is he who imposes the metaphor."[51] To Frost, who thought that human dignity was best preserved in an atmosphere of intellectual freedom, one of the poet's most sacred obligations was to challenge dominating systems of thought and offer the world a fresh perspective on life.

Two poems in particular from this volume succeed in disrupting some of Darwin's more controversial metaphors. More empirically based than some of Frost's other responses, "At Woodward's Gardens" and "The White-Tailed Hornet" employ single dramatic events to challenge Darwin's famous assertion in *The Descent of Man* that human beings and animals are closely linked on the evolutionary tree and "differ only in degree and not in kind." Darwin's major motive in writing this book was to defend natural selection by demonstrating that even human speciation was the natural outcome of evolution. Marshaling ample evidence to demonstrate the close kinship between human beings and lower primates, Darwin hoped to convince his skeptical Victorian audience that human beings were not immune to the laws of natural selection.

Although perhaps overly didactic, "At Woodward's Gardens" (1936) remains one of Frost's most straightforward challenges to this premise as well as to Darwin's ancillary assertion that man's moral sense develops naturally in response to his superior intellectual capacities. A dramatic narrative, "At Woodward's Gardens" chronicles the actions of a mischievous boy who, "presuming on" his own "intellect," conducts a "scientific" experiment on two monkeys housed in a local zoo. Though the boy already knows what the outcome will be, he attempts to "teach" the monkeys about the significance of the magnifying glass he carries with him. "Words are no good," so he employs an alternative method in his efforts to make the apes understand:

> But let him show them how the weapon worked.
> He made the sun a pin-point on the nose
> Of first one, then the other till it brought
> A look of puzzled dimness to their eyes
> That blinking could not seem to blink away.
> They stood arms laced together at the bars,

And exchanged troubled glances over life.
One put a thoughtful hand up to his nose
As if reminded—or as if perhaps
Within a million years of an idea.
He got his purple little knuckles stung.

(*CPP&P*, 267)

The attenuated cruelty in these carefully wrought lines questions Darwin's assertion that "morality is the most noble of all the attributes of man" and clearly reveals Frost's skepticism about humans' ability to find in animals a corresponding native intelligence. Rather than seeing intellectual equivalence between monkeys and humans, Frost finds a gap in intellectual ability so large that it would take nearly "a million years" for the monkeys to bridge it. Socialization, memory, language, and reinforced habit, Darwin's preconditions for morality to exist, appear in this poem to be of no help at all to either the monkeys, who can never "be made to understand," or the small boy, whose superior intelligence has provoked cruelty rather than sympathy toward a "fellow creature."[52]

Even more telling than the moral issues in this poem is Frost's appropriation of Bergson's controversial distinction between intelligence and instinct. As a means of dispelling the more disturbing elements of Darwin's mechanistic evolutionary model, Bergson proposed in *Creative Evolution* the existence of the *élan vital*, the spontaneous life force that impels all living things toward greater complexity. What distinguishes the *élan vital* from natural selection is Bergson's idea that evolution proceeds, not in a linear manner, as Darwin intimated in *The Descent of Man*, but through the divergence of the universe's creative impulse into separate lines of specialized adaptation. To prove these divergences, Bergson cites instinct and intelligence as two forms of separate adaptation that have been remarkably successful.[53] The first, which manifests itself most clearly in insects, Bergson defines as knowledge of matter. Instinct, he claims, is a bodily function, a "natural ability to use an inborn mechanism," that benefits the organism without the aid of an intervening consciousness. The second, which manifests itself in vertebrates, Bergson defines as a knowledge of a form. In contrast to instinct, intelligence is the human ability to manufacture useful instruments out of unorganized inanimate matter. According to Bergson, instinct and intelligence have their own advantages and disadvantages. Whereas intelligence can extend creative ability to an unlimited number of ingenious beneficial instruments, it is inferior to instinct in the sense that it cannot ascertain the "whole of life." The process of rationality actually distances intellect from the creative vital force that has given rise to it. On the other hand, instinct is inferior to the intellect because it is limited in function and can satisfy only the immediate needs of the organism. Those species that rely solely on instinct have no specialized creative capacity to extend instinct beyond its naturally designated function. In Bergson's framework, instinct and intelligence each lack the benefits of the other. Although an autonomous intellect can propel the imagination toward greater and more ingenious instrumental forms, it has difficulty comprehending the *élan vital*, which is more accessible through instinct. Only through intuition, a specialized adaptation of our own highly developed instincts, can we begin to comprehend a spiritual reality that continually expresses itself through matter.

That "At Woodward's Gardens" mediates between Bergson's ideas and the poet's observed experience becomes evident in the second half of the poem, where the monkeys display their innate curiosity and "snatch" the magnifying glass away from the small boy who has wandered too close to the cage. As soon as the monkeys own the glass, they begin conducting their own instinct-based "experiments":

> Precipitately they retired back cage
> And instituted an investigation
> On their part, though without the needed insight.
> They bit the glass and listened for the flavor.
> They broke the handle and the binding off it.
> Then none the wiser, frankly gave it up,
> And having hid it in their bedding straw
> Against the day of prisoners' ennui,
> Came dryly forward to the bars again
> To answer for themselves: Who said it mattered
> What monkeys did or didn't understand?
>
> (*CPP&P*, 267)

Here the reader is implicitly invited to assume, along with the narrator, that autonomous creative capacity is simultaneously a benefit and a detriment. The monkeys have no rational ability to synthesize the object's meaning into anything more than what instinct has already provided them: they test it as a source of food and finally use it as part of their "bedding straw." Because the monkeys cannot derive any intellectual significance from the glass, they cannot use it, as the boy has used it, as a tool of torment. Cruelty, Frost suggests, emerges not from natural instinct but rather from an intellect that has not developed a corresponding ethic to harness the power that knowledge may confer. The poem's final line, "It's knowing what to do with things that counts," not only reveals the gulf between human and animal consciousness but also serves as a commentary on humans' potential for cruelty in all scientific endeavors.[54] Humans' intellectual constructs, Frost suggests, can be ethical only when a corresponding moral awareness can more fully guide knowledge toward appropriate ends. The future happiness of man may in fact depend upon the further development of his intuitive faculties. As Bergson suggests, and as Frost intimates in this poem, humans' instinct can be located on an "indistinct fringe" of consciousness and, as such, can "recall its origins" and reattach itself to the "whole of life."[55]

While Frost's distinction between instinct and intelligence may appear in "At Woodward's Gardens" to be something of his final word on the subject, Frost often contradicts himself, explores a number of variations upon a single theme, and eventually questions the conclusions he has drawn in other poems. "The White-Tailed Hornet" (1936), a companion piece to "At Woodward's Gardens," is one such poem that not only calls into doubt the distinction between instinct and intelligence that Bergson and the entomologist Jean Henri Fabre adamantly defend but also challenges the scientific epistemology that has given rise to such questionable anti-Darwinian conclusions. In this poem, Frost uses Bergson's approach to knowledge as a way of challenging Bergson himself. And while there are times when Frost feels sure that Bergson and Fabre are right about the issue, he also perceives a greater melding between instinct and intelligence than Bergson is ever willing to concede.

The poem's first section extends the theme in "On A Bird's Singing in its Sleep" that instinct, courage, and native intelligence naturally provide individuals with some adequate measure of protection against external threats. Locating the initial action in the hornet's domain, Frost describes the insect in vividly mechanistic terms. The hornet's exit is "like a gun," while the hornet, who has the "power to change his aim in flight," "comes out more unerring than a bullet." So capable is the hornet of defending its own territory that the poet surmises that he could write "verses" about the infallibility of such well-honed instincts. Indeed, not only does the hornet seem well suited for combat, it appears capable of attacking the narrator where he is particularly vulnerable:

> Verse could be written on the certainty
> With which he penetrates by best defense
> Of whirling hands and arms about the head
> To stab me in the sneeze-nerve of a nostril.
> Such is the instinct of it I allow.
>
> (*CPP&P*, 253)

The playfully mocking tone of these lines indicates that the speaker does not feel threatened by the peculiar behavioral habits that so clearly differentiate the hornet's cognitive ability from his own. The easy assurance of the opening lines deteriorates, however, as soon as this visitor begins to recognize similarities between himself and the hornet. Like Fabre, whose own experiments with wasps proved conclusively to him that "instinct knows everything, in the undeviating paths marked out for it; it knows nothing outside those paths,"[56] the speaker begins to surmise that error, rather than being a fault of instinct, actually depends upon a level of intelligence beyond blind mechanism. Error, he assumes, can only exist when rationality sanctions an improper choice.

This possibility becomes prevalent in the poem's second section, where the sudden change in environment confuses both the hornet and speaker. To the speaker, the hornet, "hawking" for flies about the kitchen, appears in this domestic realm to be "at his best."[57] Yet even here the speaker cannot decide whether the wasp's actions can be attributed to slight deviations in instinct or to an intelligence that has not prepared the insect adequately for survival. In spite of the speaker's ineffectual warnings, the hornet cannot possibly comprehend its egregious mistakes:

> I watched him where he swooped, he pounced, he struck;
> But what he found he had was just a nailhead.
> He struck a second time. Another nailhead.
> 'Those are just nailheads. Those are fastened down.'
> Then disconcerted and not unannoyed,
> He stooped and struck a little huckleberry
> The way a player curls around a football.
> 'Wrong shape, wrong color, and wrong scent,' I said.
> The huckleberry rolled him on his head.
>
> (*CPP&P*, 253–54)

At last, when the hornet succeeds in attacking an actual fly, the narrator begins to make comparisons, this time suggesting that except "for the

fly," the hornet, like the poet, might have been capable of creating metaphors. By making this comparison, Frost questions the hornet's capacity
for thought and suggests that our own metaphor-making capacity may
have evolved in response to our own previous failures to acquire food.
Poetry, like the wasp's poor hunting ability, may be just another ineffective
instinct, a specialized adaptation that proves useless in a Darwinian world
of competition.

The third section of the poem calls even this interpretation into doubt
and supposes that any conclusion derived from the given observations
depends upon the relative perspective from which one makes the comparison. As the two previous sections reveal, the hornet's domain and the narrator's correspond to different subjective states that affect the quality and
kind of comparisons being made. In the first section, a "downward" comparison situates the hornet firmly within the instinct-driven realm of animals; in the second section, an "upward" comparison situates the hornet
more firmly within the realm of human intelligence. The speaker's recognition that his own subjectivity has influenced the quality of his conclusions makes him doubt the authority of the theoretical "certainties" that
have led him to the problem in the first place:

> Won't this whole instinct matter bear revision?
> Won't almost any theory bear revision?
> To err is human, not to, animal.
> Or so we pay the compliment to instinct,
> Only too liberal of our compliment
> That really takes away instead of gives.
> Our worship, humor, conscientiousness
> Went long since to the dogs under the table.
> And served us right for having instituted
> Downward comparisons. As long on earth
> As our comparisons were stoutly upward
> With gods and angels, we were men at least,
> But little lower than the gods and angels.

> (CPP&P, 254)

The subsequent "disillusion upon disillusion" that results from our having made too many "downward" comparisons can be attributed, as these
lines imply, to such cultural revolutionaries as Darwin, Freud, and Pavlov,
who successfully overthrew existing theories simply by inverting them. As
the speaker has amply demonstrated by his own example, any theory can

be "revised" if one has the courage and the insight to approach the problem from a different point of view. The poem, then, is not so much a defense of human potential against deterministic biology as it is a germane commentary on our inability to comprehend fully even the simplest of our everyday observations. Our metaphorical constructions simply will not give us complete access to the answers that we most often seek, and the supposed truths our constructs offer can be exposed as elaborate fictions. That a playful skepticism is the poem's central issue becomes clearer in the final lines, where Frost ironically parodies his skepticism: "Nothing but fallibility was left us, / And this day's work made even that seem doubtful" (*CPP&P*, 254). Such comprehensive doubt so playfully wrought would clearly have met the approval of Nietzsche, who had earlier proclaimed that scientific conclusions were merely special cases of anthropomorphic error.[58]

The pervasive skepticism that informs "The White-Tailed Hornet" forces us to examine how we can find, in the face of cognitive "fallibility," some stable redemptive structure to offset the disillusionment fostered by Darwinism. As "The White-Tailed Hornet" and other related poems indicate, Frost considered the creation of cognitive structures both a blessing and a curse, a means of erecting psychological boundaries that protected us from the external world and, paradoxically, a barrier that denied us access to the deeper realities of divine purpose. One way to overcome the loss of metaphysical certainty was to participate in what was perhaps the strangest of all paradoxes: to deconstruct the very cognitive structures one had erected. That Frost might attain a greater redemptive stability by destabilizing convention may seem like a glaring contradiction, yet this contradiction continually guides Frost out of the dark Darwinian wood. By abandoning his desire for truth, Frost poetically attempted to reattach an intuitive consciousness to a spiritual reality far more profound than intelligence could comprehend. He would not have his thought entirely systematic; instead he would trust the instinct of a bard.

Although not Darwinian in a strict sense, three of Frost's most well known poems—"Hyla Brook" (1923), "West-Running Brook" (1930), and "Directive" (1946)—challenge the legacy of scientific mechanism by devaluing the authority of scientific premises. More metaphysically oriented than any of Frost's other quasi-"scientific" empirical challenges, each of these poems is laden with images of water, most often a "brook," which serves as a metaphor for a spiritual continuum that cannot be explained or contained by rational thought. Just as Bergson often employed music as a metaphor to demonstrate how a total listening experience could blur the sharp distinctions between individual notes, Frost sometimes employs the image of the brook to subordinate under a primordial spiritual reality all explanatory concepts that have been projected onto it.[59] Each of these poems, in one form or another, asserts that the brook will continue to flow beyond our conscious scrutiny of it.

"Hyla Brook" remains one of Frost's clearest demonstrations of this belief. Situated next to "The Oven Bird" in *Mountain Interval,* this sonnet answers the conundrum of the Oven Bird, who asks "what to make of a diminished thing." Viewed as a source of spiritual energy, the brook, perhaps also a metaphor for the act of writing of a poem, exhausts itself in an array of creative processes:

> By June our brook's run out of song and speed.
> Sought for much after that, it will be found
> Either to have gone groping underground
> (And taken with it all the Hyla breed
> That shouted in the mist a month ago,
> Like ghost of sleigh-bells in a ghost of snow)—
> Or flourished and come up in jewel-weed,
> Weak foliage that is blown upon and bent.
> Even against the way its waters went.
> Its bed is left a faded paper sheet
> Of dead leaves stuck together by the heat—
>
> (*CPP&P,* 115–16)

Although the brook has literally disappeared, one can find it again if one is willing to accept the proposition that the brook survives in sustained moments of imaginative reverie, where all of the particulars of transience can be subordinated to an abstract permanence of continual change. Viewed in this Heraclitean manner, the brook never disappears; it merely diverts its creative powers toward other natural objects. As the brook takes the spring peepers underground, its waters simultaneously renew the life of the jewel-weed. Even the "faded paper sheet," an image suggesting that the book of nature is finally illegible, can be appreciated within the larger context of the natural cycle. Only an imaginative process that dissolves the temporal and transitory and fuses the past, present, and future into a single undivided unity can redeem diminishment:

> A brook to none but who remember long.
> This as it will be seen is other far

> Than with brooks taken otherwhere in song.
> We love the things we love for what they are.
>
> (*CPP&P*, 116)

Perhaps, as Frost also proposes, changing subjective states correspond to, and even participate in, the evolutionary forces affecting matter. In "Hyla Brook" the poet's consciousness mirrors the creative power of the brook.[60] Past, present, and future are simultaneously present in any given moment of consciousness, as memory and desire each flow easily into the other to form the perceptions of the present moment. Even love, Frost suggests, follows this pattern of continuous organic development. "We love the things we love for what they are," because we love them for what they have been and for what we anticipate they will eventually become. Although the actual brook, jewel-weed, or physical self must eventually succumb to change and natural decay, the creative force that impels that process, as well as consciousness and love, will exist forever. In the face of diminishment and self-extinction, we can alleviate our fear by opening ourselves up to the intuitive proposition that we take part in an eternal, spiritual reality that cannot be understood solely by rational thought.

If "Hyla Brook" transforms the world of competition and decay by invoking the aid of a redemptive memory, then "West-Running Brook," one of Frost's most celebrated poems of marriage, depends upon a loving reconciliation of opposed subjectivities to generate redemption. Here, as in "Two Look at Two," a loving couple walking in the countryside try to establish a relationship to the wilderness that will be as comforting and as meaningful to them as their relationship to each other. Frost's woman, the Eve figure of the poem, first seeks to understand the mystery of why the brook runs west when "all the other country brooks flow east." To help her solve her dilemma, her husband promptly recommends that she name the brook, which she does, and with lasting ironic consequences: men will call it West-Running Brook forever. The act of naming or taming the wilderness does not satisfy her curiosity, however. She wonders about the meaning of the brook and how her life fits into the context of a larger natural order. In the absence of any definite answers, however, her only recourse is to anthropomorphize the brook. She suggests to her husband that they surrender their separate identities to it. By doing so, they begin to humanize nature and therefore naturalize themselves:

> We've said we two. Let's change that to we three.
> As you and I are married to each other,

> We'll both be married to the brook. We'll build
> Our bridge across it, and the bridge shall be
> Our arm thrown over it asleep beside it.
>
> (CPP&P, 236)

Unfortunately the woman's suggestion does not seem at all satisfying to her husband. When she argues that the brook has endorsed her solution by "waving" back to them, the husband dismisses her idea as a projection of her own feminine subjectivity. Surprisingly, the wife, who has trusted her husband "to go by contraries," is not offended by his assertion. Secure in her own "feminine" position, she actually provokes from him a counter-response, which is as compelling as anything in Frost's poetry. Claiming that they have not evolved from any "creature," the husband asserts that their true origin lies in a creative life force that throws itself back and continually resists the onslaught of entropy. The brook, he claims,

> flows between us
> To separate us for a panic moment.
> It flows between us, over us, and *with* us.
> And it is time, strength, tone, light, life, and love—
> And even substance lapsing unsubstantial;
> The universal cataract of death
> That spends to nothingness—and unresisted,
> Save by some strange resistance in itself,
> Not just a swerving, but a throwing back,
> As if regret were in it and were sacred.
>
> (CPP&P, 237–38)

The Bergsonian and Lucretian impulses in this section unite joy and sadness, life and death, resistance and acceptance, purpose and accident, truth and fantasy into a single moment of lived experience that is bound by the desire for love and reconciliation. The delicate chiasmus in the final lines of the husband's response balances perfectly the counterforces of destruction and renewal that he has perceived in both nature and in their differing points of view:

> Our life runs down in sending up the clock.
> The brook runs down in sending up our life.
> The sun runs down in sending up the brook.
> And there is something sending up the sun.
>
> (CPP&P, 238)

The husband cannot describe the elusive something sending up the sun, any more than he can describe the "void" into which all life will expend itself. The limits of cognitive perception simply will not allow him to answer the question that his wife initially proposes. Despite his greater "scientific" knowledge of natural processes, he arrives at the point of their initial departure. He cannot solve or explain the mystery of an underlying creative reality. Their inquisitive moments have not been wasted, however, for in spite of their failed efforts to understand their ultimate relationship to the natural world, they have succeeded in further understanding each other and themselves. They recognize that each of them has paid the same tribute to the source, and this moment of reconciliation rewards them with the peaceful stasis that closes the poem. Neither nature nor the man or woman has gained the upper hand, and for the moment the threat of entropy and misunderstanding has been temporarily repelled by a delicate synthesis of opposites.

If "West-Running Brook" ameliorates the consequences of natural decay by acknowledging the existence of a renewing counterforce, then the most important instructions on how best to overcome the vast forces of history and physical decay are clearly supplied in "Directive," the most important poem of Frost's later career and the one that clearly aligns Frost conceptually to the later poetry of T. S. Eliot. As in Eliot's "Little Gidding," spiritual renewal and wholeness can be attained only when one is willing first to confront physical decay and then, paradoxically, to move beyond it. That our quest for spiritual renewal must first be conditioned by an accompanying loss of conventions is evident in the first "directive" of the poem, which playfully "backs" us out of the present and into a past that will become a proving ground for the future:

> Back out of all this now too much for us,
> Back in a time made simple by the loss
> Of detail, burned, dissolved, and broken off
> Like graveyard marble sculpture in the weather,
> There is a house that is no more a house
> Upon a farm that is no more a farm
> And in a town that is no more a town.

> (*CPP&P*, 341)

If knowledge itself has become the source of distress in our lives, the "too much for us" that we can no longer bear, then the prescription for that ill is to abandon our impulse to divide the world into arbitrary particulars that ossify into convention. Withdrawing from the world of present confusion will not be easy, however, for along the road to childhood simplicity one will inevitably be barraged with images of desertion and destruction. The poet-guide, who only has at heart our "getting lost," promises a salvation, but only if one is willing to accept the stark realities of an ephemeral existence and relinquish the desire to subdue the eroding qualities of time:

> The ledges show lines ruled southeast northwest,
> The chisel work of an enormous Glacier
> That braced his feet against the Arctic Pole.
> You must not mind a certain coolness from him
> Still said to haunt this side of Panther Mountain.
>
> (*CPP&P*, 341)

Vestiges of the Ice Age linger to create a sense of doubt and fear; human time, in comparison with geological time, is largely insignificant, yet the wear of "iron wagon wheels" suggests that others too have braved alien entanglements in an effort to find a promised land. In moments of greatest distress, when one feels most vulnerable to the elements, a vision of labor and community can offer some protection:

> Make yourself up a cheering song of how
> Someone's road home from work this once was,
> Who may be just ahead of you on foot
> Or creaking with a buggy load of grain.
>
> (*CPP&P*, 341)

Such nostalgic, imaginative gestures offer only a temporary respite from isolation. At the end of the "ladder road" the self must also deny an imaginative communion with those who can appease anguish. The end of the quest is "CLOSED" (*CPP&P*, 341) to all but the isolated individual who must confront an impending sense of mortality and the teleological end of all desire. That end, for both the physical body and the imagination, is of course the brook, the sacred water of an underlying unity that only the courageous can glimpse:

> Your destination and your destiny's
> A brook that was the water of the house
> Cold as a spring as yet so near its source,
> Too lofty and original to rage.
>
> (*CPP&P*, 342)

Volitional destination and biological destiny ironically end in the same place. As an attentive student of Dante, however, Frost will never let us achieve complete union with the source of the brook. Mortal consciousness, which separates us from whatever spiritual reality might exist, intervenes to keep the mystery and the journey intact. Yet one can travel far enough to know that beyond the grail we drink from lies a source so pure and lofty that it can never "rage." As in Eliot's *Four Quartets,* a final peace will endure for those willing to abandon desire and open themselves to the possibility of further loss.

The question of Frost's religious faith, perhaps nowhere better expressed than in "Accidentally on Purpose" (1960), makes an appropriate coda to this discussion of Frost's response to Darwin. Published in *In the Clearing* when Frost was eighty-eight years old, "Accidentally on Purpose" is interesting and important because it remains Frost's final word on his long struggle with evolution. Remarkably, as the title implies, Frost synthesizes in a single lyric the most important intellectual conflicts surrounding evolution. In this poem, accident and purpose, design and chaos, instinct and intelligence, art and science are juxtaposed in a manner that exposes the intrinsic value of each. In the opening stanza Frost acknowledges the existence of a tangible world that can serve as a material resource for metaphorical activity. As Lucretius himself might have suggested,

> The Universe is but the Thing of things,
> The things but balls all going round in rings.
> Some of them mighty huge, some mighty tiny,
> All of them radiant and mighty shiny.

> (*CPP&P,* 438)

This first stanza accomplishes poetically what Einstein could not do mathematically; Frost has fused the microcosm with the macrocosm by subordinating each particular to a larger containing boundary, which he alternately capitalizes as "Universe," "Thing," or "Omnibus."

Each particular remains equally precious, and in the face of such austere material splendor Frost cannot accept the Darwinian idea that the perceived universe can be attributed to mere accident. Darwin, he asserts, merely imposed upon natural processes an explanation that he pretentiously presumed to be absolutely true. But just as the "Universe" contains material objects, it also contains ideas:

> They mean to tell us all was rolling blind
> Till accidentally it hit on mind
> In an albino monkey in a jungle
> And even then it had to grope and bungle,
>
> Till Darwin came to earth upon a year
> To show the evolution how to steer.
> They mean to tell us, though, the Omnibus
> Had no real purpose till it got to us.
>
> Never believe it. At the very worst
> It must have had the purpose from the first
> To produce purpose as the fitter bred:
> We were just purpose coming to a head.
>
> (*CPP&P*, 438)

Frost's bald assertion that Darwin could not possibly hope to "steer" evolution is an article of faith. That fact becomes clear in the final stanzas of the poem, when Frost assumes that because purpose has come to a "head," we will never be satisfied until scientists have reached the end of their own inquiry:

> Whose purpose was it? His or Hers or Its?
> Let's leave that to the scientific wits.
> Grant me intention, purpose, and design—
> That's near enough for me to the Divine.
>
> And yet for all this help of head and brain
> How happily instinctive we remain,
> Our best guide upward further to the light,
> Passionate preference such as love at sight.
>
> (*CPP&P*, 438)

If scientific answers cannot provide the source of purpose and design (and it is doubtful to Frost that they will), then instinct—in this case an intuitive, spontaneous recognition of love—becomes the most appropriate guide toward the light. As always, Frost remains reticent about what the divine might actually be like, and it is doubtful that science or poetry, rationality or intuition, can ever come close to revealing the true source of the brook. In this context, to be fully human means for Frost accepting the paradoxical directive that we must devote ourselves wholeheartedly to truths that, because of our cognitive limitations, we can never fully understand. The universe rolls along blindly only because our aspirations and hopes exceed the power of our sight.

That paradox is finally the only acceptable way out of the dark Darwinian wood is a reflection of Frost's difficult struggle between his strong belief in the power of concepts to mediate and limit the threats of the natural world and his equally strong belief that those same concepts, once carried too far, in the end become more destructive than useful. As Frost was fond of saying, "Only in a certain type of small scientific mind can there be found cocksureness, a conviction that a solution to the riddle of the universe is just around the corner."[61] Frost wanted to avoid permanent adherence to what he called "monometaphor," to preserve something of mystery, to leave intact behind the concealing veils of metaphor something to inspire the imagination toward startling new discoveries. And more than anyone else, it was Darwin—for Frost the most threatening intellectual figure of the nineteenth century—who necessitated a new model of cognitive awareness that might counter the disturbing conclusions of scientific determinism. Although Frost was by no means the only major literary figure of the early twentieth century to question the relationship between mind and matter and so reconfigure our definitions of truth, it is this particular element of his poetry, employed in part as a means to rehabilitate the failed promises of romanticism, that makes it continuous with the poetry of the past and, ironically, clearly modern.

3. We Are Sick with Space

Space ails us moderns: we are sick with space.
Its contemplation makes us out as small
As a brief epidemic of microbes
That in a good glass may be seen to crawl
The patina of this the least of globes.

"The Lesson for Today" (1942)

WHEN ISABELLE MOODIE FROST ENCOURAGED HER SON TO ACQUIRE the telescope he had found advertised in the pages of *The Youth's Companion,* she had high hopes that his sudden enthusiasm for the stars might also awaken in him an equal enthusiasm for God.[1] For some time she had feared that her fifteen-year-old son was beginning to question his religion, so when the chance to rehabilitate his waning faith presented itself in the guise of scientific inquiry, she seized it almost immediately. She knew of course that Emerson, once a devoted amateur astronomer in his own right, had undergone a similar reaffirmation nearly a half-century earlier, and she was confident that given enough time and proper guidance, her son would eventually adopt her favorite philosopher's creed, expressed in *Nature,* that "observation of the stars" would "preserve for many generations the remembrance of the city of God."[2] Thus, after pestering enough relatives and friends into buying the requisite quota of magazine subscriptions so the telescope might be acquired at no charge, mother and son set up a makeshift observatory in an upstairs bedroom window and began searching the sky for the heavenly bodies that might inspire their religious sensibilities and bring them into the "perpetual presence of the sublime."[3]

At first, all went as Belle Frost had planned, and for a while, at least, she was pleased to see her son following the religious paths she had blazed for him. Having read about the wonders of Saturn and Sirius in Richard Anthony Proctor's *Our Place among Infinities,* a popular account of contemporary astronomical discoveries, the young Frost, his curiosity aroused, borrowed the star charts from the Lawrence Public Library and began observing the celestial events that Proctor's book had predicted. Immersed in such an intriguing body of knowledge and genuinely fascinated by his own growing command of the magnitude, position, and motion of stars, Frost publicly sang praises for his new hobby in an editorial for the Lawrence High School *Bulletin* in December 1891. "Astronomy," he wrote, "is one of the most practical as well as theoretical sciences. It is a wonderful teacher of observation and cultivator of the practical imagination."[4]

Such persistent devotion to the heavens not only continued to please his mother greatly, as it seemed to bolster her son's spirits and restore his confidence in God; it also kindled in him a strong desire to compose the first of many "astronomical" poems, several of which would attempt to integrate cosmology and theology.[5] One of the most revealing of Frost's juvenilia, "God's Garden," for example, illustrates just how deeply Frost had enmeshed himself in his mother's religion in the decade prior to 1900. Published in the *Boston Evening Transcript* in 1898, the poem's final stanza exhorts its readers to turn away from material riches and toward the stars for proper spiritual guidance:

> O, cease to heed the glamour,
>   That blinds your foolish eyes,
> Look upward to the glitter
>   Of stars in God's clear skies.
> Their ways are pure and harmless
>   And will not lead astray,
> But aid your erring footsteps
>   To keep the narrow way.
> And when the sun shines brightly
>   Tend flowers that God has given
> And keep the pathway open
>   That leads you on to heaven.
>
> (*CPP&P,* 504)

While it is impossible to tell exactly when Frost composed this poem—the style and tone indicate that it was well before 1898—its pedestrian subject, sentimental clichés, and youthful overexuberance immediately suggest why he denied writing it as late as 1946.[6] Clearly, he was embarrassed by the poem, but perhaps for reasons that had little to do with aesthetic criteria. As Lawrance Thompson has argued, Frost remained intensely guarded about his religious convictions, even long after he had modified his views, out of fear that his critical detractors might use his "antiquated" beliefs as evidence of a more pervasive intellectual shallowness.[7] Reluctant to supply his detractors with ammunition and genuinely confused about the issue himself, Frost not only hid from the public much of his early religious poetry but also habitually evaded the question of his religious faith by speaking in metaphorical tongues. Asked by John Sherrill about what God had meant to him in his poetry, Frost answered that "if you would have out the way a man feels about God, watch his life, hear his words. Place a coin, with its denomination unknown, under paper and you can tell its mark by rubbing a pencil over the paper. From all the individual rises and valleys your answer will come out."[8]

Questions of embarrassment and literary value aside, "God's Garden" is useful as a historical relic, if only because it indicates that between its composition and the publication of *A Boy's Will* in 1913 Frost descended into the first of his many valleys of despair and entered into a spiritual crisis equivalent to the one William James had experienced in the 1860s. Consider, for example, the polar differences between "God's Garden" and "Stars," one of the opening poems in *A Boy's Will*. Composed in Emily Dickinson's favorite stanzaic pattern, common measure, the poem also alludes to a Dickinsonian theological skepticism, which is reflected in the subtitle, "There is no oversight of human affairs":

> How countlessly they congregate
>   O'er our tumultuous snow,
> Which flows in shapes as tall as trees
>   When wintry winds do blow!—
>
> As if with keenness for our fate,
>   Our faltering few steps on
> To white rest, and a place of rest
>   Invisible at dawn,—
>
> And yet with neither love nor hate,
>   Those stars like some snow-white
> Minerva's snow-white marble eyes
>   Without the gift of sight.

(*CPP&P*, 19)

How appropriate that Frost would choose Minerva, Roman goddess of wisdom, culture, and the arts, as a metaphorical emblem for a universe that he now perceived as incapable of generating either wisdom or sympathy. Although the stars might have seemed to Frost more stable and less immediately threatening than drifting and accumulating snow, it is obvious that by 1913 he had completely divested them of all religious significance. In the context of his whole career such an antipodal gesture is momentous for two reasons. First, it marks the decade in which Frost matured into a poet deeply concerned about his own existential fate; and second, his religious skepticism demonstrates a remarkable congruity with his developing anti-romantic attitudes toward the natural world. Just as Frost grew more and more reluctant to detect in spider webs, woodchucks, and orchids evidence of divine design, he was now confronted by the even harsher realities of a cosmos completely emptied of its divine attributes. By 1913 the starlight he saw through his telescope was not the light of God shining through holes in the firmament, as his mother had once intimated, but rather the inevitable and predictable by-product of simple elements that reacted with one another for no apparent purpose or human benefit. No matter how often he aimed his telescope toward the heavens, or how frequently he upgraded his lenses' magnifying power, by the time Frost turned thirty-five the Emersonian certainties his mother had once found in the heavens had disappeared into the cold black emptiness of infinite space.

While it is impossible to speculate about all of the factors that may have contributed to this spiritual reversal, two distinct causes jolted Frost out of his religious complacency. The first was the personal tragedy that plagued the Frost family between 1900 and 1906. In 1900, just two years after the publication of "God's Garden," Frost's four-year-old son, Elliot, contracted cholera, was misdiagnosed by the family physician, and died suddenly two days later, leaving Frost and his wife devastated by grief.[9] Four months later, Belle Frost, who had been diagnosed with cancer, died alone in a New Hampshire sanitarium, bereaving her son of the most important religious influence in his life.[10] These misfortunes, coupled with the death in 1906 of another child, two-day-old Elinor Bettina,[11] and his intermittent estrangement from Elinor, who Frost once claimed had "come out flat-footed against God,"[12] placed tremendous pressures upon his religious faith and seemed to confirm for him the nagging suspicion that the Darwinian ideas he had absorbed at Harvard were not invented fictions, as he would have liked to believe, but the most truthful accounts of nature he had yet encountered. With the slaughter of the innocents mounting rapidly before him, and continually beset with bouts of pneumonia so severe that he often feared for his own life, it is no wonder that Frost decided long before the trip to England that a change of scenery was in order.

The second and, in this context, more important cause of Frost's changing attitude toward the stars was the simple fact that he educated himself. In addition to reading Darwin and Lyell as a special student at Harvard, Frost diligently kept abreast of the most popular astronomical models of his day, gleaning much of his knowledge from Proctor's book and from the pages of *Scientific American,* a periodical he read avidly and once touted as his favorite magazine.[13] Neither of these sources approached scientific concepts with the kind of detail that Frost might have liked, yet they did provide him remarkably well with diluted versions of the new theories, most of which were still comprehensible to an audience of nonspecialists. In addition to furnishing Frost with an above-average layman's understanding of physics, these popular forums also discussed how new developments in physics might affect culture.

Its pages filled with wonderfully detailed pen-and-ink drawings, *Scientific American* dealt primarily with practical issues. At the turn of the century the magazine devoted much of its space to the spectacular successes of the dynamo, discussing how it would eventually eliminate the drudgery of back-breaking manual labor and reduce American dependency upon coal as a source of power. Articles on the electron, the vacuum tube, the triode, and the radio reinforced the bully, progressive spirit of the age and provided the American public with remarkable new evidence that science, with its ability to manipulate nature, had a much cozier relationship with physical reality than did any competing discipline in the arts or humanities.

In contrast to *Scientific American*'s emphasis upon practical issues, Proctor's interests lay in the realm of pure rather than applied physics. *Our Place among Infinities* discusses in detail the evolution of galaxies and stars and speculates about the possibility of life in other worlds, subjects far more appealing to Frost's religious sensibilities. Frost seems to have been affected most profoundly by Proctor's method of placing all of his scientific discussions in a religious context.[14] Proctor even went so far as to set boundaries for science, suggesting in his second chapter, inauspiciously entitled "Of Seeming Wastes in Nature," that

> We may believe, with all confidence, that could we but understand the whole of what we find around us, the wisdom with which each part has been designed would be manifest; but we must not fall into the

mistake of supposing that we can so clearly understand all as to be able to recognize the purpose of this or that arrangement, the wisdom of this or that provision. Nor if any results of scientific research appear to us to accord ill with our conceptions of the economy of nature, should we be troubled, on the one hand, as respects our faith in God's benevolence, or doubt, on the other hand, the manifest teachings of science. In a word, our faith must not be hampered by our scientific doubts, our science must not be hampered by religious scruples.[15]

This passage, which Thompson cites as evidence of why Frost treasured Proctor's book, could have been written in the eighteenth rather than the nineteenth century, as many of its arguments share affinities with Enlightenment rather than Victorian assumptions about God and nature. Like Galileo and Newton, Proctor asserts that behind the changing facades of matter lies an immutable divine force that resists transformation by either perception or material processes. Conceived in this manner, the material world for Proctor is essentially a realm that evades complete scientific understanding. Although random waste appears to us as the essential condition of the universe, such a condition, he asserts, exists only within the larger context of an unknown divine purpose. "We should be content to believe," he writes, "though at present we may be quite unable to prove, *that the waste is apparent only, not real,* and to admit that we see too small a part of the scheme of the Creator to pronounce an opinion on the economy or wisdom of the observed arrangements."[16]

    This argument, which by 1900 had become a mainstay for those who still wished to preserve religious faith, gathers its authority by overtly challenging the supremacy of the empirical observer and by placing cognitive limits on perception. The passage also resonates with the distinctions between fact and value that Arnold, in his well-known defense of poetry, "The Study of Poetry," levied against T. H. Huxley just four years after *Our Place among Infinities* appeared in London. There, in an effort to keep humanistic studies at the center of a university curriculum, Arnold attempted to do for poetry what Proctor attempted to do for religion. Employing equivalent strategies, both men defended their most cherished institutions by attacking the very heart of what they perceived to be science's strength. Arguing that the scientific method, with its strict emphasis upon objectivity and precision, prevented the researcher from penetrating larger and more meaningful realms of experience, Proctor and Arnold sanctioned competing disciplines that embraced other forms of inquiry. While in their view science might tell us much about the world's physical fabric, it could neither explain why physical phenomena existed in the first place nor show how we might assimilate new scientific discoveries in our efforts to ennoble the human spirit and discover how life might be made more meaningful. Questions of value were best addressed, in Proctor's view, by religious speculation, and in the absence of religion, in Arnold's view, by the study of poetry.[17]

Although Frost was certainly attracted to this type of argument and sustained throughout his life an Arnoldian belief that the "best description of us is still in the humanities,"[18] as an attentive student of the conflict between science and religion he was also well aware that such arguments, however eloquently expressed, had done little to bolster traditional religious belief or to prevent science from usurping literature's lofty status in the university curriculum. In an intellectual milieu that had evolved to value fact more than emotion, truth more than beauty, and empirical evidence more than blind faith, Arnold's argument that poetry offered "the breath and finer spirit of knowledge"[19] was a weak defense, especially if one believed that religion could no longer be supported, as it once had been, by scientific inquiry. The same charges of irrationality could also be applied by scientists to Proctor's arguments for the existence of God. Indebted to Christian doctrine, Proctor's religious faith was in many ways incompatible with his own assessments of recent astronomical discoveries. As any Victorian scientist or clergyman would have immediately recognized, most of his book was devoted to several new astronomical theories, many of which actually militated against a traditional religious way of life.

In particular, two scientific undercurrents in *Our Place among Infinities* emerged as a source of severe anxiety for Frost. The first was Proctor's discussion of Pierre Laplace's nebular hypothesis, a widely accepted theory that saw the solar system as originating from the cooling and contracting of a large, flattened, slowly rotating cloud of incandescent gas.[20] At the time seemingly corroborated by Sir William Herschel's observations, Laplace's theory brought to a conclusion the demise of medieval Christian cosmology. The once undisputed conception of the universe as a closed, finite, and hierarchically ordered whole had finally yielded to a more comprehensive model that revealed the universe as one of unfathomable dimensions, bound together only by fundamental, mechanistic laws. Proctor's version of this theory, complete with an extensive description of how the earth had accumulated its mass by attracting matter cast off by stellar activity, reinforced rather than repudiated the more disturbing elements of cosmic mechanism. He enumerated the extent to which nineteenth-century cosmology had distanced itself from Newton and Paley's divinely ordained "clockwork universe" and, more significantly, corroborated Darwin's assertion in *The Descent of Man* that arguments for special creation lay outside the provinces of reason:

> Let it suffice that we recognise as one of the earliest stages of our earth's history, her condition as a rotating mass of glowing vapour, capturing then as now, but far more actively then than now, masses of matter which approached near enough [the earth], and growing by these continual indraughts from without. From the very beginning, as it would seem, the earth grew in this way. The firm earth on which we live represents an aggregation of matter not from one portion of space, but from all space. All that is upon and within the earth, all vegetable forms and all animal forms, our bodies, our brains, are formed of materials which have been drawn in from those depths of space surrounding us on all sides. This hand that I am now raising contains particles . . . drawn in towards the earth by processes continuing millions of millions of ages, until after multitudinous changes the chapter of accidents has so combined them, and so distributed them in plants and animals, that after coming to form portions of my food they are here present before you . . . is not the thought itself striking and suggestive, that not only the earth on which we move, but everything we see or touch, and every particle in body and brain, has sped during countless ages through the immensity of space?[21]

As Frost's poem "The Lesson for Today" (1942) suggests, the nebular hypothesis, although certainly disturbing in its own right, was only one contributing cause of a larger problem that for Frost lay at the heart of modernity itself. Convinced that the universe was "expanse and nothing else,"[22] Frost understood that the dissolution of Scholastic cosmology weakened Christianity's philosophical authority. As scientists from Copernicus to Laplace had extended the dimensions of space to indefinite and even infinite proportions, it had gradually become absurd to suppose that God had created the earth solely for human habitation and benefit. The modern universe was far too extensive to support the Aristotelian beliefs that the earth was the center of the universe and that heavenly bodies were inhabited by independent anima that controlled the direction and duration of celestial orbits. If all of the material components in the universe could be considered as ontologically equivalent, then no longer could theologians rationally envision a Dantean ascent from the dark, imperfect earth toward the illuminating perfection of the heavenly spheres. There appeared to be no definitive hierarchy, and as nineteenth-century scientists learned more and more about the true nature of physical space, it became more and more doubtful that a convincing eschatology, one that left room for divine providence and transcendent sources of value, would ever be recovered. Speaking of the shift from the "Ptolemaic geo-centric universe to the Copernican no-centric universe," Frost wrote: "It has taken me some years of my life to accept our position; but I see no way out of it. There is apparently not a soul but us alive in the whole business of rolling balls, eddying fires, and long distance rays of light. It makes any coziness in our nook here all the more heartwarming."[23]

Frost may also have been deeply troubled by Proctor's discussion of the second law of thermodynamics, the law of entropy—the "universal cataract of death," as Frost describes it in "West-Running Brook"—which demonstrated mathematically that kinetic energy within a closed system eventually dissipates in every conversion process until it finally becomes immeasurable.[24] Originally employed practically as a means for engineers to measure the horsepower and efficiency of coal-fired machines, the second law of thermodynamics, when translated to the solar system, also predicted the inevitable exhaustion of the sun's fuel, the certain cooling of the solar system, and, as a consequence, the eventual death of all organic life on earth. Although it would be nearly four decades until modern physicists, writing in the wake of Georges Lemaître's big bang theory, would postulate the thermodynamic equilibrium of the cosmos, the so-called heat death of the universe, the entropic forecast for the cosmos was just as bleak in the 1880s as it was in the 1930s. In the aftermath of entropy it became clear that despite science's profound ability to predict and sometimes control nature, humans could never completely immunize themselves against cosmic extinction. In his own discussion of entropy Proctor offered little consolation to those who were concerned about such issues. "When we look forward to the future of this earth on which we live," he wrote, "we find, far off it may be, but still discernible, a time when all life will have perished from off the earth's face. Then will she circle around the central sun, even as our moon circles, a dead though massive globe, an orb bearing only the records and the memories of former life, but, to our conceptions, a useless desert scene."[25]

In nearly every regard, then, except for a few tentative declarations of faith, *Our Place among Infinities* is not an optimistic book. Contrary to Thompson's depiction of it as a positive agent of Frost's spiritual and psychological recovery, *Our Place among Infinities* merely articulated Frost's most important philosophical problem: the growing estrangement between the human world, which emphasized moral necessity, and the natural world, which was completely indifferent to moral concerns. If the Victorian version of a godless universe was accurate, then perhaps the most rational moral response available was to "amend" nature, as John Stuart Mill suggested,[26] or, as Huxley asserted even more passionately, to "combat" nature so as to mitigate the traumatic consequences brought about by the death, disease, and predation that cosmic mechanism inevitably guaranteed.[27] The only other available alternative was to adopt the intuitive stance of the mystic, who, calmly accepting death and other cosmic absurdities as the essential conditions of the universe, saw no distinction between the civilized and natural worlds and so bridged the gulf between them.[28] In many respects, it was this latter position that Proctor unsuccessfully tried to adopt for himself. Yet despite his genuine effort to reconcile science and religion, his mystical belief had been so compromised by his scientific knowledge that he merely reaffirmed the problem Tennyson had found so disconcerting in the 1840s. God and nature were at strife, as Tennyson declared in *In Memoriam,* and the physical universe as revealed by science implied that God could not be located in the material components and mechanistic processes of nature.

Of course, had Frost been Whitman, he might have accepted Proctor's diluted romanticism with remarkable aplomb. It was Whitman, after all, who dismissed the calculations of "Learn'd Astronomers" as arrogant and then, without any vacillation, wandered "unaccountable" into the "mystical moist night-air" to "look up in perfect silence at the stars."[29] Frost, however, had none of Whitman's capacity for accepting death and "all the things of the universe" as "perfect miracles,"[30] nor could he consciously ignore the abundant scientific discoveries that had seemingly rendered a religious vision of the universe untenable. As an inheritor of a late Victorian moral sensibility, Frost was much more profoundly aware that the fin-de-siècle cosmos, newly expanded and mechanized by science, was now more than ever capable of reducing human aspirations and achievements to an almost total insignificance.

That the huge gulf between moral desire and natural fact had become for him one of the most conspicuous conflicts in his life is evident in one of his most dispiriting poems, "Desert Places" (1934). One can hardly imagine a starker contrast between Whitman's expansive, life-affirming catalogs and Frost's fear that the universe would eventually consume him:

Snow falling and night falling fast, oh, fast
In a field I looked into going past,
And the ground almost covered smooth in snow,
But a few weeds and stubble showing last.

The woods around it have it—it is theirs.
All animals are smothered in their lairs.
I am too absent-spirited to count;
The loneliness includes me unawares.

And lonely as it is that loneliness
Will be more lonely ere it will be less—
A blanker whiteness of benighted snow
With no expression, nothing to express.

They cannot scare me with their empty spaces
Between stars—on stars where no human race is.
I have it in me so much nearer home
To scare myself with my own desert places.

(*CPP&P,* 269)

As in the earlier poem "Stars," both winter and the heavens have conspired to assault the poet's sensibility; he cannot "count" either as a significant human being or as a poet, who by "counting" out the metrics of his verse might engage the imagination to amend nature and transform it into a comprehensible, less menacing place. In such a bleak moment of absent-spiritedness, the only recourse left is for Frost to engage his keen sense of detached irony; he can deflect the external threat only by conjuring up an equivalent internal threat that might neutralize the other's impending danger. As a last resort, perhaps taking his cue from Wallace Stevens, Frost summons "the violence from within" to protect himself "from the violence without."[31]

Unfortunately, however, this strategy also fails, for contrary to the apparent bravado in "They cannot scare me with their empty spaces / Between stars," the falling rhythms and faltering extra syllables of the last stanza betray the poet's posturing as his confidence gives way to a more comprehensive fear. Here, fear is not merely a projection of an overactive imagination but a highly rational response by one who has full knowledge of a world informed by science. The terrestrial and extraterrestrial environments are so threatening that the poet can no longer mentally forge adequate protective structures against them. Paralyzed by the desert places surrounding it, the mind, too, has become a desert place—notice the echo of Proctor's description of cosmic decay as "a useless desert scene"—where hope and redemption remain impossible and the threat of annihilation seems imminent.

The idea that the external universe might transform the mind from a sanctuary into a source of terror is further underscored by Frost's conscious revision of the famous quotation from Blaise Pascal's *Pensées,* "Le silence eternal de ces espaces infinis m'effraie" (The eternal silence of these infinite spaces frightens me), where Pascal describes how terror, rather than destroying his belief in God, actually leads him to ecstatic moments of religious faith.[32] As evidence of faith's rationality, Pascal offered his famous wager: If we believe in God and God does not exist, then we have lost nothing. Conversely, if we do not believe in God and God does exist, then we have committed ourselves needlessly to a lifetime of suffering. Because this argument shares strong affinities with James's belief that religious faith has a beneficial psychological component, one might assume that Frost would have welcomed Pascal's argument as an attractive complement to James. As the tone of resignation in "Desert Places" ultimately suggests, however, Pascal's wager was untenable for Frost. His fear of a barren cosmos is here so pronounced that it has crippled his ability to imagine a more secure future. Instead of leading him to religious insight, the "empty spaces between stars" lead him only to the stark realization that he is unable to reconcile the natural world's destructive processes with his own desire to preserve his ego.

While "Desert Places" suggests that hostile landscapes can transform the mind from a source of redemption into a source of terror, it would be unwise to take "Desert Places" or "Stars" as Frost's final word on the perils of astronomical phenomena. As always in Frost's poetry, discernible thematic countermovements often neutralize ideas that at first glance appear absolute. This deconstructionist propensity, which Richard Poirier has astutely identified as the "central achievement of Frost's poetry from the first volume onward,"[33] evinces itself in other poems that mediate seasonal or astronomical threats. In well-known poems such as "The Onset," "Tree at My Window," and "Take Something Like a Star," Frost stresses the idea that even though we are irreparably separated from nature by our own consciousness, it is paradoxically that same consciousness that allows us to navigate the gulf between "inner" and "outer" weather so we can "amend" nature and make it more compatible with our own needs. If nature is a destructive force that can annihilate the ego, it is also, to Frost's way of thinking, a restorative force that has paradoxically equipped us with a mind capable of creating ample protective structures. The imagination—whose volitional processes condition the mind to select the objects it wishes to perceive, to discriminate among them, to judge them good or bad, to change them for the better, or to make among them sound, responsible choices—enables us to imagine a better and more congenial future. The act of writing is thus for Frost not only the first step toward coming to terms with a hostile cosmos but also the first step toward erecting the saving structures of community, marriage, and religious faith.

In a 1961 interview with the novelist Mark Harris, Frost expounded his voluntarist tendencies, many of which had influenced his thinking since his first encounter with William James:

> The most creative thing in us is to believe a thing in, in love, in all
> else. You believe yourself into existence. You believe your marriage into
> existence, you believe in each other, you believe that it's worthwhile
> going on, or you'd commit suicide wouldn't you? . . . And the ultimate
> one is the belief in the future of the world. I believe the future *in*. It's
> coming in by my believing it. You might as well call that a belief in
> God. This word God is not an often-used word with me, but once in a
> while it arrives there.[34]

The will to believe, the capacity to transform imaginatively the disturbing elements of one's life, including threats fostered by the natural world, became for Frost such a useful redemptive method that he argued for its validity for the rest of his life.

While Frost's uncompromising belief in free will and an autonomous ego contradicts postmodern arguments that the author is nothing more than an articulator among the various discourses by which he or she is written,[35] it is necessary to remember that Frost's desire to defend free will stems partly from his profound need to rescue himself from the processes of mechanistic determinism. If human consciousness is a mediating process of continual invention, Frost reasons, then psychic activity cannot logically be bound by the same determinate laws that govern matter. Because psychic activity helps us to create rather than discover the laws of the physical world, mental processes partially elevate themselves beyond the reach of the mechanical law. Our capacity for make-believe and a deep awareness of our constantly changing subjectivity liberate us from determinism and help us create the moral foundations of our own humanity.

There is nothing terribly original in Frost's romantic faith in the autonomous ego; surely emphasis upon the poet as a maker and shaper of reality can be traced from Santayana, James, and Nietzsche all the way back to Coleridge and Wordsworth and, finally, Kant. What makes Frost's insistence on free will so surprising is that he was one of the few modernists in America to defend both free will and individual genius against the panoply of psychological, sociological, scientific, and linguistic systems that would explain them away. As Frost well knew, the laws of thermodynamics and evolution implied that people were not active agents in the world but were shaped by natural contingencies that brought them under the control of the external environment. In such a deterministic system, where physical law exerted its machinelike regularity upon people exactly as it did upon planets, combating nature's most destructive forces by imaginative processes remained impossible. Nature would run her course despite any human intervention designed to change its direction. As the scientific historian Carl Snyder wrote in 1904, "So far as the outer world is intelligible to us, the immediate portion in which we live our lives is simply a machine, so orderly and compact, so simple in its construction, that we may reckon its past and gauge something of its future with almost as much certitude as that of a dynamo or a waterwheel. In its motions there is no uncertainty. . . . This is the first fact which modern science has to offer the philosophic mind."[36]

As Thompson and Poirier have argued, it was this kind of scientific thinking that Frost found so repugnant because it failed to acknowledge the prominent role that free will and imagination played in the construction of knowledge. What Frost desired most from his immersion in science was not so much a refined knowledge of his exact relationship to the physical world but rather a version of the discipline that would be more amenable to the free play of the imagination. If it could be demonstrated, for example, that the human mind, as both Wordsworth and Coleridge argued, partially constructed rather than discovered its own universe, then a universe of constantly changing particulars might be shaped and reshaped into a realm more thoroughly compatible with one's desires for permanence and value.

To anyone familiar with the history of thought in the early twentieth century, the version of science that Frost had been looking for since his Harvard days was already well under way, even as Snyder was busy singing the praises of scientific certitude. As the nineteenth century came to a close, a revolution in physics was beginning to undermine not only the assumptions of classical physics, whose Newtonian principles had laid much of the essential groundwork for the widespread belief in cosmic mechanism, but also the two most sacred principles of the scientific method: causality and objectivity. In a span of forty years, three successive events—the refutation of a luminiferous ether as a medium for the transmission of light, the theory of special relativity, and the quantum theory of energy—corrected nearly all the core conceptions of Newtonian mechanics. Although concepts such as absolute space, time, mass, and motion could not be construed by the emerging paradigms as wrong per se, the new physics clearly demonstrated that traditional Newtonian concepts were valid only within a limited domain of experiential phenomena.[37] These unimaginable and strangely original accounts of nature also seemed to reveal the universe as one of emergent novelty and unpredictability, thus reducing the once dominant idea of cosmic mechanism to a historical oddity.

Taken together, these three events revolutionized physics. Modern scientists suddenly found themselves in a natural realm much more complex than the one the Victorians had envisioned, and as the billiard-ball model of the universe yielded to one that viewed uncertainty as an incontrovertible fact, the limitations of perception became more and more apparent, especially to the scientists themselves. Perhaps even more telling of a shift in thought was the restoration of chance and freedom to philosophical inquiry. If the universe did not depend upon a perfect determinism for its processes, then free will and chance, both of which had been accepted as conditions of the universe until Darwin, might be reconsidered in light of the new physical discoveries.

It was therefore not long before the popular press began to discuss the impact of the new physics, often distorting basic science in order to validate particular ideological, theological, or aesthetic viewpoints. Relativity and quantum mechanics, for example, were enlisted in various circles to sanction the idea that all truth was relative, that empirical observation was completely subjective; that poetry, if it was to reflect reality accurately, had to be a poetry of motion and process; and, finally, that a spontaneous free will, one that mirrored the physical world's quantum leaps, was a genuine component of humanity. Einstein himself became a celebrity almost overnight, and although only very few people actually understood relativity, a popular magazine such as the *Nation*, which once had declared relativity a theory that "psychologists, priests, and poets had known all along," could claim with impunity that the "difficulty of the subject" was greatly exaggerated and that anyone who did not "understand it [relativity] at a glance" was nothing but a "dunce and a simpleton."[38]

In addition to magazines, the most widely read newspapers also devoted ample space to Einstein, relativity, and quantum mechanics. In 1919, after Arthur Eddington proved that light could be deflected by a gravitational field, the *New York Times* ran sixteen articles and editorials in November alone, one of which declared that "light was all askew in the heavens."[39] With these and other popular accounts distorting the new physics so severely, most people failed to recognize the huge contrast between Einstein's relativity theory, which attempted to establish a new framework of absolute relations rather than relative ones, and quantum mechanics, which suggested that complete scientific certainty was untenable. Nevertheless, despite these and other misconceptions, most educated people thought that the new century's revolutionary physical paradigms had somehow reunited science, art, and philosophy after years of separation and specialization. The new physics, rather than solving the persistent physical problems of the nineteenth century, had merely created several new ones that required an entirely new set of scientific and philosophical lenses. A Pandora's box had been opened, and no one, not even Einstein, seemed able to close the lid.

One scientific popularizer who did understand relativity as well as Einstein was Arthur Eddington, a professor of astronomy at Cambridge and perhaps, with the exception of Niels Bohr, the single most important scientific influence upon Frost's later career. In a groundbreaking essay dealing with Frost's indebtedness to Eddington, Heisenberg, and Bohr, Guy Rotella argues that the source for much of Frost's astronomical knowledge was Eddington's *Nature of the Physical World* (1928), a widely popular account of the new physics that explored the impact of the new science upon social values and particularly upon religion.[40] According to Rotella, Frost was attracted to this book primarily because Eddington recognized the limitations of scientific inquiry and wrote about physics in a witty style that often employed allusions to classical poetry. A severe rationalist as well as a devout Quaker, Eddington doubted the authority of mechanistic laws and often claimed in his books that science offered an incomplete picture of reality because its conclusions were cognitive creations based upon epistemological principles, not empirical data. "All the laws of nature that are classified as fundamental," he claimed, "can be seen wholly from epistemological considerations. They correspond to *a priori* knowledge, and are therefore wholly subjective."[41] In a famous quotation, Eddington, echoing Kant's idea that we can never know the noumenal world, boldly challenged Einstein's widely shared belief that physical theories were merely economical descriptions of observed natural phenomena. Suggesting instead that theories were free creations of the human mind that were imposed upon the world in a "complex of metrical symbols," Eddington suggested that humans had found "a strange footprint on the shores of the unknown" and had "devised profound theories, one after the other, to account for its origin. At last, we have succeeded in reconstructing the creation that made the footprint. And Lo! It is our own."[42]

Taken a step farther, Eddington's idea that scientific conclusions were constructed rather than discovered meant that given the flexibility and ingenuity of the human imagination, theoretical permanence of any type was highly unlikely. Anticipating our contemporary predilection for scientific skepticism, Eddington recognized that the historical context of an era could direct the course of future scientific activity and thus exclude from the realm of possibility all ideas that had not already been partially forged in the furnaces of scientific tradition. Indeed, thirty years before Thomas Kuhn popularized the concept of the scientific "paradigm," Eddington asserted that revolution was an integral component of science and speculated that the theoretical knowledge he possessed might one day become as obsolete as Newton's theories:

> It is not so much the particular form that scientific theories have now taken—the conclusions we believe we have proved—as the movement of thought behind them that concerns the philosopher. Our eyes once opened, we may pass on to yet a new outlook on the world, but we can never go back to the old outlook.
>
> If the scheme of philosophy which we now rear on the advances of Einstein, Bohr, Rutherford and others is doomed to fall in the next thirty years, it is not to be laid to their charge that we have gone astray. Like the systems of Euclid, of Ptolemy, of Newton, which have served their turn, so the systems of Einstein and Heisenberg may give way to some fuller realization of the world. But in each revolution of scientific thought new words are set to the old music, and that which has gone before is not destroyed but refocused.[43]

One of the consequences of limiting science to a small domain of experience was that Eddington, like James and Bergson, could then postulate the existence of an unseen spiritual world that lay beyond the realm of observed physical reality. According to Eddington, if we were to know the spiritual world, we had first to attend to the "symbols of our personality" rather than to the "symbols of the mathematician" and thus develop an intuitive relationship with the spiritual world that would "not submit to codification and analysis."[44] Similar to Bergson's advice on how to recover real duration, Eddington delineated distinct boundaries for all forms of symbolic knowledge. In order to gain access to the spiritual world, we had to admit that feeling, emotion, intuition, and memory contributed to the totality of each moment of lived experience: "We recognize a spiritual world alongside the physical world," he wrote. "Experience—that is to say, the self *cum* environment—comprises more than can be embraced in the physical world, restricted as it is to a complex of metrical symbols."[45] Attention to the nonquantifiable aspects of reality reinforced the very qualities of life that made man most human. "We all know," he wrote, "that there are regions of the human spirit untrammeled by the world of physics. In the mystic sense of the creation around us, in the expression of art, in a yearning towards God, the soul grows upward and finds the fulfillment of something implanted in its nature."[46]

In addition to finding in Eddington credible arguments to support the possibility of a divine reality, Frost was also drawn to Eddington's belief that determinism could not hold true at the quantum level. As Rotella has pointed out, clear evidence that Frost was fascinated by the possibility of a flexible, indeterminate universe can be found in "Education by Poetry," an ars poetica that Frost delivered to the Amherst College Alumni Council on 15 November 1930.[47] There, in a talk that lauded metaphor as the cognitive foundation for all knowledge, Frost enlisted several physical theories to demonstrate how science, like poetry, depended upon figurative juxtapositions to explain the inexplicable complexities of natural phenomena.

In particular, references to two major developments in particle physics served his arguments well. The first was a discussion of quantum probability. Comparing quantum leaps to actuarial science, Frost rationalized that quantum events were random occurrences and could not be predicted: "You know that you can't tell by name what persons in a certain class will be dead ten years after graduation, but you can tell actuarially how many will be dead. Now, just so this scientist says of the particles of matter flying at a screen, striking a screen; you can't tell what individual particles will come, but you can say in general that a certain number will strike in a given time. It shows, you see, that the individual particle can come freely."[48]

Why Frost concentrated his attention on the "freedom" of the "individual particle" Rotella never suggests. A closer look at *The Nature of the Physical World,* however, reveals at least one plausible explanation. In the penultimate chapter, a polemical essay entitled "Causation," Eddington tackled the problem of free will and predestination. Arguing that "physics is no longer pledged to a scheme of deterministic laws," Eddington appropriated

Heisenberg's famous indeterminacy principle to show why quantum action necessitated a revision of materialist explanations for human behavior. Although Eddington was often reluctant to enlist science as proof for
religious arguments, he nevertheless postulated in this chapter that human
volition and free will were the natural outcomes of physical processes. The
"emancipation" of the mind, however, also required a concomitant emancipation of material, which for Eddington was not an obstacle:

> The materialist view was that the motions which appear to be caused
> by our volition are really reflex actions controlled by the material
> processes in the brain, the act of will being an inessential side phenom-
> enon occurring simultaneously with the physical phenomena. But this
> assumes that the result of applying physical laws to the brain is fully
> determinate. It is meaningless to say that the behaviour of a conscious
> brain is precisely the same as that of a mechanical brain if the behav-
> iour of a mechanical brain is left undetermined. If the laws of physics
> are not strictly causal the most that can be said is that the behavior
> of the conscious brain is one of the possible behaviours of a mechani-
> cal brain. Precisely so; and the decision between the possible behav-
> iours is what we call volition.[49]

If Frost actually read this passage, he may have noticed in Eddington a
familiar reluctance to formulate reality into either a purely deterministic or
a purely random cosmos. Like Frost, Eddington desired a universe that
admitted to the simultaneous existence of predetermined causation and
random chance. The universe could not be too rigid, or else emergent novelty in both natural forms and ideas would be absurd. Conversely, however,
the universe must have had some causal antecedents that could give rise to
a material reality, including the human brain. For both men, then, humans'
most propitious engagement with the physical world occurred in the dynamic interplay between matter and spirit, form and flux, necessity and
chance. The "freedom to work in one's material," as Frost often described
his poetic process, was naturally offset by the retarding forces of the material itself, and no matter how much the physical world might limit volitional
choice, it was paradoxically that material confinement that awakened the
opportunity for metaphorical activity. Freedom could be measured only by
the magnitude of its constraints; tennis could only be properly played, as
Frost liked to assert in his famous statement on free verse, with a net.

In addition to using quantum mechanics to demonstrate his ideas about
metaphor and science, Frost also enlisted Heisenberg's uncertainty princi-

ple to explain some of his ideas about poetry. Although Heisenberg had formulated the uncertainty principle only three years prior to the composition
of "Education by Poetry," Frost understood the principle well enough to use
it as an example of another "charming mixed metaphor right in the realm
of higher mathematics and higher physics." Comparing the uncertainty
principle to Zeno's problem of the arrow, Frost described one of the problems long associated with consciousness. As Frost well knew, the arrow's
flight, in Zeno's frame of reference, was a series of positions without any
corresponding motion. For Heraclitus, however, the arrow itself was pure
motion, and its discrete positions, merely a fixed series of illusions. For
Frost, the paradox was easily resolved by limiting the domain of velocity to
time and the domain of position to space. Referring directly to Heisenberg,
Frost explained the problem by suggesting that measurements were constrained by an experimental context in which time and physical space were
incompatible frameworks:

> The other day we had a visitor here, a noted scientist, whose latest
> word to the world has been that the more accurately you know where a
> thing is, the less accurately you are able to state how fast it is moving.
> You can see why that would be so, without going back to Zeno's prob-
> lem of the arrow's flight. In carrying numbers into the realm of space
> and at the same time into the realm of time you are mixing metaphors,
> that is all, and you are in trouble. They won't mix. The two don't go
> together.[50]

To Frost, who had spent most of his life searching for rational ways to
resist scientific naturalism, the idea that Eddington and Heisenberg might
limit the scope and domain of science was indeed a happy discovery. For
the first time in Frost's life, scientists, not theologians, provided him with
solutions to the problems of faith and volition that he had been struggling
with since first encountering Darwin, nearly forty years earlier. Here were
men who were willing to challenge the foundations of nineteenth-century
science and offer the world a completely modern version that demanded
new theoretical lenses. In Eddington he found rational arguments for belief
in both God and free will. In Heisenberg he found evidence that human
perception ultimately encountered physical limits that could not be crossed.
And in both he recognized an unqualified acceptance of uncertainty as a
paradoxical feature of existence.

To be sure, Eddington and Heisenberg were not the only scientists to
reassert belief in God as a valid response to the problems of existence. In

contrast to the biologists, who were then formulating the neo-Darwinian synthesis, physicists such as Max Planck, Alfred North Whitehead, Louis De Broglie, Erwin Schroedinger, James Jeans, and Wolfgang Pauli—among the most gifted scientists of the day—were in various ways contemplating the existence of God, whom they often described as a "perfect" rationality. Planck, for example, emphasized faith and intuition as integral components of scientific inquiry.[51] Heisenberg, who was heavily influenced by Pauli, advocated a Neoplatonic theory of forms and suggested that "just as in Plato, it therefore looks as if the seemingly so complicated world of elementary particles and force fields were based upon a simple and perspicuous mathematical structure."[52] Perhaps echoing the sentiments of all of these figures, James Jeans summarized the significance of the movement as follows:

> The most outstanding achievement of twentieth-century physics is not the theory of relativity with its wedding of space and time, or the theory of quanta with its apparent negation of the laws of causation, or the dissection of the atom with the resultant discovery that things are not what they seem; it is the general recognition that we are not yet in contact with an ultimate reality. To speak in Plato's well-known simile, we are still imprisoned in our cave, with our backs to the light, and can only watch the shadows on the wall.[53]

The view that shadows did exist in the realm of higher physics was also prominent in the thought of Niels Bohr, whom Frost met and dined with at Amherst College in 1923. As Thompson describes their encounter, Frost asked Bohr several questions about the structure of the atom, most of which, Thompson claims, were "far more penetrating than those questions asked by professional scientists in the dinner group."[54] What the two talked about is open to speculation, but strong circumstantial evidence suggests that they talked about recent developments in physics and how those developments reinforced the idea of free will. Given that Bohr himself had read extensively from William James, Frost may even have prodded the physicist on several Jamesian issues. In "Education by Poetry" Frost mentions Bohr in relation to the freedom of the individual particle: "I asked Bohr that particularly, and he said, 'Yes, it is so. It can come when it will and as it wills; and the action of the individual particle is unpredictable. But it is not so of the action of the mass. There you can predict.' He says, 'That gives the individual atom its freedom, but the mass its necessity.'"[55]

Just how much of this statement can be attributed to Bohr and how much to Frost is guesswork. Rotella has correctly noticed, however, that Frost alludes in this passage to Bohr's correspondence principle, an epistemological model that Bohr developed from his recognition that macroscopic classical laws broke down when they were applied to microscopic quantum numbers.[56] In the absence of a theory to unify microscopic and macroscopic phenomena, Bohr conceded that one had to accept the efficacy of both scientific frameworks. One system did not have to replace the other or assume a dominant epistemological position; both, in fact, were necessary and *complementary* descriptions of an elusive totality that could not be fully explained by the same measuring tools.[57]

We have no way of knowing whether Frost fully understood the significance of Bohr's correspondence principle. What is important here is that Frost saw in Bohr, as he did in so many other well-known physicists of the time, an epistemological skepticism incommensurable with the professed certitudes of nineteenth-century science. Scientific concepts, he learned, were not literal transcripts of reality but rather mental constructions— mathematical symbols, as Eddington called them—imposed upon matter to serve as useful guides through chaotic sensory experience. Even if supported by reasonable observation, scientific models were still only forms of thought, metaphors, as Frost so often called them, that mediated between conceptual abstraction and concrete experience. Although each of these scientists would readily admit that scientific law provided humans with the most practical means for orienting themselves to the natural world, the epistemological integrity of those laws was still a matter open for debate. Bohr himself suggested that causality might be considered just another "mode of perception by which we reduce our sense impressions to order."[58]

Frost expressed the idea a little differently. Appraising Amy Lowell's poetry just after her death, he formulated some of his most profound statements concerning scientific knowledge: "The most exciting thing in nature is not progress, advance, but expansion and contraction, the opening and shutting of the eye, the hand, the heart, the mind. We throw our arms wide with a gesture of religion to the universe; we close them around a person. We explore and adventure for a while and then we draw in to consolidate our gains. The breathless swing is between subject matter and form."[59] Composed in 1925, this brief passage amalgamates the several instrumentalist accounts of knowledge that Frost learned from James and Bergson and later found verified in theoretical physics. Here one can immediately recognize the familiar nonteleological account of creative evolution, the

Promethean desire to impel spirit deeply into matter, the futility of religious certitudes, and, finally, the hard-won belief that constructed forms can provide us with the only meaning possible in a world irreducible to rational formulation. The "breathless swing between subject matter and form" is, as always for Frost, indicative of our daring struggle to fend off death and limit nature's threat. In spite of these redeeming qualities, however, Frost acknowledges that forms, no matter how useful or beautiful, are temporal illusions, "strange apparitions of mind," as he describes them in "All Revelation," that can never assure us of their truthfulness (notice the allusion to King Hamlet's ghost) or guarantee the fulfillment of our deepest desires about how the world should be. The best they can do is provide us with brief revelations of insight, or as Frost stated more simply in "The Figure a Poem Makes," "momentary stays against confusion."[60]

The idea that poetry and science can never penetrate the surface forms of everyday experience to uncover a deeper, more meaningful realm of existence is a feature of nearly all of Frost's books from the mid-twenties until his death in 1963. That this theme did not emerge until after his encounter with Bohr, Eddington, and modern physics becomes clear when one compares Frost's account of science in "Birches" (1915) with the pervasive scientific skepticism that informs later poems such as "The Bear," "Skeptic," "All Revelation," and "Any Size We Please." The most striking difference between the earlier poem and the later group is that in the former Frost nostalgically yearns for a pristine, divinely inhabited world not yet violated by the encroachment of scientific knowledge, while in the latter, seeing no threat from science, Frost enlists its help to demonstrate an epistemological equivalence between science and poetry.

As most commentators have noticed, the controlling metaphor of "Birches" centers on the malleability and resistance of nature as it comes under the influence of the manipulating processes of human will.[61] The opening lines yoke the poem's central conflict, namely, the speaker's struggle between accepting a naturalized world immune to the human forces exerted upon it and his desire to subdue that world by imaginative reverie. The alternating pattern of natural and imaginative processes attests to the speaker's desire for balance between the two forces so that one will not dominate the other:

> When I see birches bend to left and right
> Across the lines of straighter darker trees,

> I like to think some boy's been swinging them.
> But swinging doesn't bend them down to stay
> As ice storms do.
>
> *(CPP&P,* 117–18)

As Frank Lentricchia has noticed, the speaker knows that his imagined explanation for the birches' bend cannot compete with the more believable empirical explanation. The final shape of mature birch trees cannot be attributed to human causes but rather must be attributed to natural causes such as ice storms, which subdue nature more permanently than human figuration.

The speaker's awareness that his fictional world is ephemeral, a condition that Lentricchia has labeled Frost's "ironic consciousness,"[62] becomes even more evident as the poet extends his description of material causes, in effect pleading with his readers to verify what he already knows to be true. Ultimately his scientific explanation of the birches' bend expands into a description of a modern, scientific world that has shattered religious sentiment:

> Often you must have seen them
> Loaded with ice a sunny winter morning
> After a rain. They click upon themselves
> As the breeze rises, and turn many-colored
> As the stir cracks and crazes their enamel.
> Soon the sun's warmth makes them shed crystal shells
> Shattering and avalanching on the snow crust—
> Such heaps of broken glass to sweep away
> You'd think the inner dome of heaven had fallen.
>
> *(CPP&P,* 117)

The spondaic rhythms in line ten unmistakably call attention to the double entendre of the sun as the source of both artistic inspiration and religious decay. Initially comparing the ice-coated trees to pottery, Frost also simultaneously employs images of sun and light to remind us of the consequences of material causation. One cannot help recalling here Keats's despair over Newton's prismatic diffraction of light—an experiment that, for Keats, destroyed the rainbow's beauty forever—or Copernicus's heliocentric model of the cosmos, at one time a heretical idea that discredited medieval cosmology. In a scientifically informed culture where transcendent sources of hope have been discredited, the poet must rely upon his metaphorical resources to transform the harsh objective world into an imagined reality bathed in the life-enhancing qualities he desires:

> You may see their trunks arching in the woods
> Years afterwards, trailing their leaves on the ground
> Like girls on hands and knees that throw their hair
> Before them over their heads to dry in the sun.

> (*CPP&P*, 117)

Although nature in this section stands briefly humanized by the manipulating powers of mind and will, the speaker is all too aware that his metaphorical re-creation of the world is merely a fleeting fictional gesture. As in traditional pastoral, where political strife and civic duty eventually invade the *locus amoenus* and destroy it, in this modern pastoral, science, with all of her "matter of fact about the ice storm," interrupts his reverie and demands capitulation to an empirical explanation. The speaker seems to resent science's intrusion, however, and once again he embarks upon another reverie, this one even more fantastical and teeming with images of a single, human will braving alien entanglements:

> I should prefer to have some boy bend them
> As he went out and in to fetch the cows—
> Some boy too far from town to learn baseball,
> Whose only play was what he found himself,
> Summer or winter, and could play alone.
> One by one he subdued his father's trees
> By riding them down over and over again
> Until he took the stiffness out of them,
> And not one but hung limp, not one was left
> For him to conquer.

> (*CPP&P*, 118)

Frost's attempted return to a Wordsworthian childhood, an imagined world in which the childlike vision of nature's munificence has not yet been corrupted by knowledge or doubt, obviously cannot provide him with any lasting psychological relief. Instead, far from revealing a benevolent cosmic order "recollected in tranquillity," the isolated boy who finds happiness in an activity of his own making becomes a metaphor for our necessity to subdue by any means possible an inimical natural world whose romantic possibilities have been eradicated by science. The necessity of this reparation can arise only from a poet who is entirely self-conscious about how ineffective his fictional reveries are in the face of scientific truth. While imaginative forms allow him for a brief moment to elevate his mental processes beyond the reach of cosmic mechanism, he knows that even as he imposes his fictions upon reality, nature's hard facts undermine his constructs, thus making an equivalent redeeming countervision nearly impossible.

Frost's rarely discussed later poem "Any Size We Please" (1949) serves as a strong rebuttal to the scientific positivism of "Birches." A sonnet divided into two equal parts by the period in the syllabic middle of line seven, the poem formally mirrors the radical shift in cosmology that occurred during Frost's own lifetime. The first half is clearly influenced by Euclid's parallel postulate, an idea that led not only to an unquestioned acceptance of infinite space and absolute time but also to Newton's belief in the intricate order of God's clockwork universe. Here the narrator, feeling insignificant as part of the natural order (the "he" and the "I" are the same person), holds his arms out parallel in "infinite appeal" to a universe that refuses to respond to his entreaties:

> No one was looking at his lonely case,
> So like a half-mad outpost sentinel,
> Indulging an absurd dramatic spell,
> Albeit not without some shame of face,
> He stretched his arms out to the dark of space
> And held them absolutely parallel
> In infinite appeal.
>
> (CPP&P, 359)

The consolations to be gathered from this appeal are minimal, even as the speaker seems perplexed by an exaggerated posture that he can assume only in private. In the second half of the poem, the narrator, finding this lack of celestial response a portentous "hell," immediately draws his arms around him in an effort to contain the immense size of the universe and transform it into a more manageable size:

> Then saying, 'Hell'
> He drew them in for warmth of self-embrace.
> He thought if he could have his space all curved
> Wrapped in around itself and self-befriended,
> His science needn't get him so unnerved.
> He had been too all out, too much extended.

He slapped his breast to verify his purse
And hugged himself for all his universe.

(CPP&P, 359–60)

This exploratory gesture "between subject matter and form" might have been unremarkable had Frost not grounded the sonnet's final seven lines in Einstein's curved space-time dimension, a theory based upon Riemannian geometrical models, which set limits on the boundaries of physical space. Frost's shift from one paradigm to another also suggests knowledge of Gödel's theorem, which states that while a geometrical proof validates an initial set of postulates, the postulates themselves cannot be proven within the mathematical system itself.[63] Geometrical proof in no way guarantees the truth of any set of axioms. Scientific paradigms are so prone to revision and collapse that the best we can do is explore and adventure for a while, draw in to consolidate our gains, and accept the idea that uncertainty need not paralyze our quest for meaning and purpose in the world, however unstable our answers might ultimately be.

The pervasive scientific skepticism that informs "Any Size We Please" is also a prominent feature of "The Bear," a poem that reveals how knowledge mediates among several extremes, none of which can be regarded as truer than any other. On the surface, the poem addresses a conflict between our desire to return to an unbridled primordial state and our equally strong desire to erect artificial barriers or landmarks that can guide us through the wilderness. Upon closer inspection, however, "The Bear" demonstrates how intellect, rather than liberating us from nature, merely defines the boundaries of our perception. From the outset, the poem laments the fact that human beings possess an innate curiosity and simultaneously celebrates the unbridled instinct that drives the bear's forays through the wilderness:

The bear puts both arms around the tree above her
And draws it down as if it were a lover
And its choke cherries lips to kiss good-by,
Then lets it snap back upright in the sky.
Her next step rocks a boulder on a wall
(She's making her cross-country in the fall).
Her great weight creaks the barbed-wire in its staple
As she flings over and off down through the maples,
Leaving on one wire tooth a lock of hair.

(CPP&P, 247)

In contrast to "Birches," "The Bear" focuses upon a creature that, endowed by nature to master its environment, subdues natural and artificial
barriers by brute physical force. Relatively invulnerable to any structures
standing in its way (hence leaving nothing but a lock of hair), the bear
appeals to the speaker's desire to abandon the corrupting influences of an
intellect that has imposed upon nature too many patterns, mores, and traditions. Despite the speaker's knowledge that the bear's own natural urges
negate autonomous choice, he, like the bear, seeks a more direct, instinctive
relationship to the natural world than he has yet encountered through scientific or philosophical inquiry. Emphasizing the inability of either discipline to provide any secure forms of knowledge, Frost chronicles the futility of our intellectual efforts to comprehend a natural world:

> Man acts more like the poor bear in a cage
> That all day fights a nervous inward rage,
> His mood rejecting all his mind suggests.
> He paces back and forth and never rests
> The toe-nail click and shuffle of his feet,
> The telescope at one end of his beat,
> And at the other end the microscope,
> Two instruments of nearly equal hope,
> And in conjunction giving quite a spread.
> Or if he rests from scientific tread,
> 'Tis only to sit back and sway his head
> Through ninety odd degrees of arc, it seems,
> Between two metaphysical extremes.
> He sits back on his fundamental butt
> With lifted snout and eyes (if any) shut,
> (He looks almost religious but he's not),
> And back and forth he sways from cheek to cheek,
> At one extreme agreeing with one Greek,
> At the other agreeing with another Greek
> Which may be thought, but only so to speak.
> A baggy figure, equally pathetic
> When sedentary and when peripatetic.

(CPP&P, 247)

Pacing back and forth like a caged, raging animal, Frost's frustrated man
demonstrates that truth does not reside in the literal correspondence be-

tween concepts and reality but rather in the movement between two metaphysical extremes. Platonic idealism (our "sedentary" truths) and Aristotelian processes (our "peripatetic" truths) inform our knowledge in any given historical moment and condition our interpretation of life and nature. Failing to find the correct interpretation of life through the use of one philosophical framework, we become aware of our diminutive place in space and are forced by our desire for certainty to shift our gaze to the other. Intellectual history, the poem implies, is merely a process of shifting emphasis, in which we turn from idealism to naturalism, or vice versa. In the absence of any permanent or satisfying correspondence between nature and knowledge, the best Frost's modern bear can do is "reject all his mind suggests" and begin searching anew for more comprehensive truths, which unfortunately will forever elude him.

The antipositivist account of science that informs "The Bear" invites comparison with one of Frost's most complete rejections of astronomical certainty, the perplexing poem "Skeptic" (1949). Perhaps more fully influenced by modern physics than any of his earlier astronomical poems, "Skeptic" not only doubts the hard facts of science but also offers an alternative method for comprehending the world more clearly. To understand the full significance of these esoteric stanzas, it is first necessary to understand the scientific theories that inform this poem.

Early-twentieth-century astronomers had no clear evidence that observed astronomical objects lay outside our own Milky Way galaxy. In 1912, however, the work of V. M. Slipher proved that objects resided not only outside our galaxy but a great distance from it.[64] Basing his measurements of stellar distance upon what later came to be known as the "red shift," Slipher observed that light emitted from distant stars and galaxies always shifted toward the red spectrum. In 1929 Edwin Hubble, using Slipher's theories, concluded that the red shift was proportional to a stellar object's distance from our galaxy and that the greater the distance between any two galaxies, the greater the speed at which they were separating.[65] This important observation, later termed Hubble's law, was seen by many as a confirmation of Georges Lemaître's controversial big bang theory (1927), which saw the universe as originating from a singular cosmic explosion. Although Lemaître and his theory were ridiculed by many scientists, Hubble's law implied not only that the universe seemed to be expanding uniformly toward higher states of entropy but that cosmic expansion must eventually end in thermodynamic equilibrium, the so-called heat death of the universe. Confronting these disturbing theories, Frost's speaker attempts to reconcile diminutive human experience with the vast dimensions of an indifferent cosmos:

> Far star that tickles for me my sensitive plate
> And fries a couple of ebon atoms white,
> I don't believe I believe a thing you state.
> I put no faith in the seeming facts of light.
>
> I don't believe I believe you're the last in space,
> I don't believe you're anywhere near the last,
> I don't believe what makes you red in the face
> Is after explosion going away so fast.
>
> (*CPP&P,* 353)

As in "Any Size We Please," Frost's speaker once again tries to contain the immense size of the universe by challenging the epistemological status of the poem's informing concepts. The idiomatic expression "I don't believe I believe" reflects the poet's teetering vacillation between belief and doubt, as well as his inability to discern whether the "seeming facts of light" can be attributed to either particles or waves. The dual nature of light, coupled with his own recognition that the light he sees is already far older than the light currently emitted by the star, casts doubt upon the veracity of his observations and thus prevents him from accepting any theory that claims the universe will die a "heat death."

The pervasive doubt that informs our understanding of light spills over into the second stanza, where the poet vacillates even further. While he seems able to accept the idea that the far star is not the "last" alternative galaxy in the universe, he appears reluctant to accept that the universe is continually expanding in the "after explosion" of the big bang. Calling all prior evidence into question, the speaker abandons his search for definitive answers and once again draws in to consolidate his gains:

> The universe may or may not be very immense.
> As a matter of fact there are times when I am apt
> To feel it close in tight against my sense
> Like a caul in which I was born and still am wrapped.
>
> (*CPP&P,* 353)

Evocative and completely appropriate for his need to contain space, Frost's comparison of the universe to the womb's protective membrane once again satisfies his need to transform a threatening environment with metaphorical activity. Unlike "Birches," however, where Frost's imaginative transformations are rudely interrupted by scientific knowledge, "Skeptic" maintains an easy stasis between fact and fiction, or more accurately, between one fiction disguised as science and another fiction disguised as poetry. In either case, what Frost describes here is a means by which he can satisfy his thirst for real knowledge. By calling into doubt the truth claims of all scientific theories and metaphorically transforming them into protective enclosures, Frost reveals that the only way for us to understand the universe is to measure it by its responsiveness to human need. Although scientific evidence may or may not inform us that both organic life and the universe are expanding toward an entropic death, imaginative reverie and common sense transform those discomforting "matters of fact" into more congenial ideas that rescue us from fear.

Frost elaborates upon this idea in "All Revelation" (1938), perhaps his fullest poetic meditation on the futility of speculation about the origin of matter, thought, and knowledge. An elaborate fertility ritual, the poem's union of mind and matter plays with history's most important ideas regarding the construction of knowledge. It also ponders whether the world of sensory experience can be an adequate object of knowledge if our modes of perception continually change.

In the first ten lines of the poem Frost examines at least four different epistemological theories, none of which attains prominence as *the* definitive account of how we formulate knowledge. Neither wholly active nor wholly passive, the natural world and human consciousness interact with one another, breaking down the traditional nineteenth-century dichotomy of a penetrating scientific consciousness and penetrated natural object:

> A head thrusts in as for the view,
> But where it is it thrusts in from
> Or what it is it thrusts into
> By that Cyb'laean avenue,
> And what can of its coming come,
>
> And whither it will be withdrawn,
> And what take hence or leave behind,
> These things the mind has pondered on
> A moment and still asking gone.
> Strange apparition of the mind!

(*CPP&P*, 302)

As the first five lines make plain by their obvious sexual diction (*thrust* occurs three times in the opening lines), knowledge can be conceived of as an instinctual urge, the origin and end of which must necessarily remain a mystery. Partially determined by an unknown natural force that impels consciousness into uncharted territory (the Darwinian position), cognition appears initially to be a bodily function, a purely practical mechanism that allows us to negotiate the environment in a manner that satisfies our immediate needs, values, and desires. Viewed in this manner, the rational intellect for Frost is an adaptational tool of survival. The end of our contemplation is not arbitrary; rather, nature directs our thought toward those material objects that can serve us in the most productive and protective ways.

The suggestion is strong here, however, that problems arise once mind and matter begin to interact with one another. Whether the mediating subject constructs the object of its knowledge (the romantic position), whether the subject "withdraws" from its object to complete the necessary separation of mind and matter (the empiricist position) or whether the mind will "ponder" constructs that exist independently of empirical data (the rationalist position), the end result remains ambiguous. As both the object and the subject of its contemplation, the mind can know neither its own cognitive processes nor the noumenal world that exists beyond the boundaries of perception and rationality. Frost makes clear that each method sets limits on the type of knowledge the mind can comprehend, thus relegating to the provinces of illusion ("strange apparition of the mind") any concept formulated outside one particular method. What counts, Frost seems to suggest, is not so much the integrity of our concepts as the processes by which we derive whatever meaning we can from a mysterious and "impervious" natural world.

The third and fourth stanzas extend the abstract inquiry of the first stanzas and offer a Jamesian account of how sensation actually stimulates conceptual activity. Here our excursive mediating consciousness, metaphorically compared to a "cathode ray," and the objective "geodesic" world upon which it operates conspire to produce the conceptual offspring that emerge in the poem's final lines. Frost's choice of the cathode ray to describe the interplay between conceptual abstraction and immediate experience is an exceptionally accurate illustration of Jamesian pragmatism. By using this figure, Frost implies that we have been equipped by nature to direct our mental activity toward a freely chosen object of contemplation:

But the impervious geode
Was entered, and its inner crust
Of crystals with a ray cathode
At every point and facet glowed
In answer to the mental thrust.

Eyes seeking the response of eyes
Bring out the stars, bring out the flowers,
Thus concentrating earth and skies
So none need be afraid of size.
All revelation has been ours.

(CPP&P, 302–3)

Just as a directed beam of electrons might illuminate a phosphorescent screen, so too does intellect illuminate, or "bring out," the world's more salient features. The illuminated crystals, however, constitute only a small part of the geode's interior cavity. Unable either to penetrate beyond the material world's negligible surfaces or to expand its inquiry to encompass an adequate scientific breadth, the mind is limited to concepts that are in part predetermined by environmental exigencies.

This obvious shift from abstraction to sensation reveals not only the futility of all metaphysical speculation but also the inherent wisdom of our attempts to shape the local features of experience. Our innate curiosity to know a sentient being, whether human or divine, forces us into conceptual innovation, which in turn leads to greater experiential revelation.[66] By "bringing" out the "stars" and "flowers," Frost "concentrates"—both mentally and physically—the inexplicable world and transforms it into a genial realm where he can find his bearings and contemplate life's transient beauty. As the title "All Revelation" ultimately implies, knowledge is a product of both invention and discovery, a process of creating the useful forms that reveal our relationship to the material world. And while we cannot fully recover certainty through either philosophy or science, we must nevertheless "reveal" the forms of existence to ourselves in a manner that responds to our deepest psychic needs. Only then can we begin to prosper in a difficult, immense world and strengthen, as Frost once claimed, our tentative "hold on the planet."[67]

The same epistemological skepticism keeps repeating itself in Frost's work after 1925. Scientifically based poems such as "The Star-Splitter," "A Star in a Stoneboat," "On Looking Up by Chance at the Constellations," and "Lost in Heaven," recapitulate in one form or another the antipositivist attitudes that Frost cultivated in the years following his encounters with Heisenberg and Bohr. In their metaphysical suspicion, in their exploratory mediation between abstraction and experience, and in their strong affirmation of our ability to amend the reality we perceive, these poems exhibit the means by which Frost transformed the immense, chaotic, and dark worlds that he so often conjured. Perhaps the most important distinction one can make between these and the earlier poems is that in the later poems, rather than cowering beneath science, Frost paradoxically makes use of science to surmount his anxiety over the heaven-shattering materialism that pervades so many of his earlier poems and letters. Indeed, far from being the obsessed antagonist of physics and biology that many commentators describe, Frost demonstrates in his later poems a remarkable tranquillity in the face of those disciplines. Science, he suggests, has not made the world safer or less mysterious, and, as he makes clear throughout his later work, he believes such prospects are highly unlikely.

Lack of ultimate certainty, however, need not paralyze our efforts to find meaning and value in the world. As Frost continually reminds us, uncertainty can awaken in us an unlimited opportunity to produce the radiant forms—the beautiful myths, models, and fictions of our imagination—that bring order and meaning to existence. Although we can never be completely sure whether our propositions are true, we can measure their "truthfulness" by the extent to which they guide us successfully through the chaotic flux of experience. Neither wholly optimistic nor wholly pessimistic, this twofold attitude—an acceptance of our limitations and an acknowledgment of our life-affirming capabilities—underlies Frost's mature approach toward all orders of knowledge, including science, thus marking him as one of the most eloquent spokesmen of the humanistic tradition. This skeptical attitude also helped to restore Frost's belief in divine purpose, what he often called in private moments of religious speculation a "wisdom beyond wisdom." As Frost grew older and settled his quarrel with scientific materialism, he found more reasons to be confident about the intellectual integrity of his own religious beliefs. "I despise religiosity," Frost once stated in 1949. "But I have no religious doubts. Not about God's existence, anyway."[68]

Such bald statements of belief are difficult to ignore, and one can do so only at the peril of neglecting the mature philosophical position that Frost adopted in the mid-1920s and maintained for the rest of his life. Occupying a stance that mediates halfway between the epistemologies of Bergson and James, Frost believed that man's anthropocentric creations were deceiving illusions that served as barriers to a deeper reality, ultimately hidden to consciousness (the Bergsonian view), or that man's invented forms were synecdochical parts of a much larger unity whose purpose and magnitude remained imperceptible (the Jamesian position). In several respects, Frost's vacillation between these two positions reflects his perpetual struggle over whether to relocate the fallen, pristine realm of Platonic perfection in the transcendent realm of some preconscious unity or in the immanent creative surge of Bergson's *élan vital*. This problem seems to have preoccupied Frost's thoughts toward the end of his life, and whereas early in his life he denied being a "Platonist," in his old age he admitted that many of his ideas exhibited certain Platonic characteristics. In a 1961 address to the Greek Archaeological Society in Athens, Frost explained that many of his late "romantic tendencies," as he called them, were derived from Plato. "I like to think that I'm not quite a Platonist," he claimed, "and then all of a sudden I find myself saying something that I myself trace right back to Plato. For instance, I say there's more religion outside the church than in, there's more love outside of marriage than in, and there's more wisdom outside of philosophy than in."[69] Frost's enduring faith that a larger or more benevolent reality exists beyond our intellectual creations clearly indicates that he saw religious conventions both as catalysts for civic order and as limiting orthodoxies that had to be overcome in the name of intellectual freedom. Adhering to the latter demand, Frost challenged the religious dogma he inherited from his mother, and he ardently disputed the scientific ideas that had given rise to materialism and atheism. If the truthfulness of man's invented concepts could not be grounded in anything beyond the self, Frost reasoned, why was it not possible to discredit the concepts that had purged the modern world of its religious belief?

Perhaps, in the final analysis, one can best describe Frost's poetry as an art of equipoise, his lasting achievement a body of work whose emotional gravity and formal temperance enable us always to find small moments of hope amidst life's abominations. Virtually every feature of Frost's work, from his elegant metrics to his heroic themes, from his imaginative excursions to his imaginative withdrawals, is free of the emotional excess that characterizes so much of his generation's poetry. The means by which Frost reconciled his early quarrel with science might best be described as controlled moderation. Speaking with Jonas Salk in 1956, Frost, seven years removed from his own death in 1963, offered one of his most eloquent and inclusive statements on how he regarded science and religion:

I think a scientist and anybody with an active mind lives on tentatives
rather than tenets. And that you've got to feel a certain pleasure in
the tentativeness of it all. The unfinality of it. And that's what you live
[and]—when I say that you hang around until you catch on, that
doesn't mean you hang on until you get the final answer to anything,
that you hang onto—the spirit in which we live, in which this is to
be taken, the tentativeness of things, the process of things, of the little
certainties that we get among the uncertainties, the little place we make,
the little formula we make. And those—there's faith in it, of course, the
faith that those all some way are related and may be tumbled together
somewhere, that they may make something, may make something.[70]

Perhaps Frost took this final cue from Einstein, that enigmatic, optimistic,
and dominating spirit of the age, who, only two weeks before his own death
in 1955, had confided to Bernard Cohen that because our "physical theories
were far from adequate" the fundamental mysteries of physics might always be with us.[71] To Frost, who read this account and praised it in one of
his Bread Loaf lectures,[72] Einstein's words must have been a source of incalculable comfort. Coming from a man who had spent his whole adult life
searching for a unified theory for all physical phenomena, this admission
of a "great attempt" that had so far failed must have joyfully confirmed for
Frost what he had suspected all along: that the wisest man, as Socrates once
declared, was wise simply because he knew he did not know.

4. Education by Poetry

And there are many other things I have found myself saying about poetry, but the chiefest of these is that it is metaphor, saying one thing and meaning another, saying one thing in terms of another, the pleasure of ulteriority. Poetry is simply made of metaphor. So also is philosophy—and science, too, for that matter, if it will take the soft impeachment from a friend.

"The Constant Symbol" (1946)

ONE OF THE MOST CONSPICUOUS FEATURES OF ROBERT FROST'S career is that he was one of the few American modernist poets who never wrote a single volume of literary criticism. Despite writing steadily for more than sixty years and meeting Britain's and America's most influential poets, Frost never publicly participated in the cultural conversations that ignited the modernist revolution, nor did he ever offer the adroit critical judgments that made Pound and Eliot arbiters of taste for nearly half a century. That this was the case seems largely the consequence of Frost's sensitive, and sometimes defensive, personality. Throughout his life he displayed in his letters and lectures a strong aversion to pedantry, partly because he genuinely felt threatened by his contemporaries' success, but even more because he thought that literary critics corrupted the unsullied relationship between poet and reader. Critics were too scholarly and meddlesome, too rigid in their tastes, too quick to point out a poet's minor flaws or virtues, too dogmatic in their explication, and, above all, too eager to intrude upon those special moments when writer and reader collaborated to form the brief "clarification of life" that Frost considered so necessary to any well-written poem. One consequence of this antagonistic attitude toward literary scholars was that Frost never published criticism that measured up to Eliot's *Sacred Wood,* Stevens's *Necessary Angel,* or even Pound's *ABC of Reading.* Although Frost privately expressed his insecurity over his sparse critical output, admitting once that the "very thought of reviewing scare[d] him incoherent,"[1] he tended to downplay his critical deficiencies. "Writing about writing," he claimed, was simply something he had "never done nor wanted to do."[2]

This is not to say that Frost never had anything important to say about poetry. On the contrary, he thought long and hard about his craft, and when he did muster the courage to write about it, he often elucidated in a clear and coherent manner ideas about poetry that were already in the air when he arrived on the Harvard campus in the fall of 1897. The problem in assessing Frost's contribution to modern aesthetics, however, is that so much of what he wrote or said about poetry exists only in fragments. Apart from his passing tribute to Robinson's *King Jasper* (1935) and the brief preface to his own *Collected Poems* (1939), most of Frost's pertinent ideas appear in letters, marginalia, lectures, and interviews. Furthermore, his cavalier attitude has limited our capacity to assess the sincerity of his aesthetic judgments.[3] So often does he contradict himself or feign a melange of affected postures that it is difficult to ascertain when he is serious and when he is merely fooling. Contradictions abound, and the result has been a great deal of critical inconsistency over just where and how Frost fits into the tradition of twentieth-century American poetry. In the past few years he has alternately been labeled the last poet of the nineteenth century and the first poet of the twentieth; a modernist, a classicist, and a romantic; a philosopher of the highest rank and a purveyor of "Hallmark" sentimentalities; a gifted synecdochist and an Emersonian emblemist; a salacious elder statesman and a "figure of frustrated impotence."[4] For a poet who strove to clarify life, Frost's critical reticence merely led to confusion. The sheer breadth of the disagreements over his work might well have astonished even him, though he once claimed that "no sweeter music can come to my ears than the clash of arms over my dead body."[5]

To explain some of these confusions, in this chapter I situate Frost's poetics in the intellectual context of the late nineteenth and early twentieth centuries and explain how Frost's ideas about poetry matured from a narrow consideration of aesthetics into a much broader concern for the nature and function of poetry in an age dominated by science. Central to my argument is the idea that his art emanates from an aesthetics of "surfaces and depths." By "surfaces and depths" I mean Frost's lifelong tendency to posit a sharp dichotomy between the world of ordinary experience—one that we have constructed through mental activity—and an elusive realm of confusing sensory stimuli that both precedes and necessitates our cognitive shaping of it.[6] As I hope to make clear, virtually all of Frost's significant ideas about poetry, from his early ideas about the "sound of sense" to his later definition of poetry as metaphor, depend upon this underlying principle for their rational coherence. Additionally, an aesthetics of "surfaces and depths," as I also hope to make clear, enabled Frost to reassert the cultural value of poetry. As I have been arguing throughout this book, the instrumentalist accounts of knowledge that arose in response to materialism also influenced the development of modernist poetics. The modernist propensity to investigate the relationship between concrete sensation and conceptual abstraction became one of the movement's most important features and, in turn, led to the novel idea that scientists and poets, rather than thinking differently, generated knowledge by employing the same cognitive processes. Both constructed new forms or models that established new relationships in the flux of sensory experience.[7]

That Frost developed an aesthetics of surfaces and depths is not surprising given that he fell heir to the neo-Kantian revolt that emerged in response to French positivism and British materialism. Although most nineteenth-century philosophers had agreed with Comte that knowledge required some engagement with the particulars of the physical world, many began to reject his idea that metaphysics was an obsolete subject for inquiry. Whether one complied with positivism or vitalism was, of course, largely dependent upon one's religious temperament. More scientifically inclined thinkers such as Huxley and Marx, for example, were convinced that a clear distinction could be made between objective and subjective realities and that the material world and its informing laws could be comprehended with a great deal of certainty. Thus, rather than concentrating their attention on unverifiable metaphysical or religious problems, they used the language and methods of science to mitigate the grim economic and social problems that had arisen in the aftermath of urbanization and industrialization. In general, despite drawing attention to the poverty, squalor, and disease that besieged the lower classes in England and France, the materialists and positivists were fairly optimistic. Having descended from the architects of the Enlightenment, they were convinced that reason, sensible political action, and scientific progress were the best means of ameliorating the dehumanizing conditions that industrialism had created. For them, any attempt to extend systematic inquiry beyond material phenomena to a metaphysical reality was not only a pointless and irrational enterprise but also an abdication of moral and social responsibility.

In stark contrast to the positivists and Marxists, more metaphysically inclined thinkers rejected the constructed perceptions of science, arguing that an underlying reality was more readily accessible through intuition. Echoing the romantics' rejection of science and skeptical about the accuracy of scientific conclusions, Schopenhauer and Bergson, for example, reaffirmed man's capacity to recover metaphysics, but in an antirational form that bore little resemblance to the Enlightenment's emphasis upon inductive or deductive reason. For them, "true" reality lay behind the various conventions that organized and shaped the familiar world of daily existence. To recover a deeper reality, they argued, it was necessary to divest oneself of conventional knowledge and abandon the scientist's tendency toward ratiocination. For this group of thinkers, aesthetic contemplation was thus one of the principal means of liberating the self from the blinding conventions that intervene between sense perception and direct, intuitive experience.[8] Because art in their view did not systematize, classify, or "dissect" experience (to use Wordsworth's word), it temporarily projected humans into an eternal stream of unmediated impressions that brought them closer to the true nature of reality.

When one compares these various schools with Frost's essays on poetry, it becomes clear, once the scattered fragments have been assembled, that Frost's poetics displays a confusing mediation between positivist and vitalist poles. At times, especially early in his career, Frost devalues objective knowledge and emphasizes the recovery of immediate experience. Later in his career, however, he advocates the creation of objective forms that can organize reality in an effective and practical manner. While this tightrope act between poetry as practical, stabilizing form and poetry as illusion may seem precarious, it is necessary to remember that Frost thought that by shuttling between these two epistemologies—by creating useful forms and then letting them break down before they degenerated into the kind of wisdom that "sects and cults" were built on—he had solved for himself the two problems that science presented him. First, he invented a more congenial world that suited his everyday needs, and second, he left room for a creative spiritual reality that could infuse life with greater meaning and moral purpose. In other words, temporal, secular knowledge could be revealed in poetic form, while knowledge of the absolute could be consigned to religion.

Frost's firm belief that knowledge evolved in response to changing societal exigencies expressed itself in an art that embraced the fluid correspondence he had observed between the objective and subjective realms of experience. Following James, Frost understood that no clear division existed between the objective and subjective worlds and that neither realm could be wholly subordinated to the other. Both the raw material of nature and the imagination interacted with one another in any given moment of lived experience. If art were to mirror this basic feature of life, it would thus have to be created with a view toward incorporating the objective and the subjective, the rational and the emotional, the material and the spiritual, the conventional and the radical. "Outer weather" affected "inner weather," and vice versa, in any poem that would give coherence to the confusion and chaos of daily existence. Commenting on the correspondence between nature and prosody, Frost revealed some of the rationale behind his aesthetic ideas in a letter to Katharine Bates in 1919. "Free rhythms," he wrote, "are as disorderly as nature; meters are as orderly as human nature and take their rise in rhythms just as human nature rises out of nature."[9] Unbridled poetic license was thus never a valid option for any serious artist. Just as nature necessitated and impeded the creation of new form, tradition enlivened and constrained individual talent. In breaking free from his poetic precursors Frost was thus never radical; rather, he preferred, as he himself claimed, an "old-fashioned way to be new."[10]

Frost's desire to be old-fashionedly new manifested itself not only in his effort to liberate himself from an outmoded genteel tradition but also in his efforts to extend the quality and scope of his poetics. Although it would be folly to apply a strict chronology to Frost's critical maturation, it is nevertheless possible to divide his career into three distinct periods, each of which corresponds to a set of events that inspired accompanying shifts in critical emphasis.

In the first major period, what I would call the aesthetic phase, Frost was concerned entirely with an original theory of versification, which he called "the sound of sense." Beginning about 1911, when Frost was teaching Shakespeare at the Pinkerton Academy, and culminating in a landmark discussion with F. S. Flint and T. E. Hulme in 1913, this period saw Frost distinguish his technique from both the Georgian poets, with whom he was closely affiliated, and the practices of Ezra Pound, whose "imagist" movement had already been influencing epigones in England and America for several years. During this phase of his career, Frost first recognized the dramatic possibilities inherent in colloquial speech rhythms and began to realize that James's and Bergson's distinctions between surfaces and depths might also apply to a theory of prosody. As we shall see, Frost's idea that there exists in poetry an antagonistic, though beneficial, relationship between imposed meter and rhetorical intonation is strikingly similar to Bergson's distinction in *Creative Evolution* between the retarding forms of matter and the creative forces of organic life, which would express themselves despite encountering material resistance.

The second major period in Frost's career, what I would call his metaphorical phase, began in the mid-1920s, after his encounters with Eddington, Heisenberg, and Bohr showed him that even scientists could challenge the philosophical assumptions undergirding scientific materialism. Armed with enough credible scientific evidence to establish a greater epistemological equivalence between science and poetry, Frost extended his surfaces-and-depths aesthetics into a much broader concern for poetry's cultural value. According to the Frost of this phase, metaphor was not merely an ornamental figure of speech but, as James and Nietzsche had argued, a complex psychological process by which one could arrive at a fresh understanding of life. The poet does not render an exact representation of a pre-existing reality but instead creates new metaphors, new models, or new systems of relations that might defamiliarize everyday experience and recreate it anew. In this phase of his career, Frost continually argued that poets should accept their responsibility to disrupt conventional thought. Thus, his essays from this period are filled with language that reflects a Nietzschean desire to be courageous in the face of threatening metaphysical conditions or repressive intellectual conventions.

The last major phase, what I would call Frost's expressionist phase, corresponds nicely to the poet's rejuvenation of spirit in the late 1930s, a condition that, as Donald Sheehy has argued, occurred as a result of his love affair with his secretary, Kay Morrison.[11] This last phase, which saw him resuscitate in *A Witness Tree* (1942) the lyric genius that distinguished his first four books, marks a significant withdrawal from his earlier insistence upon the poet as autonomous "maker" and upon poetry as consciously crafted form. In what is perhaps his best and best-known essay from this period, "The Figure a Poem Makes" (1939), Frost is much more receptive to the romantic notion of the poem as organic process. In this phase he repudiated the neoclassical depiction of the poet as a conduit for conventional doctrine and instead saw the poet as a lone discoverer, who, buoyed along by external forces, carefully discloses to himself and others the multivalent truths available in an open-ended world filled with possibilities. Although

Frost readily admitted that the poet served as a catalyst for creation, he believed that the poem's content, its "wildness of logic," as he called it, was in some mysterious way predetermined by an unconscious, cohering principle that revealed itself only as the imagination sought closure for its subject. By embracing a poetics of organic form, Frost, like Coleridge and Emerson before him, thus celebrated an aesthetic in which spontaneity, freedom, and acquiescence to cohering subconscious impulses became the poet's most important virtues. Although he maintained throughout his life a strong belief that external form was necessary to constrain the wild impulses of the imagination, the unpredictability of a poem's internal structure remained for him an endless source of fascination. The way Frost arrived at the point where he was able to reinstate one of the key concepts of romanticism is evidence of a remarkable maturation.

Before we consider each of these phases, it would be worthwhile to pause briefly and consider the literary marketplace that Frost encountered as he began his career. As I have been arguing throughout this book, the modern world of industry and science left little room for poets to find a place for their art. Viewed as both feminine and irrelevant to the practical ideals of modern society, the genteel poetry published in popular magazines was deemed incapable of rendering modern experience accurately. Commenting on this dilemma, Frost once told Louis Mertins that his poems from *A Boy's Will* were inferior to his later work because in his first book he had merely imitated the pedestrian style and archaic diction of his late Victorian forebears:

> When I first began to write poetry—before the illumination of what
> possibilities there are in the sound of sense came to me—I was writing
> largely, though not exclusively, after the pattern of the past. For every
> poet begins that way—following some pattern or group of patterns. It is
> only when he has outgrown the pattern, and sees clearly for himself
> his own way that he has really started to become. You may go back to all
> those early poems of mine in A Boy's Will, and some that are left out
> of it. You will find me there using the traditional clichés. Even "Into My
> Own" has an "as't were." In "Stars" there is a line "O'er the tumultuous
> snow"; while in my very first poem "My Butterfly," I was even guilty of
> "theeing" and "thouing," a crime I have not committed since.[12]

Written in hindsight, this passage reveals two significant problems that Frost struggled with during his early years as a poet. As his specific reference to "theeing" and "thouing" indicates, Frost's first concern centered on the issue of credibility: what kind of diction would be most appropriate for a poet to render the complexities of modern experience accurately? Reflecting on his work from a perspective of nearly twenty-five years later, Frost recognized that his deliberate use of antiquated words had damaged his ethos. Such self-consciously affected language, employed in most cases simply to satisfy the demands of metrical constraints, hindered the emotional and intellectual nuances he sought to express honestly. Like all poetic revolutionaries, Frost equated changes in language with changes in the larger patterns of thought and considered it essential for a poet to endure occasional metamorphoses if he would adapt to the new environmental conditions around him.

Frost's desire to find a new lexicon closely links him to the other important modernists, such as Eliot and Pound. Although he publicly derided Eliot's notion of the "dissociated sensibility," stating in his "Letter to *The Amherst Student*" (1935) that "all ages of the world are bad,"[13] his poetry indicates that he felt that human experience in the twentieth century had been radically severed from the perceived continuities of the past and therefore demanded an alternative form of expression. The poetic idiom of Palgrave's *Golden Treasury* and Jesse Belle Rittenhouse's *Little Book of Modern Verse* (1912)—popular anthologies that cultivated a refined lyric gentility—no longer seemed to Frost a legitimate vehicle to express the complexities he associated with America's transition from an agrarian to an industrial society. In this respect Frost concurred with Eliot, who recognized that "a refreshment of poetic diction similar to that brought about by Wordsworth is called for."[14]

Although Frost wrote little formal prose discussing this problem, he nevertheless fully explored the dilemma in "Pan with Us," a poem he paired with "The Demiurge's Laugh" in *A Boy's Will*:

> Pan came out of the woods one day,—
> His skin and his hair and his eyes were gray,
> The gray of the moss of walls were they,—
>   And stood in the sun and looked his fill
>   At wooded valley and wooded hill.
>
> He stood in the zephyr, pipes in hand,
> On a height of naked pasture land;
> In all the country he did command
>   He saw no smoke and he saw no roof.
>   That was well! and he stamped a hoof.

His heart knew peace, for none came here
To this lean feeding save once a year
Someone to salt the half-wild steer,
  Or homespun children with clicking pails
  Who see so little they tell no tales.

He tossed his pipes, too hard to teach
A new-world song, far out of reach,
For a sylvan sign that the blue jay's screech
  And the whimper of hawks beside the sun
  Were music enough for him, for one.

Times were changed from what they were:
Such pipes kept less of power to stir
The fruited bough of the juniper
  And the fragile bluets clustered there
  Than the merest aimless breath of air.

They were pipes of pagan mirth,
And the world had found new terms of worth.
He laid him down on the sun-burned earth
  And raveled a flower and looked away—
  Play? Play?—What should he play?

                                                   (*CPP&P*, 32)

"Pan with Us" centers on the speaker's doubt that traditional aesthetic resources are still available to any poet who has lived long enough to see the beginning of the modern world. Similar to the landscape in Eliot's *Waste Land,* the landscape in "Pan with Us" lacks the lush fecundity of the Theocritan or Virgilian countryside, a point Frost makes abundantly clear by alluding to the salted fields laid waste by Roman legions. Here the poem's inhabitants do not harmonize with one another, as they do in Greek pastoral, nor does Pan seek communion with another poet who might play his pipes, in friendly competition, with equal vigor. Indeed, one of the most conspicuous features of "Pan with Us" is that there are no people in the poem. Like Dreiser's Carrie Meeber and Fitzgerald's Jay Gatsby, the "homespun children"—those best suited to participate in the Jeffersonian agrarian ideal—are no longer inspired by the natural setting around them and, as a result, have turned to the city as the site for their stories. In stark contrast to the communion and cooperation of the past, the blue jay and the hawk circle beneath the scorching sun in a perpetual Darwinian struggle, while the poet, searching for the right music to convey the desolation he sees around him, remains isolated and paralyzed.

The last stanza forcefully extends this dilemma. Unable to participate in the "pagan mirth" of an earlier age, Frost recognizes that he must conform to the world's "new terms of worth." He can no longer simply celebrate nature; as the raveled flower suggests, he must dominate it by brute force. The "new terms of worth" demand decisive action and exploitation, impulses perhaps more appropriate for the robber baron and industrialist than for the poet, and a new language rooted in a phenomenal world filled with competition and strife. But how was the poet to participate in the world's new terms of worth when the tradition of English and American poetry had cultivated values antithetical to business, industrialism, and science? As in so many of his lyrics, Frost refuses to answer the question, not because he wishes to avoid closure, as is usually the case in his poems, but because at the time when he composed this poem, in the first decade of the century, he did not yet have one. Despite his own awareness that the poet has to find a language more appropriate for the times, Frost continues to exploit in "Pan with Us" a vocabulary more characteristic of the nineteenth century. One cannot help hearing the ghosts of Longfellow, Tennyson, and Keats lurking behind such hackneyed phrases as "stood in the zephyr," "sylvan sign," "pagan mirth," or "heart knew peace." Yet Frost, whose own science-laden sensibility was in many ways not very far removed from our own, felt compelled, in the absence of any other plausible alternatives, to use the language that had worked so well in the past.

In addition to trying to find a language that could mirror the complexities of a modern technological society, Frost also sought to engender his poetry with a more masculine diction that might help to overturn the fin-de-siècle stereotype that poetry was essentially a feminine pastime.[15] At the beginning of the twentieth century, what was left of poetry's audience often turned to the genteel, sentimental verse of poets such as Edgar Guest and James Whitcomb Riley, two "fireside" figures whose work appeared in mainstream magazines such as the *Saturday Evening Post, Harper's,* and the *Atlantic.* While the general public seems to have valued such poetry for the refuge it provided them from the harsh realities of urban life, it was generally not taken seriously by critics with more refined tastes. In populist circles, poetry was usually read for its escapist entertainment—as a brief refuge from a sixty-hour workweek—while poets themselves were thought to embody ideals antithetical to the masculine values epitomized by such figures as Andrew Carnegie and Teddy Roosevelt.[16] Roosevelt, in particular, seems to have most embodied the spirit of the times. In *The Strenuous Life*, a book filled with Darwinian motifs of competition, aggression, and struggle, Roosevelt had argued that an emerging, industrial America should exhibit "resolution, courage, and indomitable will," virtues he associated with "the iron qualities . . . of true manhood."[17] Such "bully" ideals, buoyed along by a rising tide of nationalism, conflicted with the genteel values inherent in the poetry written between 1890 and 1910, a period Conrad Aiken deplored in 1922 as "graceful, sentimental, rightly ethical, gently idealistic."[18]

It is not surprising that with so much masculine rhetoric being broadcast in nearly every quarter of American society, male poets felt uncomfortable about revealing their vocation to the public. In a society that valued hard work, industry, and decisive action, the poet was often perceived as the equivalent of Plato's "light and winged creature," a person whose emotional or physical infirmities kept him from participating in the higher, and more masculine, faculties of reason. The attitude that poetry had become a "sort of embroidery for dilettantes and women," to use Pound's phrase,[19] helps to explain why Hemingway boxed and fished, why Faulkner contrived a commission in the Canadian Air Force, why Stevens asked his wife to keep secret his first collection of poems, and why Pound felt bound to reinvigorate a masculine figure of Christ. The fear of being labeled effeminate also helps to explain why Frost felt compelled to use the language of the "blue jay" and the "hawk" and why it was wise for him to expatriate himself to establish his career. To be a man and write poetry in turn-of-the-century America was an abdication of one's responsibility to work hard, provide for a family, and make enough money to live comfortably into old age.

In a 1913 letter to Sydney Cox, Frost, feeling the pressures of a practical America, expressed at least one of the motivations behind his move to England:

> I like that about the English—they all have time to dig the ground for the unutilitarian flower. I mean the men. It marks the great difference between them and our men. I like flowers you know but I like em wild, and I am rather the exception than the rule in an American village. . . . Americans will dig for peas and beans and such like utilities but not if they know it for posies. I knew a man who was a byword in five townships for the flowers he tended with his own hand. Neighbors kept hens and let them run loose just to annoy him.[20]

The frontier image of the sturdy, self-reliant American who produces for pragmatic rather than for aesthetic ends is presented here as the antithesis of the cultivated, genteel Englishman who can create his art without fear of ridicule.

The American urge to produce practical goods and services was not just an urban phenomenon but one that had pervaded rural environments as well. It was an ethos that Frost, for a variety of reasons, could not embrace, and he felt that his reputation had suffered as a result. A conversation with Louis Mertins reveals some of the difficulty Frost had in trying to appease his artistic urges while fulfilling his obligation to work his farm well: "They would see me starting out to work at all hours of the morning—approaching noon, to be more explicit. I always liked to shut up all hours of the night planning some inarticulate crime, going out to work when the spirit moved me, something they shook their heads ominously at, with proper prejudice. They would talk among themselves about my lack of energy. . . . I was a failure in their eyes from the start—very start."[21] Constantly on the defensive and anxious to justify his art to a public that cherished the ideal of utility, Frost, along with other American male modernists, consciously sought a masculine style that would invert the feminized tradition of Victorian verse.

Closely tied to the issue of finding an appropriate style was the even more vexing problem of originality. In many respects, Frost's desire to distinguish himself from tradition, "to become," as he phrased it, can be traced, as it can for all of the modernists, to the radical individualism first championed by Wordsworth and later more fully expressed by Nietzsche. While no evidence exists that Frost ever read Nietzsche directly, Frost's well-known associations with George Santayana, H. L. Mencken, Van Wyck Brooks, T. E. Hulme, and Ezra Pound suggest that he knew Nietzsche's philosophy, albeit in a diluted form that combined an odd mixture of Marxist and democratic principles. In fact, so ubiquitous was Nietzsche's thought at the turn of the century that it had a seductive effect on an entire generation of poets and artists. In addition to influencing Pound and Hulme in Britain, Nietzsche's idea that the true artist was a Sophoclean figure who threw off the shackles of convention and took a "deep look into the horror of nature"[22] became the central creed of the Greenwich Village school, a coterie of American critics that included, in addition to Mencken and Brooks, such luminaries as Kenneth Burke, Malcolm Cowley, Max Eastman, Randolph Bourne, and Frost's good friend Louis Untermeyer. Persuaded by Untermeyer to serve as a contributing editor of *Seven Arts,* one of the short-lived progressive "little magazines" that published nontraditional verse, Frost acquainted himself with the group's aesthetic principles, most of which were inseparable from their leftist politics. As Malcolm Cowley described the "Greenwich Village Idea" in *Exile's Return* (1934), artistic originality was commensurate with unbridled liberty: "Every law, convention or rule of art that prevents self-expression or the full enjoyment of the moment should be shattered and abolished."[23]

While Frost was certainly attracted to this kind of Nietzschean rhetoric and emphasized at times the artist's need for the courage and freedom to work in one's material, he nevertheless resisted the impulse to write in radically new forms—primarily because of the aesthetic considerations that I have already discussed but also because the literary marketplace was reluctant to embrace poets whose verse did not conform to established tastes. Like Eliot, Frost felt that if a poet was to learn his craft well and distinguish himself meaningfully against tradition, he had first to be a receptive student of the "patterns" of the past. Of course, for Frost tradition meant Palgrave, and though critical consensus generally agrees that Frost is a regional poet of a distinctly American vernacular, a brief glance at his juvenilia, most of which are so similar to Wordsworth and Shelley in substance and style so as to be indistinguishable, reveals just how completely the young Frost had fallen under the anthologist's spell. To wear the title of poet, one had not only to sound like the poets in the *Golden Treasury* but also to write only in lyric forms. The public demanded such an art, and Frost knew that if he was to attract a wide audience and sell enough poems to help feed his family, he would have to respond to the demands of the literary market.

Unfortunately, responding to accepted tastes often conflicted with artistic integrity. In a 1913 letter to John Bartlett, Frost revealed his intention to make a living by writing and selling poetry:

> You musn't take me too seriously if I now proceed to brag a bit about
> my exploits as a poet. There is one qualifying fact always to bear in
> mind: there is a kind of success called "of esteem" and it butters no
> parsnips. It means a success with the critical few who are supposed
> to know. But really to arrive where I can stand on my legs as a poet and
> nothing else, I must get outside that circle to the general reader who
> buys books in the thousands. I may not be able to do that. I believe in
> doing it—don't you doubt me there. I want to be a poet for all sorts
> and kinds. I could never make a merit of being caviar to the crowd the
> way my quasi-friend Pound does.[24]

That Frost did succeed attests not only to his perseverance but also to the way he managed, at times to the detriment of his health, his conflict between external constraints and internal desires. In a recent compelling book on Frost's poetics, Mark Richardson has appropriately described Frost's conflict between originality and tradition as an "ordeal," a process by which Frost's art responds to both an "individualistic inner desire," which reinforces the primacy of the will, and the "outer forces of 'conformity' and sociality" that would constrain it.[25] While all true poets engage the burden of the past to some degree, Richardson has nevertheless exposed a contradiction in Frost's poetics that is not easily reconciled.[26] The desire both to be new and to express a world utterly changed by science, contrasted with his and others' expectations of what poetry should sound like, reveals some of the contradictions inherent not only within Frost but within the larger modernist project itself.

What enabled Frost to overcome these contradictions, to be both an original and a popular poet, was that he subverted romanticism's idealism without completely disrupting the accepted standards of literary taste. Unlike the poems of the high modernists, which often displayed a surface obscurity and a subsurface banality, Frost's poems were simple and accessible on the surface yet complex and subtle in their analysis of modern life. By composing his poems in this manner, Frost could become, as Frank Lentricchia has argued, "a poet for all kinds, but only by favoring the ordinary reader, by fashioning an accessible and seductively inviting literary surface that would welcome the casual reader of poetry . . . while burying very deep the sorts of subtleties that might please those accustomed to Pound's aesthetic caviar."[27]

While the literary marketplace certainly affected Frost's decision to make his poetry more accessible, he also had important philosophical reasons for resisting the impulse to make his surfaces opaque. Frost's celebration of poetry's aural resources and Pound's dedication to its visual resources were symptomatic of a larger divergence in the way each initially responded to the demands science had placed on them. Essentially, their quarrel centered on the issue of where one could locate a "true" reality so as to make poetry more authoritative. For Pound, poetry's truths were best conveyed when the poet rendered the objects of perception as precisely as possible. Pound thought that by presenting a series of surface images and then fixing in collage form the surprising relations between them, he could defamiliarize ordinary experience and direct the reader's attention to an objective world uncorrupted by emotional excess. By contrast, Frost located truth in the temporal rather than in the spatial elements of experience. Employing an intoned language that approximated the sequential character of music, Frost, early in his career, sought to recreate in his poetry the fluid movements of consciousness. Since visual or conceptual surfaces always served as a barrier to the dynamic processes of actual experience, the poet was to make those surfaces as transparent as possible. Only then could the reader recognize the poet's subtle changes in thought and emotion as they unfolded over time.

Surprisingly, the unlikely source for both men's visions was Bergson, whose ideas about art and language had filtered down to Frost and Pound via their mutual friend T. E. Hulme. Hulme, who had just translated Bergson's *Introduction to Metaphysics,* met with Frost and Pound on several occasions and discussed issues relevant to the new movement in poetry. Although there is some disagreement over how much influence Bergson commanded, a brief glance at his ideas suggests that it was considerable and helps to explain why Pound and Frost accord different priority to the visual and aural elements of poetry as well as to the subjective and objective sides of experience.

In general, Bergson's theory of poetry was closely tied to his conception of language. In *Time and Free Will* (1910) and *Laughter: An Essay on the Meaning of the Comic* (1911) Bergson fully formulated several ideas about language that had first germinated in *Introduction to Metaphysics* (1903). In these texts, Bergson argues that a distinct gap exists between sensation and expression. To Bergson, words, like scientific concepts, are discrete units of thought that organize in a useful manner a continuous stream of constantly changing sensations.[28] Although words help us communicate ideas, they inevitably distort consciousness by fixing the heterogeneous flux of immediate experience into imprecise generalizations: "Each of us has his own way of loving and hating; and this love or this hatred reflects his whole personality. Language, however, denotes these states by the same words in every case: so that it has been able to fix only the objective and impersonal aspect of love, hate, and the thousand emotions which stir the soul."[29] Since the writer cannot possibly translate the subtle differences of experience into language, he is bound to a difficult paradox: the artist must convey the "infinite permeation of a thousand different impressions" but can do so only by employing a medium that by its nature must distort the fluid nature of reality.

Accordingly, the goal of the writer, as Bergson envisions him, is to release us from the conventions that condition our everyday perception and restore us to a primordial consciousness that lies beneath the surface of ordinary awareness.[30] In Bergson's view, poetry should mimic the sequential character of music and avoid the excessive surface imagery of individual words and forms, which serve as barriers to real duration. The true artist is one who focuses on the mobility of consciousness and through fluid, impressionistic language provides the reader with a sustained equivalent of that experience:

> The words may then have been well chosen, they will not convey the whole of what we wish to make them say if we do not succeed by the rhythm, by the punctuation, by the relative lengths of the sentences and parts of the sentences, by a particular dancing of the sentences, in making the reader's mind, continually guided by a series of nascent movements, describe a curve of thought and feeling analogous to that we ourselves describe. . . . The words, taken individually, no longer count: there is nothing left but the flow of meaning which runs through the words, nothing but two minds, which, without intermediary, seem to vibrate directly in unison with one another.[31]

Perhaps the most obvious literary examples of the kind of discourse Bergson advocates here can be found not so much in modern poetry as in the stream-of-consciousness techniques that Joyce and Faulkner employed so successfully in the novel. Their frequent subordination of the objective world to the dreamlike processes of the mind and their honest rendering of constantly changing subjective states serve as a kind of ideal model for a Bergsonian poetics. It may seem odd, then, that even as so many modernist poets were reading Bergson, they refused to emulate the innovations of the modern novel and instead embraced Pound's dictum that poetry should be at least as "well-written as prose,"[32] by which he meant that the poet should record experience with the objectivity, coolness, and precision of the naturalist novel, and specifically Flaubert.

Contrary to Pound's belief that the image was the best medium for portraying the inner life, Frost thought the poet could best capture immediate experience by making his surfaces transparent. Frost, following Bergson, thought that by diminishing the role of surface texture and focusing on the modulations of an unfolding consciousness, he could render more accurately the subtle nuances of the psyche as it responded to different external exigencies. In a famous 1913 letter to John Bartlett, one of his former students from the Pinkerton days, Frost argued that the poet should concern himself with the poem's auditory textures, which, by virtue of their shifting intonations, could translate the poet's inner emotion and experiences more accurately. This letter, which Frost wrote only three days after a momentous meeting with Hulme and Flint on 1 July 1913 (where Frost's ideas "got just the rub they needed"), illustrates some of the key differences between Pound and Frost. It begins in typical Poundian fashion, with Frost adopting a playful, self-promoting posture:

> To be perfectly frank with you I am one of the most notable craftsmen of my time. That will transpire presently. I am possibly the only person going who works on any but a worn-out theory (principle I had better say) of versification. You see the great successes in recent poetry have been made on the assumption that the music of words was a matter of harmonised vowels and consonants. Both Swinburne and Tennyson aimed largely at effects in assonation. But they were on the wrong track or at any rate on a short track. I alone of English writers have consciously set myself to make music out of what I may call the sound of sense.[33]

Acknowledging his debt to the nineteenth century, Frost immediately announces his intention to modify rather than revolutionize the exhausted "harmonised vowels and consonants" that led Tennyson and Swinburne "on the wrong track." Implicit in this statement is Frost's objection to the highly wrought diction that both poets employed while disregarding the vitality of everyday speech. To Frost, who "could get along very well without this bookish language altogether,"[34] such inflated diction concealed the dynamic patterns of an emerging consciousness. To make a new music, one that would excite a pragmatic twentieth-century audience, "the poet has got to come down, sooner or later, to the talk of everyday life." By using the "hard everyday word of the street" or an "everyday level of diction that even Wordsworth kept above,"[35] the poet could avoid the obscuring surfaces of inflated language and reveal the recognizable patterns of various emotional states.

To illustrate what he means, Frost provides three examples that demonstrate how rhetorical intonation can capture the emotional nuances present in common experience. Here Frost asks Bartlett to imagine how his sentences would sound if he were listening to "voices behind a door that cuts off the words":

> You mean to tell me you can't read?
> I said no such thing.

Well read then.
You're not my teacher.

He says it's too late
Oh, say!
Damn and Ingersoll watch anyway.

One-two-three—go!
No good! Come back—come back.
Haslam go down there and make those kids get out of the
    track.[36]

This technique, which Pound once classified in "How to Read" as *Melo-poeia*—a type of poetry "wherein the words are charged, over and above their plain meaning, with some musical property, which directs the bearing or trend of that meaning"[37]—is clearly more closely aligned to Bergson's than to Pound's conception of poetry. Like the Bergsonian dualism in *Creative Evolution,* wherein the *élan vital* struggles to express itself despite the retarding forms of matter, the audial imagination in Frost's early poetry struggles against the metrical patterns and genres that would constrain it. The dynamic interplay between the formal constraints of his poetry and its emotional nuances—what Frost calls in his letter to Bartlett the "*abstract vitality* of our speech" (emphasis added)—constitutes for him the supreme artistic achievement. The synthesis of tone and form conveys the infinite variety of unfolding emotional states much better than the individual words that would fix them into rigid structures.

Thus, for Frost, the true artist is not one who merely pays close attention to noble or uplifting subjects but one who has an "ear and an appetite for the sound of sense," who has learned to capture the "high possibility of emotional expression" by "skillfully breaking the sounds of sense with all their irregularity of accent across the regular beat of the meter." Calling a line of poetry a "sound in itself on which other sounds called words may be strung," Frost, in a follow-up letter to Bartlett eight months later, reiterates Bergson's argument that the intellect fixes in static form those forces that are constantly seeking to express themselves. "A man is all writer," Frost writes, "if *all* his words are strung on definite recognizable sentence sounds. The voice of the imagination, the speaking voice must know certainly how to behave, how to posture in every sentence. . . . Remember, the sentence-sound often says more than the words. It may even as in irony convey a meaning opposite to the words."[38]

The excitement that Frost communicates in these early letters suggests just how important it was for him to clarify, with the help of Hulme and Flint, the aesthetic ideas that had been simmering since he taught Shakespeare at Pinkerton Academy. Although the dynamic play between meter, diction, and intonation was certainly not new to English poetry—Shakespeare himself rarely adhered to a strictly measured line—his theory of the speaking voice must have seemed to him a prosperous departure from his contemporaries as well as strong justification for the dramatic dialogues he was then writing for *North of Boston*. Perhaps the most surprising element of his new theory, however, was that with it he thought he had found the poetic corollary to Bergson's distinction between instinct and intelligence. Carefully crafted, the sentence sound, the "vital" part of the sentence, was not just a means of exploiting the dramatic possibilities of verse; it was also a useful biological adaptation, a form of expression that made poetry more accessible and meaningful to large numbers of people.

That Frost attempted to overcome the intrinsic limitations of language by focusing on tonal rather than symbolic forms is clear from a letter he wrote to Sidney Cox in December 1914. There Frost distinguishes between the "grammatical sentence," which is equivalent to Bergson's notion of concepts, and the "vital sentence," which is equivalent to the instinctive processes of real duration:

> I shall show the sentence sound saying all that the sentence conveys with little or no help from the meaning of words. I shall show the sentence sound opposing the sense of the words as in irony. And so till I establish the distinction between the grammatical sentence and the vital sentence. The grammatical sentence is merely accessory to the other and chiefly valuable as furnishing a clue to the other. . . . Just so many sentence sounds belong to man as just so many vocal runs belong to one kind of bird. We come into the world with them and create none of them. What we feel as creation is only selection and grouping. We summon them from Heaven knows where under excitement with the audial imagination. And unless we are in an imaginative mood, it is no use trying to write them, they will not rise.[39]

Like Hulme, who claims that the poet extracts visual images from the flux of the inner life, Frost here suggests that summoned "sound images," which are "definitely things as any image of sight,"[40] liberate us from conventional generalities and transpose our awareness to a deeper reality veiled by the linguistic mechanisms that condition understanding. By themselves, sentence sounds can convey connotations that exist independently of words, yet the fact that nature has endowed us with only a limited number of "vocal runs" means that the artist can elicit a variety of emotional responses only by altering the context in which those sentence sounds occur.[41] The interdependency of grammatical and vital sentences thus expands the artist's range of expressive possibilities. Outlining these ideas for a critical essay he intended to write for educators, Frost once stated in an interview with Stirling Bowen that

> [t]here are only three things, after all, that a poem must reach: the eye, the ear, and what we may call the heart or the mind. It is the most important of all to reach the heart of the reader. And the surest way to reach the heart is through the ear. The visual images thrown up by a poem are important, but it is more important still to choose and arrange words in a sequence so as virtually to control the intonations and pauses of the reader's voice. By the arrangement and choice of words on the part of the poet, the effects of humor, pathos, hysteria, anger, and in fact, all effects, can be indicated or obtained.[42]

Although Frost never wrote the critical essay he intended, this rich passage announces, perhaps more loudly than any of his discussions on the sound of sense, the key differences between his aesthetic and Pound's. While it is true that both poets employ a poetics of surfaces and depths and are clearly interested in recovering immediate experience, Frost, following Bergson, emphasizes surface clarity, rhetorical movement, sound images, and emotion, while Pound, following Hulme (and other figures, such as Remy de Gourmont), grants highest priority to surface obscurity, spatial fixation, eye images, and objective presentation. In short, although both poets employ a poetics that operates in the dialectic between form and flux, Frost attends directly to the stream of immediate experience, while Pound emphasizes the objective representation of that experience.

The "sound of sense," then, with its bold pronouncements about the "abstract vitality of speech," is as clear and profound a poetic manifesto as anything Pound ever wrote. Indebted to the nineteenth century just enough to make his poetry appear continuous with the poetry of the past, Frost's ideas about the sound of sense enabled him to solve the problems of diction and originality that had plagued him in the years prior to his trip to England. The easy, transparent surfaces of his verse, coupled with his uncanny ability to embed them with emotionally charged intonations, resulted in poems that were both highly original and psychologically penetrating accounts of the people and places north of Boston. Beyond these benefits,

Frost's emphasis upon the innate structure of various vocal sounds also provided him with a scientifically based argument for communicating with "all sorts and kinds." Like Bergson, who felt that science could never penetrate material surfaces and uncover the continual flux of reality, Frost believed that surface difficulty in poetry simply masked the basic feature of man's existence: the idea that every moment of experience is psychologically different from any other moment of experience and must be rendered accordingly by a variety of sentence sounds that represent those shifts in consciousness.

Given his already well-developed, promising literary statement, one wonders why Frost never wrote the essay he intended and why, in his later years, he rarely mentioned his theory, preferring instead to let it drift into obscurity. One recent biographer, John Evangelist Walsh, has speculated that Frost remained silent because the positive reviews of *A Boy's Will* and *North of Boston* were so encouraging that he no longer felt he had to defend his work against charges of naiveté.[43] It seems that once the London literary establishment confirmed his status as a poet of major accomplishments, Frost no longer needed to prove his intellectual merit or justify his technique.

I believe a more important reason for Frost's later reticence over the sound of sense is that he began to realize that as a coherent theory of poetry it had serious limitations. Although it had served him well as a kind of intellectual justification for the budding technique that he would eventually develop into his mature style, the theory had done little to address what was perhaps the overriding critical question of the day, namely, what was the purpose and place of poetry in an age dominated by science? Unlike Pound, who had sought to resuscitate the "dead art of poetry" by infusing it with the objectivity and precision of science, in his discussion of the sound of sense Frost had described an art in which intellect and objectivity were conspicuously absent and the subjective and emotional sides of experience assumed priority. Since the scientific community had long regarded subjectivity and emotion as threats to objectivity, truth, and reason, Frost's earliest theory of poetry had done little to justify its necessity. The very virtues that Frost ascribed to poetry were the same vices that Plato and all subsequent purveyors of rationality had been trying to purge from society for at least two thousand years.

Knowing well that his theory might be susceptible to this kind of attack, especially in America, Frost must have recognized that had he published on the sound of sense, not only might he have incurred the wrath of his contemporaries, who were then trying hard to restore poetry's cultural status, but he might also have supplied scientists with enough evidence to prove the old argument that poetry was an immature form of knowledge with little practical benefit for the modern world. That this problem began more and more to occupy Frost's thoughts is evident from two important essays that he wrote in mid-career, "Education by Poetry," which he delivered to the Amherst Alumni Council in November 1930, and "Letter to *The Amherst Student*," which he wrote and published in 1935. In each essay Frost wrestles with what he calls the "poetry nuisance" and attempts to answer some of the more disconcerting questions posed to him by colleagues in other academic disciplines: "Where does poetry come in? . . . What's it all for? and Does it count?"[44]

As its title implies, the first essay reflects Frost's lifelong preoccupation with teaching. Well known as an educational innovator, Frost had spent most of his life as a teacher, first as a high-school instructor in his mother's school and at Pinkerton Academy, later as a professor at Amherst College and the University of Michigan. It is not surprising that in "Education by Poetry" he examines the issue as a teacher might, not only pondering what kinds of ideas students might glean from their study of poetry but, more important, why it is an essential ingredient in any well-rounded life. The answer that Frost settles on is novel. To him, poetry is valuable because it trains people to construct meaningful models that serve as bulwarks against metaphysical chaos. More simply put, "education by poetry is education by metaphor":

> Greatest of all attempts to say one thing in terms of another is the philosophical attempt to say matter in terms of spirit, or spirit in terms of matter, to make the final unity. That is the greatest attempt that ever failed. We stop just short there. But it is the height of poetry. The height of all thinking, the height of all poetic thinking, that attempt to say matter in terms of spirit and spirit in terms of matter. . . . Materialism is not the attempt to say all in terms of matter. The only materialist—be he poet, teacher, scientist, politician, or statesman—is the man who gets lost in his material without a gathering metaphor to throw it into shape and order. He is the lost soul.
>
> We ask people to think, and we don't show them what thinking is. Somebody says we don't need to show them how to think; bye and bye they will think. We will give them the forms of sentences and, if they have any ideas, they will know how to write them. But that is preposterous. All there is to writing is having ideas. To learn to write is to learn to have ideas.[45]

Although bereft of Sidney's eloquence, this passage is pregnant with assertions, which, like those in the *Defence,* aspire to justify poetry's intellectual contributions to society. At first glance, Frost's ideas sound like nothing more than a blatant attack on materialism. Closer examination, however, reveals a more complex strategy, one that preserves a subject/object dualism and designates materialism as a special form of artistic figuration, as the end product of a creative spirit that has found a metaphor to "throw" its impulses into "shape and order."

In Frost's view, a metaphor is not merely an ornamental figure employed to heighten poetry's effects but a complex mental process that establishes relationships among disparate particulars and then assembles them into meaningful ideas. Since a metaphysical order always eludes our perception, we must understand that any concept, even one like materialism, is not a faithful representation of reality but instead an anthropomorphic projection that imposes onto reality only one of several possible orders. Surprisingly, it is the poet who reminds us that truth is nothing more than a special metaphor that has been codified. While such forms provide invaluable stays against confusion, Frost is quick to point out that metaphors are ephemeral. Unless people are willing to accept the tenuous quality of all knowledge, they deny themselves the psychological benefits that arise from their innate capacity to make ever new and fresh forms that meet the demands of constantly shifting external exigencies:

> Poetry begins in trivial metaphors, pretty metaphors, "grace" metaphors, and goes on to the profoundest thinking that we have. Poetry provides the one permissible way of saying one thing and meaning another. . . .
>
> What I am pointing out is that unless you are at home in the metaphor, unless you have had your proper poetical education in the metaphor, you are not safe anywhere. Because you are not at ease with figurative values: you don't know the metaphor in its strengths and weaknesses. You don't know how far you may expect to ride it and when it may break down with you. You are not safe in science; You are not safe in history.[46]

In Frost's view, then, poetry is valuable because it teaches us how to synthesize forms that help us overcome metaphysical terror *and* how to abandon them once they no longer offer us their stabilizing benefits. Responding to individual need, the poet, like the scientist or historian, disrupts convention and finds new ways to organize reality in an effective manner.

Poetry and metaphor tame "enthusiasm," the raw emotion of experience, and allow one to sort through that raw material of the world and shape it. That literal truth is unavailable in the service of such form-making activity seems small sacrifice for the enormous therapeutic benefits one derives from such activity. The dangers Frost speaks of in these passages are those that arise when we suppress our artistic drives and subordinate them to someone else's. Once we mistake someone else's fictions for literal truth, we transform ephemeral concepts into timeless Platonic essences that do nothing but deny our metaphor-making capacities. To Frost, all conceptual knowledge breaks down eventually, and it is the poet who shows us how to restore ourselves once our useful conventions no longer seem valid.

The supreme responsibility that Frost accords poets calls to mind Nietzsche's early essay "On Truth and Lies in a Nonmoral Sense" (1873). Well known among contemporary theorists for its influence on poststructuralist thought, particularly the work of Derrida and Foucault, Nietzsche's argument is one of the philosophical sources for several modern views of metaphor. Calling truth "a moveable host of metaphors, metonymies, and anthropomorphisms,"[47] Nietzsche collapses the traditional boundaries between the literal and the figurative and extols the artist, who seeks to channel his artistic energies toward the creation of new forms. By creating new models, figures, and forms, the artist not only overturns "essential" concepts and exposes them as lies, he also reorganizes our experience in a manner that is continually new and refreshing:

> The drive toward the formation of metaphors is the fundamental
> human drive, which one cannot for a single instant dispense with in
> thought, for one would thereby dispense with man himself. This
> drive is not truly vanquished and scarcely subdued by the fact that a
> regular and rigid new world is constructed as its prison from its own
> ephemeral products, the concepts. It seeks a new realm and another
> channel for its activity, and it finds this in *myth* and in *art* generally. This
> drive continually confuses the conceptual categories and cells by bringing
> forward new transferences, metaphors, and metonymies. It continually
> manifests an ardent desire to refashion the world which presents
> itself to waking man.[48]

Whether Frost ever read this passage is a matter of conjecture. What is important, however, is that he echoes many of Nietzsche's ideas in "Letter to *The Amherst Student*," a letter he wrote to the college newspaper that honored him on his sixtieth birthday. Still mourning the death of his favorite daughter, Marjorie, and perhaps feeling slightly depressed about entering his seventh decade, Frost poignantly reveals in this letter the personal struggle he endured as he coped with both his daughter's death and his wife's heart ailments. His melancholy tone, combined with a bleak view of humanity's diminished place in the universe, conveys a familiar Nietzschean metaphysical senselessness even as he argues for the necessity of external forms to stabilize ourselves against it. Like James and Nietzsche, Frost argues that our form-making ability is a natural adaptation, a biological imperative that extends nature's own creative forces:

> There is at least so much good in the world that it admits of form and the making of form. And not only admits of it, but calls for it. We people are thrust forward out of the suggestions of form in the rolling clouds of nature. In us, nature reaches its height of form and through us exceeds itself. When in doubt there is always form for us to go on with. Anyone who has achieved the least form to be sure of it, is lost to the larger excruciations. I think it must stroke faith the right way. The artist, the poet might be expected to be the most aware of such assurance. But it is really everybody's sanity to feel it and live by it. Fortunately, too, no forms are more engrossing, gratifying, comforting, staying than those lesser ones we throw off, like vortex rings of smoke, all our individual enterprise and needing nobody's cooperation; a basket, a letter, a garden, a room, an idea, a picture, a poem. For these we haven't to get a team together to play.
>
> The background is hugeness and confusion shading away from where we stand into black and utter chaos; and against the background any small man-made figure of order and concentration. What pleasanter than this should be so? Unless we are novelists or economists we don't worry about this confusion; we look out on it with an instrument or tackle it to reduce it. . . . To me any little form I assert upon it is velvet, as the saying is, and to be considered for how much more it is than nothing. If I were a Platonist I should have to consider, I suppose, for how much less it is than everything.[49]

What makes this passage so strikingly different from his earlier work is its tough-minded emphasis upon objective forms. Unlike the essays from the sound-of-sense phase, this letter, excluding the brief reference to Bergson's *élan vital* ("nature reaches its height of form and through us exceeds itself"), retains none of his earlier emphasis upon the recovery of immediate experience. Instead, the passage clearly illustrates that Frost, like Pound and Eliot before him, has begun to shift emphasis from the subjective to the objective side of experience, a move that typifies nearly all modernist poetics. The brief catalog of tangible forms—"a basket, a letter, a garden, a room, an idea, a picture, a poem"—reiterates Frost's belief that our remedies for chaos and confusion must always arise out of individual necessity. Social programs designed to ameliorate human suffering have negligible effect on what Frost called "griefs," and it is the poet, the person "most aware of such assurance," who continually reminds us that each of us has within him or her the capacity to construct new models of the world more consistent with his or her desires. That external reality is ultimately unknowable is far less important than the therapeutic benefits we derive from the "velvet" we impose upon "black and utter chaos."

But if form is "everybody's sanity," Frost also reminds us how precarious that sanity can be. Situated between the chaotic material forces that buffet us about and the timeless essences of Platonic heaven, Frost's metaphorical forms mediate between concrete sensation and conceptual abstraction without yielding completely to either. For Frost, poetry teaches us that even though the truths we impose upon reality are as ephemeral as "vortex rings of smoke," it is paradoxically their very evanescence that keeps the imagination flexible enough to create new forms so we can reduce reality to a more manageable size. Although the rings of smoke must dissipate and the "piece of ice on a hot stove . . . must ride on its own melting,"[50] the metaphors we create—in science, history, or poetry—temporarily stabilize us against the entropic forces of nature that conspire against us.

Frost's beautiful poem "The Onset" indicates that he was already developing his ideas about metaphor as early as 1923. In what is perhaps the best example of what scholars usually refer to as the Frostian turn, "The Onset" shows us how agile consciousness can be when it seeks to free itself from the mechanistic processes of materialism. By exercising the imagination and envisioning a better future, the poet transforms nature into something more manageable and translates that process in an objective form that momentarily withstands the onslaught of matter and entropy.[51] The dark encounter with nature, particularly those terrifying moments when the poet feels most vulnerable, awakens in the poet an opportunity for redemption. The fear of annihilation, whether real or projected, activates our metaphor-making capacities and exposes those qualities that make us most human. Certainly, this type of encounter with nature informs the opening stanza of "The Onset":

Always the same, when on a fated night
At last the gathered snow lets down as white
As may be in dark woods, and with a song
It shall not make again all winter long
Of hissing on the yet uncovered ground,
I almost stumble looking up and round,
As one who overtaken by the end
Gives up his errand and lets death descend
Upon him where he is, with nothing done
To evil, no important triumph won,
More than if life had never been begun.

(CPP&P, 209)

The inevitable return of winter (which is also symbolic of the return of evil and our inability to vanquish it completely)[52] sets the dark, self-destructive mood that the poet must inevitably resist if he is to survive nature's assault. Confronted with the onset of winter, the speaker describes his feelings and compares them to old age and its propensity for final resignations. Perhaps more terrified than he ought to be, the speaker exaggerates his claims and, looking backward through time, records not only his personal failure to defeat evil and complete unfinished tasks but also, more poignantly, the futility of the entire human race to do so. At the end of the first stanza, evil and death seem to triumph.

The second stanza, however, shows us Frost at his metaphorical best. Opening the second half of the poem with the line "Yet all the precedent is on my side," Frost reiterates the power of the imagination to envision a better future and transform nature's assaults into monuments that resist death and decay. Although there is in fact no precedent for thinking that one can overcome evil and death, the speaker nevertheless musters enough courage to transform a threatening landscape into familiar, nonthreatening forms. Composed like a palindrome, the second stanza looks forward to the future:

Yet all the precedent is on my side:
I know that winter death has never tried
The earth but it has failed: the snow may heap
In long storms an undrifted four feet deep
As measured against maple, birch, and oak,
It cannot check the peeper's silver croak;
And I shall see the snow all go downhill
In water of a slender April rill

That flashes tail through last year's withered brake
And dead weeds, like a disappearing snake.
Nothing will be left white but here a birch,
and there a clump of houses with a church.

(*CPP&P*, 209)

What follows in this second stanza is a series of metaphors that diminish the threat of the initial scene. Even though snow may engulf the trees temporarily, it cannot "check the peeper's silver croak." Placed strategically between the opening lines of the stanza and the ensuing vision of a better future, the line serves as a metaphor for the poet's voice and its potential for forging a stable metaphorical order against natural chaos.

As winter gives way to spring and renewal, the poet recognizes that at times the natural order and the human order can achieve a peaceful stasis. Such moments are temporary, however, and he realizes that eventually one order will inevitably succumb to the other. Although the speaker transforms the threatening four-foot snow into a "slender April rill" that disappears "through last year's withered brake," he knows that the evil and his accompanying dark mood will return again on a fated night at the same time next year. Equally important, however, is Frost's recognition that what is most meaningful in life emerges from his conflict with nature. Frost makes this point clear in the closing couplet of the poem. The "white" birch and "clump of houses with a church," though still tainted with the evil, nevertheless coexist peacefully. Furthermore, even though the church can be viewed as a traditional symbol of Christianity's efforts to overcome evil, it also symbolizes any "individual enterprise" or institution that would ameliorate confusion and reduce chaos into something more manageable. As the last lines clearly reveal, salvation for Frost depends, not upon orthodox religion, but rather upon the mind's capacity to remain flexible enough to forge saving structures. Without those saving structures, without the stable landmarks that can lead one to safety, the poet is in danger of becoming completely engulfed by material forces.

In a 1931 comment to Elizabeth Sergeant, Frost remarked that when other writers began calling themselves "Imagists or Vorticists," he started calling himself a "synecdochist."[53] This term, ripe as it is with religious connotation, is an apt description of the way metaphor actually operates in Frost's mature poetry. Although he often uses the word to mean comparison or correspondence (e.g., "every thought is a feat of association"), Frost also suggests that the forms we carve out of nature extend beyond simple figures and feats of association and, in some mysterious way, connect to the whole of reality. Taking his cue from Emerson's belief that "there is no fact in nature which does not carry the whole sense of nature," Frost sometimes finds more significance in natural forms than most Frostians give him credit for. "I believe," Frost once claimed, "in what the Greeks called synecdoche: the philosophy of the part for the whole; skirting the hem of the goddess. All an artist needs is samples." Such samples occur not only in "The Onset" but also in other *New Hampshire* poems, such as "I Will Sing You One-O" and "Fragmentary Blue." In each of these poems Frost's metaphors acquire a spiritual significance beyond their usual linguistic tropes. The word "one" in "I Will Sing You One-O," for example, not only refers to the sound of the clock tower as it strikes one o'clock but also to the poet's imagined cosmic unity, "beyond which God is." Although Frost always remains much more skeptical than Emerson about humans' ability to interpret the symbols they observe or construct, he nevertheless retains something of Emerson's legacy, believing sometimes that it is possible for one to perceive a "passing glimpse" of an elusive unity. If one is at home with figurative values and understands the limitations and benefits of the fragile metaphors one creates, then the possibilities for faith, as James argued, remain open to those who are willing to look for it. "The person who gets close enough to poetry . . . "is going to know more about the word belief than anybody else knows, even in religion nowadays. . . ," Frost wrote. Now I think—I happen to think—that those three beliefs that I speak of, the self-belief, the love-belief, and the art-belief, are all closely related to the God-belief, that the belief in God is a relationship you enter into with Him to bring about the future."[54]

The Jamesian ideas that Frost expresses in "Education by Poetry" predict the final phase of Frost's career, which was marked by a significant retraction of some of his earlier enthusiasm for the primacy of the will and its ability to forge metaphor. Unfortunately, as Frost learned through his own trials by existence, there are moments when an individual becomes lost to larger "excruciations," when the material world resists the will and exerts counterforces that have profound effects on the quality of life. Sometimes these forces have a dangerous, seductive quality to them, and there are moments when Frost's work reflects a strong desire to surrender to the brute forces of nature as one way of eliminating their threat. The alluring landscape of "Stopping by Woods on a Snowy Evening," for example, presents us with a figure of the will confronting alien entanglements so large that they actually invite the poet to unlock their deepest secrets. However inviting those secrets may be to one who has grown "overtired" of his struggle with nature, Frost is equally aware that natural imperatives can also be beneficial. Just as nature has an intrinsic capacity to increase entropy, it also has synthetic powers of regeneration and self-organization that, when left to their own creative devices, terminate in beautiful structures that are both pleasing and protective.

The idea that certain forces in nature enable us to create our own protective sanctuaries informs "The Figure a Poem Makes" (1939), Frost's introduction to *Collected Poems* and perhaps his greatest single statement on poetry. In this essay, for the first time in his career, Frost advocates the notion of organic process, a theory that envisions the poem's final form as evolving out of a unique synthesizing principle.[55] Assimilating diverse materials and adapting them to suit its own needs, this process, which is largely spontaneous and unconscious, reveals its motives only after the poem has been completed. Thus, what inheres in the "seed" of the synthesizing principle, in the subconscious desires of the poet, amalgamates the poem's individual parts, which are subordinated to the needs and function of the whole. Frost clearly has organicism in mind when he speaks of the "wildness" of any true poem. Although he never offers a formal definition, context suggests that the term refers to the spontaneous freedom the poem engenders once one refuses to impress upon it a predetermined form. In what is perhaps his most famous passage on poetry, Frost defines the poetic process as an act of revelation:

> It should be the pleasure of a poem itself to tell how it can. The figure a poem makes. It begins in delight and ends in wisdom. The figure is the same as for love. No one can really hold that the ecstasy should be static and stand still in one place. It begins in delight, it inclines to the impulse, it assumes direction with the first line laid down, it runs a course of lucky events, and ends in a clarification of life—not necessarily a great clarification, such as sects and cults are founded on, but in a momentary stay against confusion. It has denouement. It has an outcome that though unforeseen was predestined from the first image of the original mood—and indeed from the very mood. It is but a trick poem and no poem at all if the best of it was thought of first and saved for the last. It finds its own name as it goes and discovers the best waiting for it in some final phrase at once wise and sad—the happy-sad blend of the drinking song.[56]

For someone who early in life argued for the primacy of the will and for the "freedom" to work in one's material, these lines demonstrate a significant departure. If the poet's primary impulse is to preserve or even aggrandize the self through the willed creation of metaphor, then an equally important impulse is for the poet to surrender the self to what Frost calls the "harsher discipline from without."[57] The gesture is Coleridgean, especially in its emphasis upon the inexhaustibility of new forms, yet it is also a frank admission that there are limitations to both artistic agency and the power of the will to overcome material, social, and intellectual forces that cumulatively remain greater than the self. As a person who is constantly being inscribed by those forces, the poet has relatively little power to stay confusion for any measurable length of time. One constantly remains tied to physical and social reality, even though the spirit that suffuses an author's texts often aspires to transcend them.

The balance between spirit and matter that Frost advocated in this last phase of his career is perfectly realized in his last important sonnet, "The Silken Tent." Presented to Kathleen Morrison in 1939 under the title "In Praise of Your Poise," the poem's remarkable single sentence and controlling metaphor capture not only the perfect poise of a woman who understands the constraints and rewards of love but also how matter and spirit integrate fully to form the woman's identity. Frost's comparison of the woman to a silken tent, a gesture that rivals the most extravagant of metaphysical conceits in either Donne or Eliot, heightens our understanding of the bondage and freedom that love demands:

> She is as in a field a silken tent
> At midday when a sunny summer breeze
> Has dried the dew and all its ropes relent,
> So that in guise it gently sways at ease,
> And its supporting central cedar pole,
> That is its pinnacle to heavenward
> And signifies the sureness of the soul,
> Seems to owe naught to any single cord,
> But strictly held by none, is loosely bound
> By countless silken ties of love and thought
> To everything on earth the compass round,
> And only by one's going slightly taught
> In the capriciousness of summer air
> Is of the slightest bondage made aware.
>
> (*CPP&P*, 302)

The central cedar pole, metaphorically compared to the woman's soul, is the animating principle that supports and unites the woman's steadfastness and dignity. As it remains hidden behind the soft fabric and aspires heavenward, the guy ropes both tie her to the material world and keep the shelter from collapsing when her "capriciousness" compels her to exceed the constraints that love and thought have imposed upon her. The guys that constrain the soul and keep it stable, however, are those she has willingly chosen, and in the end they do not fail her. All of the parts of the tent, from the central pole that initially erects the structure to the silken fabric and guys that tie it down, work together to form the perfect equipoise that Frost so admires. Her willingness to exercise her will to power, to aggrandize and protect the self by erecting her own structures, and her equal willingness to submit graciously to the "silken ties of love and thought" that constrain perfect freedom combine to create her identity. Neither her will nor the material world assumes priority; they interact to form a properly balanced and stable life.

The kind of balance between matter and spirit, between the objective and subjective realms of experience, and between form and meaning that Frost seeks to recover in "The Silken Tent" is ultimately a prescription not only for a healthy and stable life but also for a healthy and meaningful art in an age dominated by science. Like Sidney, Frost seeks a correlation between reason and emotion, and it is no coincidence that in "The Figure a Poem Makes" he echoes Sidney's assertion that poetry's purpose is to "teach and delight." The wisdom that Frost speaks of is not the same as Sidney's culturally ordained virtues, however, nor is delight equivalent to Wordsworth's sublime tranquillity. On the contrary, delight and wisdom for Frost are variable states that become manifest in the figures we impose upon reality. Paradoxically, Frost's honest concession that poetry cannot do what its Renaissance or romantic forebears thought it could do actually bolsters rather than detracts from his credibility as a poet. Perhaps one of the reasons Frost has continued to command such a wide audience in an age when audiences of poetry have been steadily declining is that his poems are neither highly prophetic, excessively emotional, nor systematic accounts of life but instead articulations of typical and recognizable human experiences. The personal in Frost resonates with the shared perceptions of the nation, while his self-imposed restrictions on the truth make his poems more, rather than less, believable.

5. The Risk of Spirit in Substantiation

But God's own descent
Into flesh was meant
As a demonstration
That the supreme merit
Lay in risking spirit
In substantiation.

"Kitty Hawk" (1963)

ROBERT FROST'S PROLONGED RESIDENCE IN THE MOUNTAINS OF
Vermont and New Hampshire might suggest that his art bore little witness
to the technological innovations that supported the modernist revolution
in poetry. As a man who preferred the serenity of "West-Running Brook"
to the clamor of Brooklyn, Frost, so we are often told, retreated from the city
and showed little inclination to examine how the world of girders and gears
had influenced human consciousness in the early twentieth century. While
a case can certainly be made that most of Frost's poems are set far from the
city and resonate loudly with a Melvillian and Thoreauvian emphasis upon
the individual's direct confrontation with nature, he does not avoid technology, nor does he refrain from demonstrating how the machine's inva-
sion into the New England woods has affected rural life. Occasionally in-
terrupting his pastoral sequences, technology in Frost's poetry has both
positive and negative attributes. If machines have the potential to dehu-
manize and sever the bonds of human relations, they can also provoke an
imaginative spirit that seeks expression in novel ideas and forms. In a larger
sense, Frost's ambivalent and changing attitudes toward technology are
representative of his attitudes toward science in general. Initially fearful of
technology's capacity to destroy human dignity, Frost gradually reconciles

his quarrel with technology and closes his career by celebrating its pioneering spirit.[1]

Frost's incorporation of machines into his poetry is not surprising given that America's transformation from a horse-and-buggy society to one dependent upon industry had affected American consciousness so thoroughly. By the turn of the century skyscrapers, steel bridges, and coal-driven factories were common in the city, while in remote areas rail and telegraph lines had expanded at such a rapid pace that it would have been rare for even an isolated individual not to have witnessed the felling of a local balsam grove to make way for progress. Between the city and the country, in America's mid-sized cities and emerging suburbs, technology had made its greatest impact in the home. Gas lighting, sewage systems, electrical appliances, and automobiles slowly became standard features in nearly every household, thus outdating such marvelous inventions as the outhouse, the candle, and the washboard.[2] As men read about the latest inventions and marveled at the pen-and-ink drawings in *Scientific American,* women too were inundated with images of machines. As Cecelia Tichi has argued, popular magazines such as *Cosmopolitan, Harper's Weekly, Collier's, The Ladies' Home Journal,* and *Good Housekeeping* were so filled with pictures of labor-saving devices and appliances that a young bride who could afford to purchase such items could be fairly confident that, with the aid of these machines, her prospects for a happy marriage were quite good.[3] So pervasive was the proliferation of technology at the beginning of the century that no one, not even a rural poet, could be immune to its values, architecture, and vast potential for making life easier and more satisfying. As Stephen Kern suggests in *The Culture of Time and Space,* "Many writers welcomed the collapse of the old palisades and viewed the new speed [technology] favorably as a symbol of vitality, a magnification of the possibilities of experience, or an antidote to provincialism."[4]

Perhaps even more awe-inspiring than the physical presence of technology was the enormous impact that machines had on the way people thought. As scientific discoveries in the third quarter of the nineteenth century prepared the way for a deterministic vision of the cosmos, the vocabulary used to define humans' relationship with nature gradually shifted from one that described nature as a sanctuary to one that described it as little more than an efficient, orderly, vast, and complex machine. Even organic life, at one time thought to be exempt from the laws of inert matter, could be explained in the language of thermodynamics, combustion, and mechanics. In the aftermath of natural selection, people began to realize that they could no longer perceive nature as a divinely ordered unity from which an optimistic vision of the world might be derived.[5] Instead, the peaceful pastoral landscape for which so many eighteenth- and nineteenth-century writers yearned was transformed in the twentieth century into little more than an aggregate of machinelike components that worked together to form the interactive particulars of the phenomenal world. Although describing matter as a collection of discrete parts had been habitual since Lucretius, in the nineteenth century Darwin himself made the equation of nature with machines fashionable. An excerpt from *The Various Contrivances by Which Orchids Are Fertilized by Insects* provides a case in point:

> Although an organ may not have been originally formed for some special purpose, if it now serves for this end, we are justified in saying it was specially adapted for it. On the same principle, if a man were to make a machine for some special purpose, but were to use old wheels, springs, and pulleys, only slightly altered, the whole machine, with all its parts, might be said to be contrived for its present purpose. Thus, throughout nature almost every part of each living being has probably served, in a slightly modified condition, for diverse purposes, and has acted in the living machinery of many ancient and distinct specific forms.[6]

That the language Darwin uses here is echoed by several contemporary evolutionary theorists (Daniel Dennett and Richard Dawkins immediately come to mind) testifies to the long dominance of a technology-based system of values. Although the machine's formidable position has since been usurped by the computer (in 1999 Microsoft surpassed General Electric as the most valuable commodity on the stock market), the utilitarian ethos the machine inspired lingers in the language we use today to describe our relationship with nature. And while nature may continue to inspire, it does so not because we are often stirred by its sublime majesty but because we understand and are amazed by the intricacies of its systems, components, and ingenious adaptations.

While the description of nature as machine continued to reinforce America's technological imperatives, in general, the custodians of high culture had serious misgivings about technology and modernization. As I argued in chapter 4, the modernist idea that poetry was an isolated activity, far removed from both the provinces of truth and the practical lives of ordinary people, perpetuated the notion that it also lacked value. Malcolm Cowley was one of the first to make this point. In *Exile's Return* Cowley argued that a country of "efficiency, standardization, mass production, [and] the machine" could not support its artists.[7] Van Wyck Brooks was even more pessimistic about the prospects for poetry. In the "The Literary Life," one of the essays he wrote for Harold Stearns's *Civilization in the United States,* Brooks argued that the most striking feature of contemporary American literature was "the singular impotence of its creative spirit."[8] In part, Brooks's negative assessment of American letters issued from his belief that the country lacked an indigenous culture conducive to art. Because America was a heterogeneous mixture of different cultures and traditions, a nation inundated with an austere Puritan heritage, her writers had never had the latitude "to escape the importunities of bourgeois custom."[9]

The more immediate cause of American writers' being "too generally pliant, passive, acquiescent, [and] anemic," however, was the erosion of spirituality, which, Brooks argued, was the most debilitating consequence of the modern, industrial world. The ubiquity of spiritually bankrupt workplaces, combined with a strong propensity among American businessmen to forsake ethical principles for monetary gain, seemed to Brooks the most enduring characteristic of the age and the most prominent cause of American literature's poverty:

> That traditional drag, if one may so express it, in the direction of the
> practical, which has been the law of our civilization, would alone
> explain why our literature and art have never been more than half-
> hearted. To abandon the unpopular and unremunerative career
> of painting for the useful and lucrative career of invention must have
> seemed natural and inevitable to Robert Fulton and Samuel Morse.
> So strong is this racial compulsion, so feeble is the hold which Ameri-
> cans have upon ultimate values, that one can scarcely find to-day a
> scientist or a scholar who, for the sake of science or scholarship, will
> refuse an opportunity to become the money-gathering president
> of some insignificant university. Thus our intellectual life has always
> been ancillary to the life of business and organization.[10]

While Brooks's diagnosis of American literature may seem severe in light of the accomplishments of Twain, Dreiser, James, Dickinson, and Whitman, he nevertheless exposed in 1922 a problem that contemporary academics in the liberal arts still struggle with. What makes Brooks's account even more incisive is that he also names science as a victim of this cultural malaise. As his references to Robert Fulton and Samuel Morse suggest, most Americans' knowledge about science centered more on technological achieve-ment than on the remarkable discoveries in the natural sciences. By the turn of the century, for example, nearly everyone in America could name Thomas Edison as the inventor of the light bulb and the phonograph, but very few people could name Albert Michelson as the only American ever to have won a Nobel Prize in physics. The distinction that Brooks makes between basic science and technology is thus important, for he was one of the few intellectuals of his day to notice that basic science, like the arts, was also severely constrained by technology, commerce, big business, and the bottom line.

If America's technologically driven ethos was not conducive to serious art, then by far the most appalling consequence of modernization was the widespread exploitation of labor and the accompanying degradation of human dignity that followed. Because design improvements in the high-pressure steam engine had made it possible for engineers to produce power independently of wind or water, and because the immigrant labor pool had grown rapidly between 1850 and 1900, manufacturers could not only build more factories but also easily locate them next to burgeoning, poverty-stricken populations willing to work for a pittance. With such abundant re-sources readily available and an expanded commodities market eager to accommodate America's growing appetite for material goods, between 1860 and 1920 industrial employment in the United States grew nearly tenfold, while the income generated from manufacturing surpassed that of agricul-ture to make up nearly one-third of America's gross national product.[11] Unfortunately, the result of such unbounded prosperity was the exacerba-tion of the same problems that had plagued Britain during its own indus-trial revolution. Alienated from the product, isolated from other human beings, and denied creative potential, the average factory employee at the turn of the century—a man, a woman, or a child, who usually worked twelve- to fourteen-hour days in often dangerous and filthy conditions—was often left physically weakened, spiritually bankrupt, and virtually pow-erless to oppose or escape the vast machinery of industrialization. As Rebecca Harding Davis described the situation as early as 1861,

> Not many even of the inhabitants of a manufacturing town know the vast machinery of system by which the bodies of workmen are gov-erned, that goes on unceasingly from year to year. The hands of each mill are divided into watches that relieve each other as regularly as the sentinels of an army. By night and day the work goes on, the unsleep-

ing engines groan and shriek, the fiery pools of metal boil and surge. Only for a day in the week, in half-courtesy to public censure, the fires are partially veiled; but as soon as the clock strikes midnight, the great furnaces break forth with renewed fury, the clamor begins with fresh, breathless vigor, the engines sob and shriek like "gods in pain."[12]

Despite these grim conditions, however, not everyone was willing to sound the death knell for poetry. As Walt Whitman and Hart Crane surmised, another strategy might prove more successful. If the poet could bridge the chasm between art and technology by showing people that the two were not isolated activities but instead creative endeavors that shared a cognate ethos, perhaps the poet might recapture some of the prestige he had lost. In America, Whitman was the first to recognize a creative affinity between the two activities. In "Song of Myself" (1855), "A Song for Occupations" (1855), "Song of the Broad-Axe" (1856), and "Passage to India" (1871), Whitman celebrates technology as the product of the imagination. His rich, effusive catalogs not only venerate subjects usually excluded from poetry but also exalt the engineer's capacity to turn the imagination's fictions into tangible realities.

"Passage to India" makes the case in point. Celebrating the 1869 completion of the Suez Canal, the transcontinental railroad, and the transatlantic cable, Whitman envisions a world made vibrant and whole by the communion of past and present. In this poem he weaves mythology and science to form a tapestry that testifies to the energy and democratic spirit of America. The opening immediately announces how the movement of America's influence from west to east has linked the modern to the ancient world:

> Singing my days,
> Singing the great achievements of the present,
> Singing the strong light works of engineers,
> Our modern wonders, (the antique ponderous Seven
>   outvied,)
> In the old world the east the Suez canal,
> The New by its might railroad spann'd,
> The seas inlaid with eloquent gentle wires,
> Yet first to sound, and ever sound, the cry with thee O soul,
> The Past! The Past! The Past![13]

Whitman's muse infuses the products of innovation to such a degree that his rhetoric here sounds almost convincing. Yet even as Whitman celebrates the accomplishments of technology, he cannot resist the impulse to ennoble the poet, who, unlike the engineer, is the only person capable of "justifying" to "fretted children" the ways of God, nature, and science. Thus, the engineer, even in Whitman's most fawning moments, occupies a position subordinate to the poet's:

> After the seas are all crossed (as they seem already cross'd,)
> After the great captains and engineers have accomplish'd
>   their work,
> After the noble inventors, after the scientists, the chemist,
> the geologist, ethnologist,
> Finally shall come the poet worthy that name,
> The true son of God shall come singing his songs.[14]

Whitman's hope that a poet "worthy that name" might one day assimilate the concepts and innovations of science has gone unfulfilled. Nevertheless, his optimism that poets might one day appropriate technology spilled over into the Progressive Era and its obsession with reform. Emerging writers such as Pound, Williams, and Hemingway tended to view the machine as a symbol of efficiency.[15] The engineer's efforts to produce the most work with the fewest resources, combined with the functional beauty of suspension bridges, railroad stations, and subway trestles, provided poets with a visual representation of an aesthetic that saw economy as the artist's most important virtue. Pound's definition of the vortex as "the point of maximum energy," which generates "the greatest efficiency," Williams's idea that poet should convey "no ideas but in things," and Hemingway's search for a "clean, well-lighted place" all speak to the modernist desire to create great works of art without burdening them with overwrought rhetoric.

The influence of technology, then, was both beneficial and detrimental to American writers and critics. On the one hand, poets could celebrate scientific creativity because it seemed analogous to literary creativity. The engineer's inventiveness and the fact that he valued energy, structure, mechanism, and motion were admired qualities that would eventually be expressed as the catchwords for modernist poetry. On the other hand, while poets sometimes celebrated the aesthetic and intellectual contributions of technology, they often deplored the deleterious social values it espoused. Industrialism's daily assaults upon sensibility—its emphasis upon a shoddy and cheap materialism, its exploitation of human labor solely for remunerative advantage, and its devaluation of other forms of knowledge, including basic science and art—were viewed by poets as the primary causes of America's spiritual and artistic poverty. As Frost himself recognized, "Whenever I am in the city I hear people say they want to go to the country—to the open places. People are sick of each other. The beat, beat of their many contacts wears them down. There are too many late nights. Furthermore, the city is no place for children. There is too little of that feeling of the old time for children. The country is the place for children."[16]

One consequence of technology's dual nature was that American writers were often torn between their own contradictory attitudes toward it. In trying to figure out how they might appropriate technology as a way of bolstering their own prestige, poets also felt obligated to immunize society against its ill effects—in short, to restore beauty and value to a world laid waste by machines. For some, the contradictions were so vast as to seem irreconcilable. To those who could not find a compromising position the choices were fairly clear: the poet could either retreat into an intellectual aestheticism, as did Wallace Stevens, or embrace technology, with all of its marvels and pitfalls, as did William Carlos Williams. In either case, it seemed nearly impossible for one to condemn or celebrate technology fully without also feeling a round measure of guilt that his position was extreme. Just as Stevens worried in the 1930s that his art was too hermetic, too far removed from the harsh reality of daily urban life, Williams worried in the mid-1920s that his style was too "scientific" and plodding, too lacking in the traditional forms necessary to sustain a lasting and beautiful art.

In Frost's poetry the contradictions are equally apparent. As a man who had witnessed firsthand the emergence and cultivation of America's technological ethos, he confronted similar ambivalent feelings about the positive and negative effects of machines. Most of Frost's negative attitudes toward technology appear in his work through *A Further Range* (1936). These poems either question technology's bold intrusion into nature or challenge its disruption of stable human societies. While it is certainly true that poems such as "Mowing" (1914), "Mending Wall" (1914), "The Grindstone" (1916), "The Line-Gang" (1916), and "The Star-Splitter" (1923) depict laborers or friends in a happy communion with each other or their work, Frost's characters in these early works are still closely tied to the earth. Using only primitive tools such as scythes or grindstones to control and order nature, they are able to enjoy their work and each other precisely because neither nature nor culture eclipses the other. An easy stasis between cultural evolution and biological evolution obtains to create the balance that Frost finds most conducive to human happiness. The desired harmony between technology and nature is especially evident in "Mowing" (1913), where the correspondence between the mower, the scythe, the grass, and the woods seems so natural as to go almost unnoticed. The satisfactions the speaker derives from physical labor and artistic creation are equivalent forms of what Frost calls an "earnest love."[17]

Trouble arises in Frost's poems, however, when the machine disrupts humans' place in the natural order by placing demands on them that are incompatible with their biological imperatives. As the extended family and other meaningful relationships become stressed by manufacturing and labor, a blatant disregard for the intrinsic value of human life emerges as a grim consequence. Nowhere is the devaluation of human life more apparent than in "The Self-Seeker" (1914), which demonstrates how a human being who has been maimed by a machine becomes an expendable component in the vast machinery of big business.

As in many of Frost's technological poems, the subject and theme of "The Self-Seeker" can be traced directly to a specific biographical incident. In 1895, while the Frosts were vacationing in Allenstown, New Hampshire, Carl Burell, Frost's friend since childhood, suffered a serious accident that Lawrance Thompson claims "nearly cost Burell his life."[18] Burell, who was operating a mill saw that cut boards for wooden boxes, caught his sleeve in a leather pulley belt and smashed both feet so badly against the ceiling of the mill that the doctors thought they might have to amputate them. Frost visited his convalescing friend at his boardinghouse on several occasions and witnessed the insurance transaction that paid Burell a small sum as compensation for the accident. Although Frost protested the amount, complaining to Burell that it could never compensate him for his crippled condition, Burell, who had no financial means to pursue further litigation, settled in hopes that he might get on with his life without any further distractions. Unfortunately, however, both Frost and Burell knew that because of the severity of the injury, Burell would never walk well again and thus never finish the book he had begun on the orchids of New Hampshire.

As a tribute to his friend, Frost modeled the central character of "The Self-Seeker" after Burell and his misfortunes. A dramatic dialogue among four principal characters, each of which represents a type, the poem pays homage to working-class individuals. "The Broken One," a stand-in for Burell, represents a type whose archaic idealism prevents him from grasping the serious and practical consequences of his condition. More interested in pursuing his beloved orchids than in working in a box factory, The Broken One is an anachronism, a throwback to the nineteenth-century naturalist who collects, identifies, and marvels at the adaptational complexity of such remarkable plants. Serving as a foil to The Broken One, the lawyer is a figure of the modern-day manager, who is completely constrained by deadlines, schedules, and bureaucratic red tape. Carrying a satchel and a watch whose case is "cunningly devised to make a noise / Like a small pistol when he snapped it shut" (*CPP&P,* 98), the lawyer has no capacity for sympathy and callously calls The Broken One's tender conversation with Anne nothing but a "pretty interlude." Willis, who functions in the poem as the voice of pragmatic action and justice, excoriates both The Broken One, for not having the sense to demand more than five hundred dollars, and the lawyer, for not offering his friend more money to compensate his crippling condition. Unable to persuade either the lawyer or his friend that justice has not been served, Willis departs the boardinghouse, but only after he derides the lawyer and his "stockholders in Boston." Finally, Anne, Willis's young daughter, who has collected a bouquet of orchids for The Broken One, represents a new generation. She is a child caught between agrarian and modern worlds, and, as Frost makes clear, she is to be educated in the traditions of the past and protected from the injurious values the lawyer represents.

These differing points of view conflict with one another from the poem's outset. Willis, whose visit to his healing friend has been unexpected, tries to convince The Broken One that his value can be quantified in monetary terms. Willis alludes to the orchid book his friend wishes to finish and reminds him that his ability to walk will prevent him from achieving that goal. Frost's deliberate punning on the word *soul* in this section reveals not only the kind of witty repartee that Frost and Burell must have at one time engaged in but also how the soul-sole connection is crucial to our understanding of The Broken One. His feet and their activity are literally an extension of his true vocation:

> 'Willis, I didn't want you here today:
> The lawyer's coming for the company.
> I'm going to sell my soul, or, rather, feet.
> Five hundred dollars for the pair, you know.'
>
> 'With you the feet have nearly been the soul;
> And if you're going to sell them to the devil,
> I want to see you do it. When's he coming?'
>
> 'I half suspect you knew, and came on purpose
> To try to help me drive a better bargain.'

'Well, if it's true! Yours are no common feet.
The lawyer don't know what it is he's buying:
So many miles you might have walked you won't walk.
You haven't run your forty orchids down.
What does he think?—How are the blessed feet?
The doctor's sure you're going to walk again?'

(*CPP&P*, 93)

The Broken One's response to his friend is curious. Similar to Prufrock's description of himself as a "pair of ragged claws / Scuttling across the floors of silent seas,"[19] Burrell's comparison of his condition to a "starfish laid out with rigid points" suggests that, as a student of nature, he indeed has more than adequate knowledge of the natural world. Unlike Prufrock, who objectifies his consciousness by envisioning only the crab's most violent body parts, The Broken One equates himself with a creature whose limbs regenerate when injured. This unflagging optimism enables him to endure his condition, even as it infuriates the more practical-minded Willis. The Broken One, however, also suspects that he has deserved his misfortune, that he is being punished for his Promethean desire to control the machine in such a way that he violates his own nature. In explaining to Willis why such a random accident might have occurred, The Broken One personifies the machine, endowing it with fire:

'They say some time was wasted on the belt—
Old streak of leather—doesn't love me much
Because I make him spit fire at my knuckles,
The way Ben Franklin used to make the kite-string.
That must be it. Some days he won't stay on.[']

(*CPP&P*, 94)

Yet even as The Broken One laments his condition, he also realizes that his factory work, like his orchid hunting, is another extension of himself. As the mill saws "Caterwaul" through his bedroom window, his desire to return to a normal life intensifies, and he laments the fact that everything "goes the same without me there." He knows he will never again be part of the mill's or the town's prosperity; nevertheless, he stoically accepts his condition. Part of his rationale for not fighting the settlement is that he knows the cash cannot change his predicament. "I just want to get settled in my life," he says. "Such as it's going to be and know the worst, / Or best— it may not be so bad" (*CPP&P*, 95).

Willis, however, cannot in good conscience accept his friend's position. Yet although he derides the lawyer's brazen attempt to place a monetary value on his friend's feet, he unknowingly shares the lawyer's business ethic. Willis tries to convince The Broken One that his future inability to collect wildflowers should merit some kind of punitive compensation, if only so the "firm" will be punished for requiring its labor force to work in unsafe conditions. The Broken One, however, realizes that no cash amount can ever compensate him for his vocation. Like poetry writing, collecting wildflowers can serve no practical purpose; it can only enhance the spiritual quality of one's life. The conflict between pragmatism and idealism reaches stasis in the few moments before the lawyer arrives on the scene:

> 'But your flowers, man, you're selling out your flowers.'
>
> 'Yes, that's one way to put it—all the flowers
> Of every kind everywhere in this region
> For the next forty summers—call it forty.
> But I'm not selling those, I'm giving them,
> They never earned me so much as one cent:
> Money can't pay me for the loss of them.
> No, the five hundred was the sum they named
> To pay the doctor's bill and tide me over.[']

(CPP&P, 95)

Later in the exchange, The Broken One makes clear that his quixotic endeavors have value only for a few potential friends who might want to know something about the local flora. Although the narrator makes clear that The Broken One has received some accolade from John Burroughs, the famous American naturalist who chronicled in many popular books his spiritual appreciation for nature, the scientific significance of The Self-Seeker's work is, at best, minor:

> 'But what about your flora of the valley?'
>
> 'You have me there. But that—you didn't think
> That was worth money to me? Still I own
> It goes against me not to finish it
> For the friends it might bring me. By the way,
> I had a letter from Burroughs—Did I tell you?—
> About my *Cyprepedium reginae:*
> He says it's not reported so far north.[']

(CPP&P, 95)

The Broken One values the showy lady's-slipper precisely because it is as rare as those potential friends with whom he might share his love and respect for the natural world. The uncommon beauty he finds in his orchids he also finds in Anne, whom he has tutored in the ways of the natural world. Here Frost's sense of the dramatic displays itself prominently, as both she and the lawyer enter the room simultaneously. Barefoot, shy, and self-deprecating, Anne enters the room bearing orchids, while the lawyer, with his "baritone importance," enters bearing only a satchel filled with the legal documents The Broken One must sign. The poem's tone shifts dramatically at this point as The Broken One assumes a playful, teasing posture that endears him to the young girl. It would be difficult to imagine, given the Frost children's great affection for their father's friend, that the voice here could be anyone's other than Burell's. The dialogue between them is at once both clever and mockingly serious:

> 'But, Anne, I'm troubled; have you told me all?
> You're hiding something. That's as bad as lying.
> You ask this lawyer man. And it's not safe
> With a lawyer at hand to find you out.
> Nothing is hidden from some people, Anne.
> You don't tell me that where you found a Ram's Horn
> You didn't find a Yellow Lady's Slipper.
> What did I tell you? What? I'd blush, I would.
> Don't you defend yourself. If it was there,
> Where is it now, the Yellow Lady's Slipper?'
> 'Well, wait—it's too common—it's too *common*.'
>
> 'Common?
> The Purple Lady's Slipper's commoner.'
> 'I didn't bring a Purple Lady's Slipper.
> To you—to you I mean—they're both too common.'

> (*CPP&P*, 97)

Part of this section's appeal is that readers can infer Anne's blushing response from only half the dialogue. Like The Broken One, she insists upon the romantic idea that each individual flower has innate value and is to be cherished according to its rarity. She cannot possibly present The Broken One with her most prized possession without simultaneously violating all of the principles he has taught her. Nor can she desecrate the orchid bog by removing all the "four or five" examples of each type. She will allow the growth cycle to continue and leave enough plants to reproduce naturally. While this lesson may run counter to her most humanitarian impulses—certainly she would like to present The Broken One with a bouquet—her education prevents her from engaging her most basic instincts. As a delicate Eve figure who "lifts their [the flowers'] faces by the chin to hers / And says their names, and leaves them where they are" (*CPP&P*, 98), she respects and protects the delicate species around her. The Broken One understands her well and realizes that she too must be protected from the ethos of indifference that characterizes the modern, industrial world. "Pressed into service," he suggests about Anne, "means pressed out of shape" (*CPP&P*, 98). Like an orchid that is pressed and preserved between the pages of a book, the child is in danger of having her native personality distorted by both The Self-Seeker and the lawyer.

Frost makes this point clear when he suddenly banishes her, and the obsolete romanticism she represents, and we are once again in the realm of contracts, big business, and hurried existence. Suggesting that the exchange between The Broken One and Anne is nothing but a "pretty interlude," the lawyer refuses to let Willis read the final contract for fear that he will interfere and jeopardize the settlement. As The Broken One signs the settlement without even reading the document, Frost brings together the poem's central conflicts and characters:

> The lawyer gravely capped his fountain pen.
> 'You're doing the wise thing: you won't regret it.
> We're sorry for you.'
>
> > Willis sneered:
> 'Who's we?—some stockholders in Boston?
> I'll go outdoors, by gad, and won't come back.'
>
> 'Willis, bring Anne back with you when you come.
> Yes. Thanks for caring. Don't mind Will: he's savage.
> He thinks you ought to pay me for my flowers.
> You don't know what I mean about the flowers.
> Don't stop to try now. You'll miss your train.
> Good-by.' He flung his arms around his face.
>
> > > > > (*CPP&P*, 100)

Though perhaps a little melodramatic and one-dimensional, the closing scene suggests that those who are so caught up in a sentimental or diluted form of romanticism are ill-equipped to adapt to a society driven by financial competition. "The Self-Seeker," then, is a poem about not only how technology can suddenly cripple the individual life but also how it has affected our capacity to empathize with others. Those who ignore the stark realities of a mechanistic world and insist upon preserving an untenable romantic framework are doomed to be destroyed. On the other hand, as Frost's condemnation of the lawyer implies, those who succumb to a mechanistic ethos will remain incapable of forging the important and meaningful relationships that make schedules and deadlines tolerable. Perhaps the only character who is suited for the future is Anne. Trained by both her father and The Self-Seeker, she apparently will mature into a woman who exhibits both practical and idealistic qualities. She will naturalize spirit and spiritualize matter in such a way that she should be able to adapt well to all threatening situations.

Not all threats can be avoided, however, a point that Frost makes clear in "Why Wait for Science" (1947). Taken to the extreme, science without ethical constraints presents the stark possibility of what was once unthinkable during Frost's own boyhood: the total annihilation of the earth at the hands of nuclear technology. Frost does not dwell at length on this issue, yet the poem expresses his fear that humankind may already be on the brink of its own destruction:

> Sarcastic Science, she would like to know,
> In her complacent ministry of fear,
> How we propose to get away from here
> When she has made things so we have to go
> Or be wiped out.

(CPP&P, 359)

For Frost, the way to counteract science's destructive potential is to constrain its headlong pursuit of knowledge with proven ethical traditions. We can do this only by taking the time to contemplate science's potentially damaging effects and by consulting the philosophical, literary, and theological traditions that have informed the present. Only then can the human imagination thwart its own destructive urges. The stabilizing benefit of tradition is also the reason for Frost's insistence upon preserving a literary education. Science cannot describe us. The "best description of us is the humanities from of old, the book of the worthies and unworthies."[20] The poet has the primary responsibility of reminding scientists that speed, knowledge, and power should not be the only goals of innovation. Frost makes this point clear in "Some Science Fiction" (1955), a poem in which he imagines being banished from a Plato-like republic for being hostile to scientific progress. He embraces his role, however, and whimsically delights in the havoc a poet is capable of wreaking:

> And some of them may mind
> My staying back behind
> To take life at a walk
> In Philosophic talk;
>
> Though as yet they only smile
> At how slow I do a mile,
> With tolerant reproach
> For me as an Old Slow Coach.
>
> But I know them what they are:
> As they get more nuclear
> And more bigoted in reliance
> On the gospel of modern science,
>
> For them my loitering around
> At less than the speed of sound
> Or even the speed of light
> Won't seem unheretical quite.
>
> (*CPP&P,* 473–74)

As the moral conscience of society, the poet is obliged to test new developments in science against proven ethical traditions and to remind scientists that seemingly inconsequential discoveries might one day prove fatal for humankind. Although the poet may have to endure ridicule or reproach, any failure on his part to accept that responsibility may have grim consequences.

While each of the poems I have discussed to this point might suggest that Frost's attitude toward technology was overtly hostile, such a view, I believe, ignores the gradual change of heart toward machines that Frost was evincing as early as 1928. In an interview with Benson Y. Landis in June 1931 Frost openly admitted that it was impossible for one to retreat into an outdated agrarianism. "I'm not a back-to-the-lander," Frost claimed. "I'm not interested in the Thoreau business. Only a few can do what Thoreau did. We must use the modern tools at our disposal."[21] Frost makes these sentiments clear in "The Egg and the Machine" (1928). Although Yvor Winters once cited this poem as evidence of Frost's "sentimental hatred for the machine,"[22] to my mind the poem is instead a fine example of what William

Pritchard has called Frost's "elevated play."²³ The poem also sardonically plays on Thoreau's call in *Walden* for a "champion" who will meet the "devilish Iron Horse" at "the Deep Cut and thrust an avenging lance between the ribs of the bloated pest."²⁴ Frost's careful framing of the poem—he begins with an impotent gesture, "He gave the solid rail a hateful kick," and ends with an equally ineffectual response, "Will get this plasm [i.e., egg] in its goggle glass"—actually shows us how ineffectual a sentimental hatred of machines can be. Technology is simply another one of the "larger excruciations" that the poet is powerless to thwart once its machines have been set in motion.

More fable-like than most of Frost's technology poems, "The Egg and the Machine" begins with a play on the phrase *deus ex machina;* rather than lowering a god onto the stage of the poem to save the speaker from technology's assaults, Frost bestows the train with the characteristics of an angry god. Here the mock-heroic speaker personifies the train by projecting onto it his own anthropocentric fears. Frost tacitly comments on this stance by suggesting that the speaker is primitive. As he looks around for a weapon, he can find only rudimentary tools:

> His hate had roused an engine up the road.
> He wished when he had had the track alone
> He had attacked it with a club or stone
> And bent some rail wide open like a switch
> So as to wreck the engine in the ditch . . .
> Then for a moment all there was was size
> Confusion and a roar that drowned the cries
> He raised against the gods in the machine.
> Then once again the sandbank lay serene.
>
> (*CPP&P,* 248)

The iron horse the speaker would derail remains immune to such petty threats. As a metaphor for power and progress, the train hurtles, like one of the Four Horsemen of the Apocalypse, headlong down the track despite the speaker's mounting paranoia that the machine will eventually destroy all life. Technology seems uncontrollable, overwhelming, and fully indifferent to the individual.

Had Frost ended the poem on this note, one would almost have to agree with Winters's indictment of it as sentimental and didactic. But Winters misses Frost's implicit irony. What makes the poem memorable is not the silly threat mounted by an environmental extremist but the speaker's complete lack of concern for life's tenacious hold on the planet. Indeed, in the second half of the poem Frost suggests that the machine is not to blame for the destruction of habitat; rather it is the fault of a person whose solipsism disables his awareness of other meaningful forms of life. So caught up is he in his self-righteous zealotry against the machine that he completely misses the ingenuity of nature's own technological designs.[25] Rather than seeing the turtle eggs for what they are—durable and efficient incubators—the speaker views them primarily as weapons:

> The traveler's eye picked up a turtle trail,
> Between the dotted feet a streak of tail,
> And followed it to where he made out vague
> But certain signs of buried turtle's egg;
> And probing with one finger not too rough,
> He found suspicious sand, and sure enough,
> The pocket of a little turtle mine.
> If there was one egg in it there were nine,
> Torpedo-like, with shell of gritty leather
> All packed in sand to wait the trump together.

> > (*CPP&P*, 248)

The poem's irony lies in the fact that it is the machine, and not the "probing" speaker, that has made possible the hospitable nesting environment. The abrupt change in tone, as we overhear the lone traveler's invective against the train, problematizes an easy reading of the ending:

> 'You'd better not disturb me anymore,'
> He told the distance, 'I am armed for war.
> The next machine that has the power to pass
> Will get this plasm in its goggle glass.'

> > (*CPP&P*, 248)

The juvenile voice of these last four lines complicates interpretation because the action here is so unbelievable. Are we to take the speaker at his word and envision a direct confrontation between technology and organic life? Or has the speaker's discovery of the eggs culminated in an epiphany, thus making his final statement the ironic expression of his newly found knowledge that he is powerless in the face of the machine? The latter interpretation seems more plausible and consistent with Frost's usual habit of subverting his own poems with a subtle and playful turn of phrase. Like a young boy who has just been pummeled by the neighborhood bully, the speaker waits until the source of danger is well out of earshot before he inveighs against it. Such an explicit posture of false bravado suggests to me that by the end of the poem the speaker knows that since he is powerless to stop technological progress, he must resign himself to it. He has also learned another, more important lesson. In his accidental discovery of the turtle eggs the speaker immerses himself more deeply in the world's material particulars, and in this process of deepening his engagement with nature he finds an important analogy to his own threatened condition and his need to survive. Although he knows that technology is capable of destroying individuals, he discovers that nature has bestowed her creatures with the adaptational equipment necessary to ensure the longevity of the entire species. Like the train, organic processes will continue long into the future, despite disruptions, and secure their tenacious hold on the planet in any number of remarkable ways. Life's vital force seems equal to the challenge of brute, technological force.

The sustained equivalence between organic and technological processes in "The Egg and the Machine" serves as a useful transition to "Kitty Hawk" (1956). Along with "Directive" and "All Revelation," "Kitty Hawk" represents the best of Frost's work from the last twenty years of his life. Written when Frost was in his early eighties, the poem is a lengthy meditation on complex scientific issues, many of which never appeared anywhere else in mid-century American poetry. More important, however, "Kitty Hawk" represents a summing up of sorts, a last testament to Frost's attitudes toward humankind's miraculous creative capacities and a poem that clearly reveals a man who, no longer tormented by the agonizing questions of his youth, appears to have reconciled his quarrel with science and technology.

Frost structures "Kitty Hawk" around the stories of two flights, the first an unsuccessful flight from jilted love, the second a fiftieth-anniversary celebration of the Wright brothers' 1903 achievement. Contrasting the success and failure of each flight, Frost concludes part 2 with an invocation to the "God of the machine" for endowing both the artist and the scientist with the capacity to project meaning onto the natural world. Surprisingly, it is the Wright brothers—Frost's ideal scientists—who teach him about the meaning of flight. Throughout the poem, their plane serves as an instructive metaphor for free will, for our distinctly human ability to elevate our mental processes above mechanical processes. Although Frost makes clear that our imagination will always encounter material resistance, our mental activity makes "a pass at the infinite" precisely because we recognize that our creative actions, whether scientific or poetic, are imbued with divine qualities. Both God and scientists risk "spirit in substantiation" and, as a result, animate and redeem matter.

Like many of Frost's technological poems, "Kitty Hawk" can be linked to events in Frost's youth. Part 1 recalls his 1894 flight to the Dismal Swamp, in Virginia, after Elinor White, then a student at Saint Lawrence University, jilted him and his gift of poems in favor of Lorenzo Dow Case.[26] Frost, who had traveled to Saint Lawrence with the sole intention of presenting his future wife with a privately published collection of his poems, was so devastated by her rejection that he decided to kill himself in what he imagined the most dramatic way possible: by walking through the treacherous Dismal Swamp until a water moccasin, bobcat, or bear might make his return home an unlikely event. Surprisingly, Frost made it through the Dismal Swamp virtually unscathed and was rescued by a party of duck hunters, with whom he eventually traveled to Nags Head and Kitty Hawk. Frost's memory of these events informs an opening catalog of personal failures that he claims prevented him from realizing his full potential as a poet. The opening lines reveal a despairing young man who is "Out of sorts with Fate":

> Kitty Hawk, O Kitty,
> There was once a song,
> Who knows but a great
> Emblematic ditty,
> I might well have sung
> When I came here young
> Out and down along
> Past Elizabeth City
> Sixty years ago.
> I was, to be sure,
> Out of sorts with Fate,
> Wandering to and fro
> In the earth alone,
> You might think too poor-
> Spirited to care
> Who I was or where
> I was being blown
> Faster than my tread—
> Like the crumpled, better

> Left-unwritten letter
> I had read and thrown.
>
> (*CPP&P*, 441)

Like ill-fated Aeneas, the poet in these lines describes himself as being buffeted by deterministic forces so severe that he feels powerless to thwart them. He is tossed and discarded like the "Dear John" letter he has just read, and he is frustrated because his poetic entreaties to the heavens are not answered. "Aries and Taurus, / Gemini and Cancer" simply mock him, while the poem he had intended to write remains nothing but a dream "of Dark Hatteras."

The reminiscing speaker, however, is honest about the causes of his earlier artistic failures. He blames his poetic silence not upon controlling external forces but rather upon his own dolor and sloth. Describing himself as a "young Alastor" (Shelley's poetic hero who searches alone and in vain for some kind of commerce with divinity), the speaker in "Kitty Hawk" realizes that his isolation and lethargy are the primary causes of his melancholy condition. His epiphany occurs shortly after the duck hunters befriend him. Although he portrays them as kind and nurturing, he cannot participate in their drunken revelry or in their sentimental weeping over life's miseries. He sees in the hunters a portrait of what he might himself become, and the image that emerges is not conducive either to writing poetry or to resolving the problem of his failed quest for love:

> They included me
> Like a little brother
> In their revelry—
> All concern to take
> Care my innocence
> Should at all events
> Tenderly be kept
> For good gracious' sake.
> And if they were gentle
> They were sentimental.
> One drank to his mother
> While another wept.
> Something made it sad
> For me to break loose
> From the need they had

> To make themselves glad
> They were of no use.

(CPP&P, 444)

In this scene, Frost describes the poet's vocation as one of isolation and loneliness, a condition caused by an urgent need to engage the world in a sophisticated manner. Although the speaker seems genuinely to care for the men who have befriended him, he cannot remain in their company for long. They are simple-minded and compassionate and do not understand that the most basic human imperative is to vitalize matter, to give it form and meaning through conscious acts of mind. Although Christian dogma has tried to "censure / Our instinctive venture / Into what they call / The material," Frost suggests that our insatiable drive toward knowledge is not hubristic, as Raphael tells Adam in *Paradise Lost,* but instead a glorifying attribute that pays homage to divinity. Our greatest human fear, as the hunters' actions attest, should not be a fear of enlightenment but instead a fear of intellectual stagnation. Our fall from grace is thus paradoxical, for our separation from God makes possible the wonders of a creative consciousness:

> Ours is to behave
> Like a kitchen spoon
> Of a size Titanic
> To keep all things stirred
> In a blend mechanic
> Saying that's the tune,
> That's the pretty kettle!
> Matter mustn't curd,
> Separate and settle.
> Action is the word.

(CPP&P, 452–53)

Thus, the poet's flight from the hunters at the end of part 1 is a welcome escape for a young man whose mind must remain active and facile. Although it is clear that the "young Alastor" has failed in his attempt to create a meaningful poem about his forsaken love, he has nevertheless acquired through his isolation and suffering a more useful form of knowledge. The speaker elaborates upon his discovery in the closing lines of part 1. Once the poet-hero departs the company of the hunters, he speaks to a lone coast guard and recounts an imaginary conversation between the ocean and an "inner sound." Like Wallace Stevens's boundaries between the imagination and reality in "The Idea of Order at Key West," Frost's inner sound refers not only to Albemarle Sound, the actual body of water along which he walks, but metaphorically to his desire to have meaningful converse with physical reality. Once mind and matter reciprocate, the youthful poet is able, for the first time in the poem, to recite a line of poetry. At this moment, life for the young poet becomes more meaningful, and he discovers that he is happy:

> So it was in talk,
> We prolonged the walk,
> On one side the ocean,
> And on one a water
> Of the inner sound;
> "And the moon was full,"
> As the poet said
> And I aptly quoted.
> And its being full,
> Small but strong and round,
> By its tidal pull
> Made all being full.

(CPP&P, 445)

Although the line of poetry he quotes is Tennyson's and not his own, the poet realizes that he has been given a second chance at life. His suicidal impulses have been allayed by his poetic venture into the material, and his presence at Kitty Hawk, fifty years later, attests to the saving qualities of his art.

In part 2 Frost extends his Bergsonian theme and applies it to the Wright brothers' pioneering flight, which he sees as a parallel "risk of spirit in substantiation." Although the "leap" is as insignificant as "the hop from grass / Of a grasshopper," the gesture itself animates matter and reveals to us that even though we cannot create "One least germ or coal," we "may get control / If not of the whole / . . . / We can give the part / Wholeness in a sense." The synechdocal forms Frost celebrates for their ingress to external reality are, however, contingent first upon the preeminence of a vital spirit—the *mens animi*, as Frost calls it—that precedes and impels all creation forward:

> Spirit enters flesh
> And for all it's worth

Charges into earth
In birth after birth
Ever fresh and fresh.
We may take the view
That its derring-do
Thought of in the large
Was one mighty charge
On our human part
of the soul's ethereal
Into the material.

(*CPP&P*, 447)

Frost's vision here is remarkably consistent with Bergson's philosophy in *Creative Evolution*. As the *élan vital* moves through matter and beyond, it expends itself in the emergent novelty of new forms. And despite the enormous capacity for our technological prowess to annihilate the earth, Frost, near the end of his life, remains confident that human beings will endure. With such an uncanny knack for survival, we should not ground our flight toward "the infinite"; rather, we should keep humankind starring in the "royal role":

["]Go you on to know
More than you can sing.
Have no hallowing fears
Anything's forbidden
Just because it's hidden.
Trespass and encroach
On successive spheres
Without self-reproach."

(*CPP&P*, 448)

It may seem odd that this final imperative issues from a man who early in his youth excoriated science for attempting to purge us of our religious delusions. But talk of God and metaphysics is prominent here, and Frost seems unafraid, for the first time in his poetry, to reassert the romantic idealism that his mother had so carefully taught him. More soaring and hopeful than any of Frost's philosophical poems, more far-reaching in its vision of the future, "Kitty Hawk" comes full circle and reacquaints us with Emerson, the father of American philosophy, from whom every modernist had tried so diligently to win independence. "There seems to be a necessity in spirit to manifest itself in material forms," Emerson once wrote. "A fact is the end or last issue of spirit."[27]

The Emersonian impulse that Frost pays homage to in "Kitty Hawk" suggests, in the final analysis, that Frost's career parallels the careers of those modernists who would sustain success into old age. Just as Eliot saw the follies of his early life and, in response to them, resurrected Whitman in *Four Quartets*, Frost fully embraces in his later work some of the romantic idealism that he had been so reluctant to accept as a young man. Such a transformation could only have occurred in an era of rapid intellectual change. As the view that saw mind as a separate and subordinate accident of matter came to be seen by twentieth-century physicists as an outdated epistemology, some modernist poets suddenly found themselves able to revive some of the hope that had expired in the last quarter of the nineteenth century. To those such as Frost, Eliot, and Moore, all of whom were sensitive to shifts in sensibility, the old Poundian imperative to make poetry more akin to materialism had exhausted its influence within a few decades. The cosmos was more mysterious than they had supposed, and the result was a body of poetry more redeeming than anyone at the end of the nineteenth century might have predicted.

In addition to resurrecting optimism, the creative imperatives in "Kitty Hawk" serve as a metaphor for a man who endured enormous suffering and still found the courage to keep risking "spirit in substantiation." There is, however, an irony surrounding Frost's artistic longevity. While literary criticism has steadily elevated Frost's stature in American letters since his death in 1963, he himself remained insecure about his accomplishments and worried that he had not used his gifts to their fullest potential. Bereft of the Nobel Prize, still chastised by the political left, and jealous of Eliot's accomplishments, Frost often wondered whether his poetry was strong enough to defeat time. In a 1946 sermon to the Rockdale Avenue Temple in Cincinnati, Ohio, Frost publicly revealed his fears more fully than he ever had: "Now religion always seems to me to come round to something beyond wisdom. It's a straining of the spirit forward to a wisdom beyond wisdom. Many men have the kind of wisdom that will do well enough in the day's work. . . . But if they have religious natures they constantly, inside, they constantly tremble a little with the fear of God. And the fear of God always has meant the fear that one's wisdom, one's own wisdom, one's own human wisdom is not quite acceptable in His sight."[28]

In retrospect, it looks as though Frost had been thinking about "Kitty Hawk" long before he wrote it, for in this boldly religious confession Frost celebrates human creativity as the end and purpose of life. Here we do not find a Frost terrified of a material universe so devoid of sentience as to seem meaningless; rather we see a man whose faith in a "something beyond wisdom" is so strong that he faults himself for never having quite comprehended it. In Frost's poetry, the desire to know this elusive "wisdom beyond wisdom," to resurrect a God who had been buried beneath an oppressive scientific materialism is, to my mind, the central *agon* of Frost's career and the main source of his incalculable suffering. Yet Frost's separation from God also provided him with his greatest opportunity. In a lecture he delivered at Dartmouth only two months before his death in 1963, Frost defined the poem as an "extravagance about grief."[29] What he meant was that the poet's business is to engage the "irremediable" sadness that a human being often seems powerless to thwart. Yet despite Frost's claim that sadness is "irremediable," he provides us with a method to alleviate human suffering: "Every poem is a symbol small or great of the way the will has to pitch into commitments deeper and deeper to a rounded conclusion and then be judged for whether any original intention it had has been strongly spent or weakly lost. . . . Strongly spent is synonymous with kept."[30]

In Frost's view, we can defeat our cosmic loneliness and reclaim nature only by projecting onto it the saving structures that infuse it with meaning and order. As the source of all freedom, hope, and redemption, this basic human activity initiates and organizes all human inquiry and enables us to stay ourselves momentarily against confusion. As Frost's own life of suffering attests, such saving acts of mind exact a high cost. The risk of spirit in substantiation can neither disclose the true nature of an indivisible reality nor permanently protect us from the external world. Our mental acts, however, can, by their very power to elevate themselves beyond material processes, reaffirm our faith in an unseen spiritual reality. Such a provisional deliverance from the excrutiations of scientific determinism may seem meager in the disabling world we inhabit, but for Frost this measured assurance was compensation for a life strongly spent.

Notes

INTRODUCTION

1. Thompson, *Robert Frost: The Early Years*, 88–89.

2. See, e.g., Emerson's claim in "Nature" that "if a man would be alone, let him look at the stars. . . . One might think the atmosphere was made transparent with the design, to give man, in the heavenly bodies, the presence of the sublime" (Emerson, "Nature," in *Selections from Ralph Waldo Emerson*, 23).

3. Pearce, *Continuity of American Poetry*, 253.

4. Frost, *Collected Poems, Prose, and Plays*, 33. All subsequent references, abbreviated as *CPP&P*, are to this edition, which is based on Frost's *Complete Poems* (1949) and *In the Clearing* (1963).

5. The Royal Society's hostility toward poetry and rhetoric is generally indicative of the prevailing attitudes of nineteenth-century scientists toward poetry. According to Thomas Sprat, the Royal Society's historian, poetry was not only an irrational form of knowledge, it was a tool for evil: "And in few words, I dare say: that of all the Studies of men, nothing may be sooner obtain'd, than this vicious abundance of Phrase, this trick of Metaphor, this volubility of Tongue, which make so great a noise in the World. But I spend words in vain; for evil is now so inveterate, that it is hard to know whom to blame, or where to begin reform. We all value one another so much, upon this beautiful deceit; and labour so long after it, in the years of our education: that we cannot but ever after think kinder of it than it deserves" (Sprat, *History of the Royal Society*, 112–13).

6. Peacock, *Works of Thomas Love Peacock*, 8:23–24.

7. Many mistakenly use *materialism* and *positivism* as if they were the names of equivalent conceptual systems. There are, however, distinct differences between the two schools. By *materialism* I mean to suggest that all natural phenomena may be reduced to matter and the dynamic interrelationships between material events. Positivism, on the other hand, is characterized by a rejection of metaphysics, by the idea that all knowledge should be confined to what can be experienced directly, and by a belief that a phenomenon can be subsumed under one or more laws of which it is merely an instance. Materialists thus argue that any mental or spiritual entity (includ-

ing God) must be attributed to purely material causes, while the positivists argue that any attempt to move beyond phenomena to a "metaphysical" reality is simply an unjustifiable and useless enterprise. Both systems contend that science establishes the ideal form of knowledge. For an excellent discussion of materialism, positivism, and idealism see chapter 1 of Maurice Mandelbaum's *History, Man, and Reason.*

8. I am indebted here to Sanford Schwartz for his excellent discussion concerning the rise of instrumental philosophy in *The Matrix of Modernism,* 12.

9. Ibid., 15.

10. Nikolai Lobachevski and Janos Bolyai independently found alternatives to Euclidean geometry. Their "hyperbolic" geometry was based on a contrary to Euclid's fifth postulate, which stated that if a straight line crossed two other straight lines so that the sum of their interior angles on one side was less than two right angles, then the two straight lines should eventually cross on the same side. The work of Lobachevski and Bolyai was largely ignored until 1866, when Jules Hoüel made their work known in France.

11. James, *The Meaning of Truth,* 40.

12. Schwartz, "Henri Bergson," 47.

13. Bergson, *Time and Free Will,* 14.

14. Lawrance Thompson indicates that Frost developed a special bond with Hulme and spoke frequently with him about poetry and theology (see Thompson, *Robert Frost: The Early Years,* 441; and Walsh, *Into My Own,* 118).

15. Lawrance Thompson has extracted several important passages from *Creative Evolution* that Frost appropriated in "West-Running Brook." See *Robert Frost: The Early Years,* 579–81.

16. Bergson, *Creative Evolution,* 237.

17. Quirk, *Bergson and American Culture,* 1.

18. James, *Pluralistic Universe,* 265–66.

19. Quirk, *Bergson and American Culture,* 45.

20. Poe, "Poetic Principle," in Poe, *Complete Works,* 14:272.

21. Christopher Clausen has argued that most poets in the nineteenth century responded to the challenges from science in one of two ways: either they argued that the poet has intuitive access to a supernatural realm that the scientist does not, thus making the truths of poetry just as valid as those of science, or they argued that the poem is a hermetic system that provides aesthetic pleasure (*Place of Poetry,* 1). Poe clearly aligned himself with the latter group.

22. See Frost, "The Figure a Poem Makes," in *CPP&P,* 777.

23. Frost, "On Extravagance: A Talk," in ibid., 902.

24. Moore, "Poetry."

25. Williams, *Paterson,* 14.

26. Lathem, *Interviews,* 13.

27. Frank Lentricchia has argued that Frost, following Kant, justified the existence of poetry based on his belief that it satisfied a psychological need rather than a cognitive function: "When we grasp Frost's landscape, the personal world shaped by the poet's consciousness in and through language, a world answering to the psychic

needs of its shaper, we are not gaining a form of sharable knowledge of a common public reality. What we gain, initially, is a 'better nature,' a shaped vision which we, too, find therapeutic (hence the fiction's affective value)" (see Lentricchia's *Robert Frost*, chap. 1). While Frost certainly acknowledged the psychological benefits of shaping a material reality, I am arguing that Frost sought a stronger defense than the "poetry as therapy" argument could provide. Unlike Kant, who continued to privilege the cognitive and rational functions of science, Frost eventually saw both poetry and science as epistemologically equivalent disciplines whose cognitive functions were limited by perception.

28. Frost, "Education by Poetry," in *CPP&P*, 720.

29. Lentricchia, for example, claims that Jamesian pragmatism is the unifying force that binds Frost's tendencies toward realism and romanticism. "James' philosophy," writes Lentricchia, "defines the self as the redeemer of brute fact and chaos into human value, pattern, and significance" ("Robert Frost and Modern Literary Theory," 322).

30. Poirier, *Poetry and Pragmatism*, 149.

31. Frost, *Selected Letters*, 467.

32. Bergson, *Introduction to Metaphysics*, 39–40.

33. Frost, "The Future of Man," in *CPP&P*, 870.

34. Sidney, *Defence of Poetry*, 8.

35. Frost, "The Future of Man" (unpublished version), in *CPP&P*, 870–71.

36. Thomas Kuhn and Hans-Georg Gadamer both insist that scientific understanding always involves some form of historically determined prejudice. For Kuhn, scientific revolutions occur when one paradigm replaces another and introduces a completely new set of theories and linguistic terms of analysis. The notion of a paradigm-centered scientific community meshes nicely with Gadamer's belief that all understanding is bound by one's "effective-history," which provides the contextual grounds for human thought and action. Although neither Kuhn nor Gadamer denies the importance of scientific understanding, both believe that one must counter cultural encoding by questioning received scientific traditions. Sir Arthur Eddington made much the same argument thirty years prior to Kuhn. In *The Nature of the Physical World*, a book that Frost read enthusiastically, Eddington wrote that "[i]t is not so much the particular form that scientific theories have now taken—the conclusions we believe we have proved—as the movement of thought behind them that concerns the philosopher. Our eyes once opened, we may pass on to yet a new outlook on the world, but we can never go back to the old outlook. . . . If the scheme of philosophy which we now rear on the advances of Einstein, Bohr, Rutherford and others is doomed to fall in the next thirty years, it is not to be laid to their charge that we have gone astray. Like the systems of Euclid, of Ptolemy, of Newton, which have served their turn, so the systems of Einstein and Heisenberg may give way to some fuller realization of the world. But in each revolution of scientific thought new words are set to the old music, and that which has gone before is not destroyed but refocused" (353). For other sympathetic accounts of scientific hermeneutics, see Kuhn,

Structure of Scientific Revolutions, chap. 1; Gadamer, *Truth and Method,* 239, 245–47; and Putnam, *Meaning and the Moral Sciences,* 72.

37. Frost, "Why Wait for Science," in *CPP&P,* 359.

38. Thompson, *Robert Frost: The Years of Triumph,* 658–60, 729.

39. Hiers, "Robert Frost's Quarrel with Science and Technology," 183.

40. Faggen, *Robert Frost and the Challenge of Darwin,* 246–47.

41. Frost, "'Sermon' at Rockdale Avenue Temple," *CPP&P,* 792.

42. Cook, *Robert Frost: A Living Voice,* 178.

43. Guy Rotella argues that quantum mechanics provided Frost with an instrumentalist epistemology that revealed "not the world but models of the world, metaphors." Additionally, Darrel Abel demonstrates how Frost's engagement with Bergson and James led to his repudiation of positivist epistemology and his movement toward an acceptance of the view that scientific concepts are simply projections of the human mind upon reality (see Rotella, "Comparing Conceptions," 184; and Abel, "Instinct of a Bard"). Ronald E. Martin, from whom the quotation in the text comes, confirms these views in *American Literature and the Destruction of Knowledge,* 137.

44. Hayles, *Cosmic Web,* 22–23.

45. Bronowski, *Science and Human Values,* 19.

46. C. P. Snow contends that because of traditional hostility and hyperspecialization, scientists and humanists are incapable of communicating with one another (see *Two Cultures,* chap. 1).

1. A NARROW CHOICE THE AGE INSISTED ON

1. Russell, "The Free Man's Worship," 32.

2. James, *Pragmatism,* 76.

3. Ibid.

4. Holland, *Brain of Robert Frost,* 23.

5. Jones, "Cosmic Loneliness of Robert Frost."

6. Frost, Notebooks, Special Collections, Dartmouth College Library.

7. Stevens, "Sunday Morning," in *Wallace Stevens: The Collected Poems,* 70.

8. Thompson, *Robert Frost: The Early Years,* 246. Later, in *Robert Frost: The Years of Triumph,* 562, Thompson contradicts himself and asserts that Frost's skepticism was merely a "means of protecting his religious belief from the criticism of others," an assertion that I cannot agree with.

9. My discussion here is indebted to Ronald E. Martin's excellent discussion of force and nineteenth-century scientific materialism in *American Literature and the Universe of Force,* 6–31.

10. Feynman, *Six Easy Pieces,* 4.

11. The first law of thermodynamics can be stated mathematically as $\Delta E = q - w$, where ΔE is the change in internal energy of an enclosed system, q is the heat added (or subtracted, if the value is negative), and w is the work done. For an excellent general description see ibid., 69.

12. Tyndall, *Fragments of Science,* 2:4.

13. Emerson, "Nature," 25.

14. Wordsworth, "The Tables Turned."

15. Swedenborg, *Divine Love and Wisdom,* quoted in Thompson, *Robert Frost: The Early Years,* 70.

16. Darwin summarizes the theory of natural selection at the end of chapter 4 of *On the Origin of Species:* "If during the long course of ages and under varying conditions of life, organic beings vary at all in the several parts of their organization, and I think this cannot be disputed; if there be, owing to the high geometric powers of increase of each species, at some age, season, or year, a severe struggle for life, and this certainly cannot be disputed; then considering the infinite complexity of the relations of all organic beings to each other and to their conditions of existence, causing an infinite diversity of structure, constitution, and habits, to be advantageous to them, I think it would be a most extraordinary fact if no variation ever had occurred useful to each being's own welfare, in the same way as so many variations have occurred useful to man. But if variations useful to any organic being do occur, assuredly individuals thus characterized will have the best chance of being preserved in the struggle for life; and from the strong principle of inheritance they will tend to produce offspring similarly characterized. This principle of preservation, I have called, for the sake of brevity, Natural Selection" (Darwin, *On the Origin of Species,* 127).

17. Martin, *Harvest of Change,* 8n.

18. Spencer, *First Principles,* 396.

19. Huxley, *Collected Essays,* 1:41.

20. Winters saw Frost as "an Emersonian who has become skeptical and uncertain" and asserted that "his relativism, apparently since it derives from no intense religious conviction . . . resulted mainly in ill-natured eccentricity and in increasing melancholy" ("Robert Frost," 564–67).

21. Pound, *Collected Shorter Poems,* 208.

22. Stevens, "Of Modern Poetry," in *Wallace Stevens: The Collected Poems,* 239.

23. T. E. Hulme, "Romanticism and Classicism," in Hulme, *Collected Writings,* 68.

24. Pound, *Literary Essays,* 76.

25. Pound, "This Hulme Business."

26. Bawer, "Fictive Music of Wallace Stevens," 73.

27. Stevens, "The Sail of Ulysses," in *Wallace Stevens: Collected Poetry and Prose,* 463.

28. Stevens, "The Snow Man," in *Wallace Stevens: The Collected Poems,* 10.

29. See, e.g., Brower's reading of this poem in *Poetry of Robert Frost,* 136–39, and Lentricchia's reading in *Robert Frost,* 129–30.

30. Howe, "Robert Frost," 27–28.

31. Frost, *Selected Letters,* 324.

32. James, *Will to Believe,* 51.

33. Schiller, *Aesthetical and Philosophical Essays,* 110.

34. Frost, quoted in Oster, *Toward Robert Frost,* 57.

35. Frost, "*Paris Review* Interview with Richard Poirier," in Frost, *CPP&P,* 890.

36. Frost, *Selected Letters,* 583.

37. Frost, Notebooks, Special Collections, Dartmouth College Library.

38. In *The Critique of Judgment* Kant asserts that all aesthetic judgments are not merely based upon taste or opinion but upon an integration of imagination, perception, and understanding, a process that provides pleasure. Though Kant does not necessarily ascribe cognitive value to aesthetic activity, he does value art's ability to engage the imagination for purposes other than the formation of concept.

39. Frost, "Education by Poetry," 723–24.

40. Frost, "The Figure a Poem Makes," 778.

41. Haeckel, *Riddle of the Universe*, 261.

42. The second law of thermodynamics implies that all processes must operate at less than 100 percent efficiency because of wasted heat thrown off through the processes of friction. Mathematically, the concept of entropy can be stated as $\Delta S = \Delta q/t$, where S is the increase in entropy, q is the amount of heat added, and t is the absolute temperature.

43. Einstein's famous paper "Zur Elektrodynamik Beweater Körper" (On the electrodynamics of moving bodies) (1905) contested Newtonian mechanics on the basis of two simple principles, one a relativity principle, the other a light principle. The first principle postulated that all of the laws of physics must take the same form in any inertial frame. The second principle asserted that there is an inertial frame in which the speed of light is independent of the motion of its source. Together, these two principles contested Newtonian mechanics, which did not work for objects approaching the speed of light.

44. T. E. Hulme, "The International Philosophical Congress at Bologna," in Hulme, *Collected Writings*, 110. See also Quirk, *Bergson and American Culture*, 13.

45. William James, quoted in Miller's introduction to *American Thought*, xxxv.

46. Guy Rotella has admirably tracked down most of the sources of Frost's knowledge of physics in "Comparing Conceptions," 167–89.

47. Frost, Notebooks, Special Collections, Dartmouth College Library.

48. Ibid.

49. See, e.g., Angyal, "From Swedenborg to William James."

50. Cook, *Dimensions of Robert Frost*, 149.

2. DARWIN

1. Thompson, *Robert Frost: The Early Years*, 88–92.

2. Although Tennyson published *In Memoriam* nearly a decade before *On the Origin of Species* appeared, he was nevertheless affected by several evolutionary models that were then being debated. In particular, the ideas Tennyson found in Lyell's *Principles of Geology* (1830), especially those concerning the extinction of species, were especially disturbing. W. H. Hudson recorded his reaction to *On the Origin of Species* in his autobiography, *Far Away and Long Ago*, 328.

3. Frost, Lecture, University of Detroit, 14 November 1962, Archives and Special Collections, Amherst College Library.

4. Frost, in *Lawrence (Mass.) High School Bulletin* 13, no. 9 (May 1892): 4.

5. Social Darwinists held the opposite view and often drew upon the work of

Spencer to justify nationalism, militarism, eugenics, and robber-baron industrial practices. Although Social Darwinism had more adherents in Europe than in the United States, several prominent Americans, including Andrew Carnegie and Daniel A. Thompkins, were devoted disciples of Spencer's idea that modern cultures should not stop "the natural process of elimination by which society continually purifies itself" (*Study of Sociology*, 344–45). For a more complete introduction to Social Darwinism, see Richard Hofstadter's *Social Darwinism in American Thought*, 171–97; and Irvin G. Wyllie's "Social Darwinism and the Businessman." More recently, Cynthia Eagle Russett has challenged the view that Social Darwinism was a pervasive phenomenon in American society. Suggesting that most businessmen were "Christians bound to observe the 'Golden Rule,'" Russett argues that very few American thinkers felt obligated to accept Spencer's advocacy of desperate competition and exploitation. She also notes that Social Darwinists' belief in eugenics was a distortion of Darwin's ideas since Darwin himself argued throughout his career that all species had evolved from a common ancestor. Russett does note, however, that Darwinism in its purest form helped to facilitate widespread belief in determinism and a widespread decline in the romantic idea of free, autonomous choice (see Russett's *Darwin in America*, 8–14, 89–98).

6. Daniel C. Dennett admirably shows how extensively Darwin's ideas have affected culture. Claiming that natural selection is a "universal acid" that eats through our most cherished cultural foundations, Dennett clearly explains how natural selection is incompatible with the Enlightenment assumptions that America's founding fathers took for granted (see Dennett, *Darwin's Dangerous Idea*, 17–39).

7. May, *End of American Innocence*, 9–51; Quirk, *Bergson*, 32–33.

8. Santayana, *Winds of Doctrine*, 1.

9. Martin, *American Literature and the Universe of Force*, 59–95.

10. In the absence of Mendelian genetics, neo-Lamarckists proclaimed themselves to be a distinctively American school of evolution. Founded in 1866 and spearheaded by Alpheus S. Packard Jr., this group of scientists thought they had answered two main objections to Darwin: the lack of intermediate forms in the fossil record and the lack of sufficient time to account for species diversity. For a complete discussion of this school, see Edward J. Pfeifers's essay, "United States."

11. May, *End of American Innocence*, 12.

12. Several scholars have emphasized nineteenth-century America's desire to emancipate culture from British authority. In addition to May's *End of American Innocence*, see J. Meredith Neil's *Toward a National Taste*; Jackson Lears's *No Place of Grace*; and Lisa Steinman's *Made in America*.

13. See Steinman, *Made in America*, 14–15; and Branch, "Indexing American Possibilities," 285.

14. Dr. James McKey, quoted in Branch, "Indexing American Possibilities," 285.

15. See David L. Hull's comments on Agassiz in *Darwin and His Critics*, 445–49; see also Edward Lurie's "Louis Agassiz and the Idea of Evolution."

16. Joseph Le Conte, quoted in Russett, *Darwin in America*, 11.

17. Darwin, "The Origin of Species by Means of Natural Selection," in Gray, *Darwiniana*, 10.

18. *Modern synthesis* was Sir Julian Huxley's term for the fusion of Darwin's natural selection and Mendelian genetics. Based on the work of Theodosius Dobzhansky, Julian Huxley, and Ernst Mayr, the modern synthesis was fully established in the 1940s as the most important theory of evolution. For a complete discussion of this development, see Huxley's important work *Evolution: The Modern Synthesis.*

19. For a general introduction to Frost's Harvard years, see Thompson, *Robert Frost: The Early Years,* chap. 20; and Pritchard, *Robert Frost,* 47–52.

20. Santayana, *Interpretations of Poetry and Religion,* 8.

21. Ibid., 270.

22. I am inclined to agree with Thompson, who suggests in *Robert Frost: The Early Years* (244–45) that Frost disliked Santayana for religious reasons. Although it is arguable whether Frost thought Santayana's lectures "blasphemous," as Thompson suggests, ample evidence exists to suggest that Frost, while liking Santayana's poetry, disliked the philosopher's metaphysical temperament. Louis Mertins, for example, corroborates Thompson's belief and suggests that Frost thought Santayana a "confused man" and a "lost soul" (see Mertins, *Robert Frost,* 354–55). Pritchard, on the other hand, suggests that Frost may also have disliked Santayana primarily because of the philosopher's style and manner (see Pritchard, *Robert Frost,* 50–51).

23. James to George H. Palmer, 2 April 1900, in James, "Familiar Letters," 307.

24. One of the most consistent features of Frost's career is his reluctance to displace tradition. His use of traditional poetic forms, his conservatism in politics, and his acknowledgment of a physical reality existing independently of mind all corroborate Frost's idea that constructed forms serve as guides through the sensory flux of experience and necessarily militate against emotional excess in poetry, ethical relativism in society, and imaginative delusion in thought. Perhaps Frost's clearest statement about the dangers of radical revisions can be found in his introduction to Robinson's *King Jasper.* There Frost writes that "science put it into our heads that there must be new ways to be new," but there is "such a thing as being too willing to be different" (see Frost, *CPP&P,* 741). Commenting on these lines, John Hiers argues that for Frost, "the reckless striving for change obscures the proven values of tradition and replaces these illuminating guides with the illusion that human nature can be perfected through constant research" ("Robert Frost's Quarrel with Science and Technology," 189).

25. Thompson, *Robert Frost: The Early Years,* 247.

26. Shaler summarizes his response to Darwin in *The Autobiography of Nathaniel Southgate Shaler,* 181.

27. Danielle Green, of the Harvard University Archives, reports that Frost took two introductory philosophy courses during his brief stay there. Philosophy 1a, taught by Hugo Munsterberg and assisted by Dr. Benjamin Rand and George Herbert Palmer, was a class in logic, psychology (particularly William James), and the relations of the philosophical sciences. Philosophy 1b, team-taught by Santayana and Royce, was a class in the history of philosophy and the theory of philosophical inquiry. Such an

odd marriage of teachers may have contributed to Frost's confusion over Darwin, as his teachers' ideas were diametrically opposed to one another's. Surprisingly, neither Thompson nor Pritchard mentions Frost's instruction under Royce, from whom he would have been exposed to German idealism.

28. My discussion on Royce is indebted to John E. Smith's treatment of Royce in *The Encyclopedia of Philosophy.* See also Royce's *Religious Aspect of Philosophy,* 238–45.

29. Royce, "Problem of Christianity," 333.

30. Ibid., 330.

31. Ibid., 332.

32. My discussion here is indebted to Sanford Schwartz's excellent discussion of the rise of instrumental philosophy in *The Matrix of Modernism,* 12–49.

33. Santayana and Bergson, for example, were very skeptical of conceptual truth, whereas Royce and James believed that conceptual knowledge had the potential to be true. Metaphysically, Santayana occupies one end of the spectrum, and Bergson and Royce the other. Santayana did not believe in the existence of any deity or principle beyond the chaotic flux of experience. Bergson and Royce, on the other hand, acknowledged a deeper or greater spiritual reality beyond the flux of matter. Metaphysically, James occupied a position between Bergson and Santayana.

34. It is ironic that William James, the best-known of the pragmatists, cited natural selection as proof of a nondeterministic universe even as he was questioning scientific epistemology in general. Such a strategy reflects a common tendency among Americans to accept portions of the Darwinian framework that were congenial to their beliefs and to reject those that were not.

35. Frost, "Education by Poetry," 721.

36. I agree with Hildegard Hoeller, who claims that "Frost was intrigued by the vagueness and fluidity of existence, which he saw represented in the evolutionary model. But whereas Darwin tries to master that vagueness, Frost follows James's call in *Psychology the Briefer Course* for the 'reinstatement of the vague and inarticulate to its proper place in our mental life' and agrees with Bergson that 'the role of life is to insert some indetermination into matter'" ("Evolution and Metaphor in Robert Frost's Poetry," 129).

37. Frost, "Education by Poetry," 721–22.

38. Frost's resistance to Darwin, Marx, and Freud is a common feature throughout the notes and letters, much of it predicated by Frost's belief that these thinkers were responsible for formulating the systems of thought—metaphors, Frost called them— that reduced the autonomy of the creative ego to determinant "systems" of thought. Perhaps the best example of Frost's tendency to react strongly against "systematic" metaphors can be found in a letter of 25 November 1936 to Louis Untermeyer: "The national mood is humanitarian. Nobly so—I wouldn't take it away from them. I am content to let it go at one philosophical observation: isn't it a poetical strangeness that while the world was going full blast on the Darwinian metaphors of evolution, survival values and the Devil take the hindmost, a polemical Jew in exile was working up the metaphor of the State's being like a family to displace them from mind and give us a new figure to live by? Marx had the strength not to be overawed by the

metaphor in vogue. Life is like battle. But so is it also like shelter. Apparently we are now going to die fighting to make it a secure shelter. The model is the family at its best. At the height of the Darwinian metaphor, writers like Shaw and Butler were found to go to the length of saying even the family within was strife, and perhaps the worst strife of all. We are all toadies to the fashionable metaphor of the hour. Great is he who imposes the metaphor. From each according to his ability to each according to his need. Except as ye become as good children under a good father and mother! I'm not going to let the shift from one metaphor to another worry me. You'll notice the shift has to be made rather abruptly. There are no logical steps from one to the other. There is no logical connection." For the complete text of the letter, see *CPP&P,* 753–54.

39. Frost often worried that his deepest fears were imaginative projections, a tendency he revealed in letter of 27 October 1917 to Louis Untermeyer: "The conviction closes in on me that I was cast for gloom as the sparks fly upward, I was about to say: I am of deep shadow all compact like onion within onion and the savor of me is oil of tears. I have heard laughter by daylight when I thought it was my own because at that moment when it broke I had parted my lips to take food. Just so I have been afraid of myself and caught at my throat when I thought I was making some terrible din of a mill whistle that happened to come on the same instant with the opening of my mouth to yawn. But I have not laughed. No man can tell you the sound or the way of my laughter. I have neighed at night in the woods behind a house like vampires. But there are no vampires, there are no ghouls, there are no demons, there is nothing but me." For the complete text of this letter, see Frost, *Selected Letters,* 221.

40. Trilling, "A Speech on Robert Frost," 449.

41. The best discussions of "Design" can be found in Richard Poirier's *Robert Frost,* 245–52; Randall Jarrell's "To the Laodiceans," 42–45; and Reuben Brower's *Poetry of Robert Frost,* 104–8. For a good discussion of "Design"'s structural elements, see Dorothy Judd Hall's *Contours of Belief,* 69–71.

42. See Dennett, *Darwin's Dangerous Idea,* 59.

43. T. H. Huxley, "Criticisms on 'The Origin of Species,'" in Gray, *Darwiniana,* 82.

44. James, "Sentiment of Rationality," in *Collected Essays and Reviews,* 86–87.

45. Brower, *Poetry of Robert Frost,* 11.

46. In part 2 of *The Descent of Man* Darwin devotes an entire chapter (11) to describing the sexual and reproductive characteristics of butterflies and moths (see *Descent of Man,* 304–26)

47. I agree with Robert Faggen, who argues that in "Frost's insect world beauty is not its own excuse for being but, instead, an ephemeral instrument in a wasteful scheme of propagation" (*Robert Frost and the Challenge of Darwin,* 73–73).

48. Darwin, *Descent of Man,* 304.

49. Poirier, *Robert Frost,* 230–31.

50. Ibid., 231.

51. Frost to Louis Untermeyer, 25 November 1936, in *CPP&P,* 754.

52. Darwin cited four essential conditions that must be present before "good" behavior could become a real component of everyday rational existence. These condi-

tions are articulated in chapter 4 of *The Descent of Man,* titled "Comparison of the Mental Powers of Man and the Lower Animals": "The following proposition seems to me in a high degree probable—namely, that any animal whatever, endowed with well-marked social instincts, the parental and filial affections being here included, would inevitably acquire a moral sense or conscience, as soon as its intellectual powers had become as well, or nearly as well developed, as in man. For, firstly, the social instincts lead an animal to take pleasure in the society of its fellows, to feel a certain amount of sympathy with them, and to perform various services for them. . . . Secondly, as soon as the mental faculties had become highly developed, images of all past actions and motives would be incessantly passing through the brain of each individual; and that feeling of dissatisfaction, or even misery which invariably results . . . would arise as often as it was perceived. . . . Thirdly, after the power of language had been acquired, and the wishes of the community could be expressed, the common opinion of how each member ought to act for the public good, would naturally become in paramount degree the guide to action. Lastly, habit in the individual would ultimately play a very important part in guiding the conduct of each member" (95–96).

53. Bergson, *Creative Evolution,* 139–51.

54. Robert Faggen argues that "At Woodward's Garden," rather than highlighting the gulf between human and animal consciousness, plays upon the idea that greater intellectual similarities exist between humans and animals. According to Faggen, "We investigate the natural world hoping to confirm our power of intuition or to find revelation or divinity. What we find is either limitation of our perception or an awareness that we are a part of an animal world that we cannot transcend" (*Robert Frost and the Challenge of Darwin,* 91). While I am sympathetic to Faggen's notion of limited perception, it seems to me that the primary impulse of the poem here is to challenge the Bergsonian notion of the contrast between instinct and intelligence.

55. Bergson, *Creative Evolution,* 193.

56. Fabre, *Hunting Wasps,* 211.

57. B. J. Sokol has argued that Frost's description of the White-Tailed Hornet "hawking" for flies is "deliberate linguistic confusion" derivative from a conflation of "white-tailed hawk" and "white-headed hornet," two species that Sokol claims are native to North America. Since the white-tailed hawk is indigenous only to Mexico, it is more likely that Frost's description derives from Fabre's *Hunting Wasps,* which uses similar language to describe the wasp's hunting: "The Wasp has to pounce upon her prey unawares, without considering how she shall attack or calculating her blows, just as the Goshawk does when hunting in the fallows. Mandibles, claws, sting, every weapon must be employed simultaneously in the fierce fray so as to put an end as early as possible to a contest in which the least hesitation would give the victim time to escape" (301). Such a similar description suggests that Frost had first-hand knowledge of Fabre's text, which was published in translation two years after Bergson's *Creative Evolution.* Sokol also suggests that it is very likely that Frost read much more than the first quarter of *Creative Evolution,* as Ronald Bieganowski has suggested. Such an argument makes good sense, as many of the images in "West-

Running Brook" derive from passages that occur much later in Bergson's text. I disagree, however, with Sokol's contention that Frost was not deeply influenced by Bergson. Despite some of the negative commentary in Frost's marginalia, to my mind Frost remained throughout his life a strong believer in a deep spiritual reality very similar to Bergson's *élan vital* (see Sokol's "Bergson, Instinct, and Frost's 'The White-Tailed Hornet,'" 44–55; and Bieganowski's "Sense of Time in Robert Frost's Poetics," 184–93).

58. Nietzsche, *Will To Power*, 314–15.

59. Bergson also employs the image of water as a metaphor for consciousness. Clearly Bergson is the source for Frost's images: "Life as a whole, from the initial impulsion that thrust it into the world, will appear as a wave that rises, and which is opposed by the descending movement of matter. In the greater part of its surface, at different heights, the current is converted by matter into a vortex. At one point alone it passes freely, dragging with it the obstacle which will weigh on its progress but will not stop it: at this point is humanity; it is our privileged situation. On the other hand, the rising wave is consciousness, and like all consciousness it includes potentialities without number which interpenetrate and to which consequently neither the category of unity nor that of multiplicity is appropriate, made as the both are for inert matter" (*Creative Evolution*, 250).

60. Unlike Bergson, who extends the idea of "real duration" from an explanation of the psyche in *Time and Free Will* (1889) into the *élan vital*, an evolutionary principle, Frost starts with the *élan vital* and extends it into an explanation of consciousness and love.

61. Frost, interview by Allen Schoenfield, 11 October 1925, in Lathem, *Interviews*, 64.

3. WE ARE SICK WITH SPACE

1. See Thompson, *Robert Frost: The Early Years*, 90–93.

2. Emerson, "Nature," 23.

3. Ibid.

4. Frost, in *Lawrence (Mass.) High School Bulletin* 13, no. 4 (December 1891): 4.

5. Frost once claimed that nearly a third of all of his poems were "astronomical." Thompson records that Belle Frost, as a way of coaxing her son toward astronomy, often quoted a line from Edward Young's *Complaint or Night Thoughts on Life, Death, and Immortality*: "An undevout astronomer is mad" (see Thompson, *Robert Frost: The Early Years*, 92–93).

6. Thompson claims that Frost admitted authorship of this poem to Charles R. Green, the librarian of the Jones Public Library in Amherst, Massachusetts, and then retracted that statement, out of embarrassment, in 1946. Most Frost scholars, including Richard Poirier, now attribute the poem to Frost (see Thompson's note on this poem in ibid., 540).

7. Ibid., 593–94.

8. Lathem, *Interviews*, 149.

9. Thompson, *Robert Frost: The Early Years*, 258.

10. Ibid., 265.

11. Ibid., 340.

12. The sharp contrast between Robert's and Elinor's religious views is highlighted in a letter Frost wrote to Louis Untermeyer on 21 March 1920 (see Frost, *Selected Letters*, 244).

13. Mertins, *Robert Frost*, 326.

14. Much of the evidence that Frost liked Proctor's book comes from a letter Mrs. Frost wrote to Mrs. Edna Romig on 4 February 1935, in which she noted that Frost, attracted to the book's religious element, had read *Our Place among Infinities* several times about 1890 (See Thompson, *Robert Frost: The Early Years*, 501). In spite of Frost's attraction to *Our Place among Infinities*, his obsession with science in his prose and poetry clearly indicates that Proctor did not resolve Frost's conflict with science. Not until Frost encountered Bergson in 1912 and Eddington, Heisenberg, and Bohr in the early 1920s did he begin to find plausible arguments against materialism.

15. Proctor, *Our Place among Infinities*, 37–38.

16. Ibid., 39–40, emphasis added.

17. Arnold, *Works*, 4:2.

18. Frost, "The Future of Man" (unpublished version), 870–71.

19. Arnold, *Works*, 4:2–3.

20. In 1796 Laplace published *Système du Monde* (World system), which contained his nebular hypothesis as well as a general account of Newtonian mechanics. Though the nebular hypothesis had been postulated earlier by Swedenborg and Kant, Laplace's theory had become the dominant cosmology by 1820.

21. Proctor, *Our Place among Infinities*, 9–10.

22. Frost, quoted in Mertins, *Robert Frost*, 326.

23. Frost, Notebooks, Special Collections, Dartmouth College Library.

24. Postulated by Rudolf Clausius in 1865, the second law of thermodynamics states that all processes must operate at less than 100 percent efficiency because of wasted heat thrown off through the processes of friction. Mathematically, the concept of entropy can be stated as $\Delta S = \Delta q/t$, where S is the increase in entropy, q is the amount of heat added, and t is the absolute temperature. Frost often talked about the concept of entropy by invoking Yggdrasil, the great ash tree in Norse mythology, which extended its roots and branches through the universe, holding it together: "But all growth is limited—the tree of life is limited like a maple tree or an oak tree—they all have a certain height, and they all have a certain life-length. And our tree, the tree Yggdrasil, has reached its growth. It doesn't have to fall down because it's stopped growing. It will go on blossoming and having seasons—I'd give it a hundred or two hundred million years" (Frost, "The Future of Man" [published version], 868).

25. See Proctor, *Our Place among Infinities*, 41–44.

26. Mill, "Nature," 381.

27. Huxley, *Evolution and Ethics*, 83.

28. I am indebted here to Christopher Clausen's ideas concerning what he terms the moral and the mystic imagination, which he claims are two distinct but anti-

thetical responses to nineteenth-century science. Viewing the later Hopkins as representative of the moral imagination and Whitman as the supreme representative of the mystic imagination, Clausen explains Whitman's influence on Hopkins and why Hopkins, harboring severe misgivings about finding god in the natural world, repudiated his earlier mystical stance ("Whitman, Hopkins, and the World's Splendor," 175–78).

29. Whitman, *Leaves of Grass*, 228.

30. Ibid., 18.

31. Stevens, "The Noble Rider and the Sound of Words," in *Wallace Stevens: Collected Poetry and Prose*, 665.

32. Pascal, *Pensées*, 61.

33. Poirier, *Robert Frost*, 267.

34. Lathem, *Interviews*, 271.

35. I am speaking chiefly of Michel Foucault, who describes the author as a function within the larger discourse of poststructuralists who deny the author agency (Foucault, "What Is an Author?").

36. Snyder, *World Machine*, 465.

37. According to Newtonian mechanics, once the forces and initial conditions are specified, it is possible to calculate the motions of particles into the indefinite future. Basing his predictions upon his law of force, $F = ma$ (force equals mass times acceleration), and his inverse square law of gravitation, $F = G(m_1 m_2)/r^2$ (force is directly proportional to the product of the masses and inversely proportional to the square of the distance between them), Newton postulated that the course of the universe was fixed and calculable. Newton, however, had difficulty specifying an absolute state of motion or rest, a fixed frame of reference, which was necessary in order to observe these conditions. To solve this problem, Newton argued that God had provided him with the absolute frame of reference necessary for his mechanics to work. Einstein disputed this claim by suggesting that there could be no absolute state of motion or rest, only relative motion. While Newtonian mechanics worked well to describe the motions of relatively slow-moving objects, it failed once those objects approached the speed of light. For an excellent general discussion of the differences between Newtonian and Einsteinian physics, see Jeremy Bernstein's *Einstein*, 29–31.

38. I am here indebted to Carol Donley and Alan Friedman's informative discussion of the impact of physics on popular culture in *Einstein as Myth and Muse*, 13. The issue of *The Nation* they refer to is that of 7 April 1920, p. 503.

39. Donley and Friedman, *Einstein as Myth and Muse*, 10.

40. Rotella, "Comparing Conceptions," 174.

41. Eddington, *Philosophy of Physical Science*, 56.

42. Eddington, *Space, Time, and Gravitation*, 201.

43. Eddington, *Nature of the Physical World*, 353.

44. Ibid., 353.

45. Ibid., 288–89.

46. Ibid., 327.

47. Rotella, "Comparing Conceptions," 167.

48. Frost, "Education by Poetry," 721.

49. Eddington, *Nature of the Physical World,* 311.

50. Frost, "Education by Poetry," 720.

51. Planck, *Where Is Science Going?* 214.

52. Heisenberg, *Across the Frontiers,* 26.

53. Jeans, *Mysterious Universe,* 150–51.

54. Thompson, *Robert Frost: The Years of Triumph,* 617.

55. Frost, "Education by Poetry," 721.

56. Rotella, "Comparing Conceptions," 179–80.

57. Bohr's earliest elucidation of the correspondence principle occurs in "Über die Anwendung der Quantentheorie auf den Atombau" (On the application of quantum theory to atomic structure), 141.

58. Bohr, *Atomic Theory and the Description of Nature,* 116–17.

59. Frost, "The Poetry of Amy Lowell," in *CPP&P,* 712.

60. Frost, "The Figure a Poem Makes," 777.

61. To my mind, the best reading of "Birches," to which my own reading is indebted, is still Frank Lentricchia's explication of the poem in *Robert Frost,* 107–12.

62. Ibid., 7.

63. This idea may be indebted to Kurt Gödel's Incompleteness theorem (1931), which states that the axioms in any given mathematical system cannot be proven from the axioms within that system itself.

64. Bernstein, *Einstein,* 157.

65. Ibid., 158.

66. Frost's ideas here are very similar to Derrida's notion that throughout history Western philosophy has attempted to find a privileged truth, what Derrida terms the "transcendental signified," which exists outside of language, consciousness, history, and time. For Derrida, such an attempt is futile, as no self-evident truth or metaphysics of presence can exist outside of discourse.

67. Frost, "Our Hold on the Planet," in *CPP&P,* 317.

68. Frost, quoted in Rodman, "Robert Frost," 41.

69. Thompson and Winnick, *Robert Frost: The Later Years,* 291.

70. John Lancaster, curator of Amherst College Special Collections, reports that the original transcript of this interview, upon which this version is based, was loaned to Amherst by William Britton Stitt, Amherst College class of 1918 (see Frost, "Interview with Jonas Salk," Archives and Special Collections, Amherst College Library, 15).

71. Cohen, "Interview with Einstein," 69.

72. See Cook, *Robert Frost: A Living Voice,* 100.

4. EDUCATION BY POETRY

1. Frost to Lewis Gannett, 3 February 1927, Special Collections, Columbia University Library.

2. Frost to Ashley Thorndike, 25 January 1916, ibid.

3. Barry, *Robert Frost on Writing,* 9.

4. Examples of the diverse critical opinions I mention here can be found in Logan,

"The Other Other Frost," 21; Sheehy, "Measure for Measure," 76–77; Lentricchia, *Modernist Quartet*, 77–83; Oster, *Toward Robert Frost*, 105–10; Bagby, *Robert Frost and the Book of Nature*, 39–52; Meyers, *Robert Frost: A Life*, xiv–iv; and Kearns, *Robert Frost and a Poetics of Appetite*, 3.

5. Frost, *Selected Letters*, 583.

6. I have culled the phrase "surfaces and depths" from Sanford Schwartz's illuminating study *The Matrix of Modernism*, 4–7. In his introduction Schwartz suggests that a "sharp opposition between conscious 'surfaces' and unconscious 'depths' is an important feature of Modernism that informs several areas of knowledge including poetry, psychoanalysis, linguistics, ethnology, and philosophy."

7. Ibid., 5.

8. Schopenhauer is especially important in this regard, as he argues that art allows us temporarily to escape the processes of individual will that lead to the formation of abstract concepts. For Schopenhauer, the function of art, as Keats suggested in "Ode on a Grecian Urn," is to "tease us out of thought" and our drive toward the formation of concepts: "If, raised by the power of the mind, a man relinquishes the common way of looking at things . . . if he thus ceases to consider the where, the when, the why, and the whither of things, and looks simply and solely at the *what*; if, further, he does not allow abstract thought, the concepts of the reason, to take possession of his consciousness, but instead of all this, . . . lets his whole consciousness be filled with the quiet contemplation of the natural object actually present . . . then he who is sunk in this perception is no longer individual, for in such perception the individual has lost himself; . . . he is *pure*, will-less, painless, timeless *subject of knowledge*" (Schopenhauer, *World as Will and Idea*, 3:34, emphasis original).

9. Frost, *Selected Letters*, 242.

10. Frost, "Introduction to E. A. Robinson's *King Jasper*," in *CPP&P*, 741.

11. Sheehy, "(Re)figuring Love," 179–80.

12. Mertins, *Robert Frost*, 197.

13. Frost, "Letter to *The Amherst Student*," in *CPP&P*, 739.

14. Eliot, "Music of Poetry," 28.

15. For the most recent discussions of masculinity, modernist poetry, and Frost's response to this problem, see Rotundo, *American Manhood*, 257; Richardson, *Ordeal of Robert Frost*, 22–52; Lentricchia, *Modernist Quartet*, 79–83; and Steinman, *Made in America*, 15–17.

16. Steinman, *Made in America*, 15.

17. Roosevelt, *Strenuous Life*, 257.

18. Conrad Aiken, "Poetry," in Stearns, *Civilization in the United States*, 215.

19. Ezra Pound, "I Gather the Limbs of Osiris," in *Ezra Pound: Selected Prose*, 41.

20. Frost, *Selected Letters*, 71–72.&

21. Mertins, *Robert Frost*, 78.

22. In his analysis of Greek culture Nietzsche sought to overturn the Enlightenment's view of the Greeks as a people of balance and moderation. Citing Aeschylus and Sophocles as the standard against whom other artists should be compared, he

praises them for having the courage to look into the abyss of nature and still create great art (See Nietzsche, *Genealogy of Morals,* 209–10).

23. Cowley, *Exile's Return,* 60.

24. Frost, *Selected Letters,* 98.

25. Richardson, *Ordeal of Robert Frost,* 6.

26. I am sympathetic to Richardson's view that Frost sees both Dionysian and Apollonian impulses simultaneously present in a single individual. What I am suggesting here, however, is that Frost vacillates between these two poles and moves from a vitalist aesthetic to a pragmatist aesthetic in response to developments in nineteenth-century philosophy. While it is certainly true that Frost briefly engages the libertarian principles of the Greenwich Village school, he considered these issues at Harvard and in England long before Untermeyer ever introduced him to the *Seven Arts* circle. The Nietzschean, Bergsonian, and Jamesian imperatives to assert the individual will arose in response to nineteenth-century materialism and, as such, influenced not only Mencken and Brooks in America but also Hulme and Pound in Britain and Remy de Gourmont in France. Thus, the Apollonian and Dionysian dichotomy that Richardson refers to is a natural outcome of a subtle shift in our perception of how consciousness operates. Perhaps more appropriately labeled a dichotomy between form and flux, the new model for consciousness also prominently influenced not only art and literature but also psychology and ethnology.

27. Lentricchia, *Modernist Quartet,* 70.

28. Schwartz, "Henri Bergson," 56.

29. Bergson, *Laughter,* 186.

30. Schwartz, "Henri Bergson," 57.

31. Bergson, "Soul and the Body," 56–57.

32. Ezra Pound, "Affirmations," in *Ezra Pound: Selected Prose,* 375.

33. Frost, *Selected Letters,* 79. That Frost's ideas concerning the "sound of sense" have their basis in Bergson is apparent from a passage in Bergson's *Creative Evolution.* In chapter 3 Bergson contrasts the poet and the mathematician and suggests that reading a poem leads one to a deeper engagement with immediate experience: "When a poet reads me his verses, I can interest myself enough in him to enter into his thought, put myself into his feelings, live over again the simple state he has broken into phrases and words. I sympathize then with his inspiration, I follow it with a continuous movement which is, like the inspiration itself, an undivided act. Now I need only relax my attention, let go the tension that there is in me, for the sounds, hitherto swallowed up in the sense, to appear to me distinctly, one by one, in their materiality. In proportion, as I let myself go, the successive sounds will become the more individualized; as the phrases were broken into words, so the words will scan in syllables which I shall perceive one after another. Let me go farther still in the direction of dream: the letters themselves will become loose and will be seen to dance along, hand in hand, on some fantastic sheet of paper. I shall then admire the precision of the interweavings, the marvelous order of the procession, the exact insertion of the letters into the syllables, of the syllables into the words and of the words into the sentences. . . . The more we perceive, symbolically, parts in an indivisible whole,

the more the number of the relations that the parts have between themselves necessarily increases, since the same undividedness of the real whole continues to hover over the growing multiplicity of the symbolic elements into which the scattering of the attention has decomposed it" (209–10).

34. Frost, "The Unmade Word," in *CPP&P,* 694.

35. Frost, *Selected Letters,* 83–84.

36. Ibid., 80. The impulse to infuse poetry with a common vernacular was also one of the agendas of the Georgians, with whom Frost was closely affiliated. In particular, Lascelles Abercrombie, Frost's good friend and confidant, seems to have had a marked influence on Frost's ideas concerning poetic diction. In an essay delivered to the English Association in February 1914 Abercrombie outlined his reasons for preferring a poetic diction close to speech: "There is always a tendency, a dangerous tendency, as literature accumulates, for poetry to develop a language of its own. It is dangerous, because a conventional select poetic vocabulary is apt to be apart from the rough and tumble of spoken life: it only has such spoken life as the poet can imagine for it. A word in traditionally poetic language may get plenty of use—of use in poetry; but this kind of use by itself is not good for a word, but rather very bad for it. The word tends to be put more and more to a precisely identical use: and this, far from enriching its suggestive power, will very soon exhaust it. It is use in connection with action—with the continual slight variations in what we roughly call the same action—that keeps a word electric, charged with the implications we call poetic power. Poetry, then, for its staple language must rely on the words which common speech keeps newly magnetized" (see Abercrombie, *Poetry and Contemporary Speech,* 9–10).

37. Pound, "How to Read," in *Literary Essays,* 25.

38. Frost, *Selected Letters,* 113.

39. Ibid., 140.

40. Ibid., 191.

41. The idea that the poet communicates in a more direct, nonsymbolic sense is evident in a passage from an interview Frost had with William Stanley Braithwaite in February 1915: "If we go back far enough we will discover that the sound of sense existed before words, that something in the voice or vocal gesture made primitive man convey a meaning to his fellow before the race developed a more elaborate and concrete symbol of communication in language. I have even read that our American Indians possessed, besides a picture language, a means of communication . . . by the sound of sense. And what is this but calling up with the imagination, and recognizing, the images of sound" (Lathem, *Interviews,* 6–7).

42. Frost, "Poet on the Campus of the University of Michigan." In this passage Frost reiterated the arguments he first stated in a 1915 interview with Morris P. Tilley, professor of English at the University of Michigan: "There is the visual appeal of poetry. We all recognize so-called poetic words that visualize pictures for us. As this is the appeal to the eye, so there is a more important appeal to the ear. The music of poetry is not like the music of an instrument, however. It is something different. Music in poetry is obtained by catching the conversational tones which are the spe-

cial property of vital utterances. There is the sense the words convey, and there is also an emotional quality, an interpretative quality, in the tone in which the words are uttered. To gather these because they are significant and vital and carry through the ear an appeal of sincerity, is a main effort in poetry. . . . Conversational tones are numerous in dramatic poetry. As a result, the dramatic is the most intense of all kinds of poetry. It is the most surcharged with significance" (Lathem, *Interviews*, 25).

43. Walsh, *Into My Own*, 123.

44. Frost, "On Extravagance: A Talk," 902.

45. Frost, "Education by Poetry," 723–24.

46. Ibid., 719–22.

47. Nietzsche, "On Truth and Lies in a Nonmoral Sense," in *Philosophy and Truth*, 86.

48. Ibid., 88–89.

49. Frost, "Letter to *The Amherst Student*," in *CPP&P*, 740.

50. Frost, "The Figure a Poem Makes," 778.

51. Frost's desire to recreate the world anew is similar to Freud's conception of the artist. In *Civilization and Its Discontents*, Freud argues that "[t]he Hermit turns his back on the world and will have no truck with it. But one can do more than that; one can try to re-create the world, to build up in its stead another world in which its most unbearable features are eliminated and replaced by others that are in conformity with one's own wishes. But whoever, in desperate defiance, sets out on this path to happiness will as a rule attain nothing. Reality is too strong for him" ("Civilization and Its Discontents," in *Freud Reader*, 732).

52. John Lynen argues that Frost's use of snow as a symbol for evil is indebted to both Melville and Milton (Lynen, *Pastoral Art of Robert Frost*, 42–43).

53. Sergeant, *Robert Frost*, 325.

54. Frost, "Education by Poetry," 726.

55. The modernist emphasis upon organic form is derived from Coleridge. In his "Lectures on Shakespeare," unpublished during his own lifetime, Coleridge outlined his conception of proper poetic form: "The form is mechanic when on any given material we impress a predetermined form, not necessarily arising out of the properties of the material, as when to a mass of wet clay we give whatever shape we wish it to retain when hardened. The organic form, on the other hand, is innate; it shapes as it develops itself from within, and the fulness of its development is one and the same with the perfection of its outward form. Such is the life, such the form. Nature, the prime genial artist, inexhaustible in diverse powers, is equally inexhaustible in forms" (see Coleridge, "Lectures on Shakespeare," 409).

56. Frost, "The Figure a Poem Makes," 777.

57. Frost, "The Constant Symbol," in *CPP&P*, 789.

5. THE RISK OF SPIRIT IN SUBSTANTIATION

1. I disagree with John Hiers, who contends that Frost saw technology as the eroding agent of traditional ethics and therefore as a threat. On the other hand, I also disagree with Robert Faggen's claim that Frost's only quarrel with technology was with

scientists' belief that they could master and control nature. To my mind, Frost occupies a position between these two extremes. Certainly, Frost did quarrel with technology because it threatened to supplant traditional ethical systems. On the other hand, technology had the capacity to enhance Judeo-Christian values (see Hiers, "Robert Frost's Quarrel with Science and Technology," 181–86; and Faggen, *Robert Frost and the Challenge of Darwin*, 149).

2. For a more complete description of household technological innovations, see Giedion, *Mechanization Takes Command*, 40–44.

3. Tichi, *Shifting Gears*, 19–26.

4. Kern, *Culture of Time and Space*, 128.

5. Steinman, *Made in America*, 27.

6. Darwin, *The Various Contrivances by Which Orchids Are Fertilized*, 284.

7. Cowley, *Exile's Return*, 94.

8. Brooks, "The Literary Life," in Stearns, *Civilization in the United States*, 179.

9. Ibid., 187.

10. Ibid., 186.

11. "History of Manufacturing," 5.

12. Davis, "Life in the Iron Mills," 1871.

13. Whitman, "Passage to India," 275.

14. Ibid., 278–79.

15. Tichi, *Shifting Gears*, 90.

16. Lathem, *Interviews*, 78.

17. I agree with Thompson, who suggests that "the sweetest dream that occurs to the mower is that love and work combine to give form and purpose and satisfaction to experience" (Thompson, *Fire and Ice*, 102).

18. Thompson, *Robert Frost: The Early Years*, 220.

19. Eliot, " Love Song of J. Alfred Prufrock," 5.

20. Frost, "The Future of Man" (unpublished version), 870–71.

21. Lathem, *Interviews*, 78.

22. Winters, "Robert Frost," 577.

23. Pritchard, *Lives of the Modern Poets*, 114.

24. Thoreau, *Walden*, 181–82.

25. Robert Faggen was the first to notice the connection between natural and human technology in "The Egg and the Machine." "The observant eye," he writes, "capable of perceiving the analogy and the persistent foundation of technology in all life, enables the individual to transcend the crude exceptionalism and hatred that the protagonist in 'The Egg and the Machine' displays" (*Robert Frost and the Challenge of Darwin*, 155).

26. For a complete description of the events informing "Kitty Hawk," see Thompson, *Robert Frost: The Early Years*, 173–89.

27. Emerson, "Nature," 36.

28. Frost, "'Sermon' at Rockdale Avenue Temple," in *CPP&P*, 792–93.

29. Frost, "On Extravagance: A Talk," 904.

30. Frost, "The Constant Symbol," 786.

Bibliography

MANUSCRIPT COLLECTIONS

Amherst College Library, Amherst, Mass. Archives and Special Collections. Robert Frost Collection.

　"Interview with Jonas Salk." MS 358.

　Lecture, University of Detroit, 14 November 1962.

Columbia University Library, New York. Special Collections.

　Robert Frost to Lewis Gannett, 3 February 1927.

　Robert Frost to Ashley Thorndike, 25 January 1916.

Dartmouth College Library, Hanover, N.H. Special Collections.

　Carl Burell to Mrs. Edna Romig, 5 March 1935.

　Robert Frost. Notebooks.

PUBLISHED WORKS

Abel, Darrel. "The Instinct of a Bard: Robert Frost on Science, Logic, and Poetic Truth." *Essays in Arts and Sciences* 9 (1980): 59–75.

Abercrombie, Lascelles. *Poetry and Contemporary Speech.* English Association Pamphlet No. 27. London, 1914.

Agassiz, Louis. "Evolution and the Permanence of Type." *Atlantic Monthly* 33 (January 1874): 92–101.

Angyal, Andrew. "From Swedenborg to William James: The Shaping of Frost's Religious Beliefs." *Robert Frost Review,* fall 1994, 69–81.

Arnold, Matthew. *The Works of Matthew Arnold.* 15 vols. London: Macmillan, 1903–4.

Bagby, George. *Robert Frost and the Book of Nature.* Knoxville: University of Tennessee Press, 1993.

Barry, Elaine. *Robert Frost on Writing.* New Brunswick, N.J.: Rutgers University Press, 1973.

Bawer, Bruce. "The Fictive Music of Wallace Stevens." In *Prophets and Professors,* 61–75. Brownsville, Oreg.: Storyline, 1995.

Bergson, Henri. *Creative Evolution.* Translated by Arthur Mitchell. New York: Henry Holt, 1911.

———. *An Introduction to Metaphysics.* Translated by T. E. Hulme. New York: Putnam, 1912.

———. *Laughter: An Essay on the Meaning of the Comic.* Translated by Cloudesley Brereton and Fred Rothwell. London: Macmillan, 1911.

———. "The Soul and the Body." In *Mind-Energy: Lectures and Essays,* translated by H. Wildon Carr. New York: Henry Holt, 1920.

———. *Time and Free Will.* Translated by F. L. Pogson. New York: Harper & Row, 1960.

Bernstein, Jeremy. *Einstein.* New York: Viking, 1973.

Bieganowski, Ronald. "Sense of Time in Robert Frost's Poetics: A Particular Influence of Henri Bergson." *Resources for American Literary Study* 13 (1983): 184–93.

Bohr, Niels. *Atomic Theory and the Description of Nature.* Cambridge: Cambridge University Press, 1934.

———. "Über die Anwendung der Quantentheorie auf den Atombau" (On the application of the quantum theory to the structure of the atom). *Zeitschrift für Physik* 13 (1923): 117–65.

Branch, Michael. "Indexing American Possibilities: The Natural History Writing of Bartram, Wilson, and Audubon." In *The Ecocriticism Reader: Landmarks in Literary Ecology,* edited by Cheryll Glofelty and Harold Fromm, 282–302. Athens: University of Georgia Press, 1996.

Bronowski, Jacob. *Science and Human Values.* New York: Harper & Row, 1965.

Brower, Reuben. *The Poetry of Robert Frost: Constellations of Intention.* New York: Oxford University Press, 1963.

"Child Labor." In *The Grolier Encyclopedia.* New York: Grolier Electronic Publishing, 1993. CD-ROM.

Clausen, Christopher. *The Place of Poetry.* Lexington: University of Kentucky Press, 1981.

———. "Whitman, Hopkins, and the World's Splendor." *Sewanee Review* 105 (1997): 175–78.

Cohen, I. Bernard. "An Interview with Einstein." *Scientific American* 193, no. 1 (1955): 61–74.

Coleridge, Samuel Taylor. "Lectures on Shakespeare." In *The Norton Anthology of English Literature,* edited by M. H. Abrams et al., 406–9. 4th ed. New York: Norton, 1979.

Cook, Reginald. *The Dimensions of Robert Frost.* New York: Holt, Rinehart & Winston, 1958.

———. *Robert Frost: A Living Voice.* Amherst: University of Massachusetts Press, 1974.

Cowley, Malcolm. *Exile's Return.* New York: Viking, 1951.

Dampier, W. C. *A History of Science and Its Relations with Philosophy and Religion.* Cambridge: Cambridge University Press, 1989.

Darwin, Charles. *The Descent of Man and Selection in Relation to Sex.* Chicago: Rand, McNally, 1874.

———. *On the Origins of Species by Means of Natural Selection.* London: Murray, 1859.

————. *The Various Contrivances by Which Orchids Are Fertilized.* 1862. Reprint, Chicago: University of Chicago Press, 1984.

Davis, Rebecca Harding. "Life in the Iron Mills." In *Heritage of American Literature*, edited by James E. Miller Jr., 1:1867–90. New York: Harcourt Brace Jovanovich, 1991.

Dennett, Daniel. *Darwin's Dangerous Idea: Evolution and the Meanings of Life.* New York: Simon & Schuster, 1995.

Donley, Carol, and Alan Friedman. *Einstein as Myth and Muse.* Cambridge: Cambridge University Press, 1985.

Earle, William James. "William James." In *The Encyclopedia of Philosophy*, edited by Paul Edwards, 3:240–49. New York: Macmillan, 1967.

Eddington, Arthur Stanley. *The Nature of the Physical World.* New York: Macmillan, 1933.

————. *The Philosophy of Physical Science.* Cambridge: Cambridge University Press, 1939.

————. *Space, Time, and Gravitation.* New York: Harper & Brothers, 1959.

Einstein, Albert. "Zur Elektrodynamik Beweater Körper" (On the electrodynamics of moving bodies). *Annalen der Physik* 17 (1905): 891–921.

Eliot, T. S. "The Love Song of J. Alfred Prufrock." In *Collected Poems, 1909–1962*, 3–7. New York: Harcourt Brace Jovanovich, 1963.

————. "The Music of Poetry." In *On Poetry and Poets*, 17–33. New York: Farrar, Straus & Cudahy, 1957.

Emerson, Ralph Waldo. *Selections from Ralph Waldo Emerson.* Edited by Stephen E. Whicher. Boston: Houghton Mifflin, 1957.

Fabre, Jean Henri. *The Hunting Wasps.* Translated by Alexander Teixiera De Mattos. New York: Dodd, Mead, 1919.

Faggen, Robert. *Robert Frost and the Challenge of Darwin.* Ann Arbor: University of Michigan Press, 1997.

Feynman, Richard. *Six Easy Pieces.* New York: Helix Books, 1995.

Foucault, Michel. "What Is an Author?" In *Language, Counter-Memory, Practice*, edited by Donald F. Bouchard, translated by Sherry Simon, 113–38. Ithaca: Cornell University Press, 1977.

Freud, Sigmund. *The Freud Reader.* Edited by Peter Gay. New York: Norton, 1989.

Frost, Robert. *Collected Poems, Prose, and Plays.* Edited by Richard Poirier and Mark Richardson. New York: Library of America, 1995.

————. "A Poet on the Campus of the University of Michigan." *Detroit News*, 27 November 1921, sec. 7, 1.

————. *Selected Letters of Robert Frost.* Edited by Lawrance Thompson. New York: Holt, Rinehart & Winston, 1964.

Gadamer, Hans Georg. *Truth and Method.* Translated by Joe C. Weinsheimer and Donald G. Marshall. New York: Continuum International Publishing Group, 1990.

Giedion, Siegfried. *Mechanization Takes Command: A Contribution to Anonymous History.* New York: Oxford University Press, 1948.

Gray, Asa. *Darwiniana: Essays and Reviews Pertaining to Darwinism.* New York: Appleton, 1876.

Haeckel, Ernst. *The Riddle of the Universe: At the Close of the Nineteenth Century.* Translated by Joseph McCabe. New York: Harper & Brothers, 1900.

Hall, Dorothy Judd. *Contours of Belief.* Athens: Ohio University Press, 1984.

Hartley, Marsden. *Adventures in the Arts.* New York: Boni & Liveright, 1921.

Hayles, N. Katherine. *Cosmic Web: Scientific Field Models and Literary Strategies in the Twentieth Century.* Ithaca: Cornell University Press, 1985.

Heisenberg, Werner. *Across the Frontiers.* Translated by Peter Heath. New York: Harper & Row, 1974.

Hemingway, Ernest. "The Big Two-Hearted River: Part II." In *The Short Stories of Ernest Hemingway,* 221–32. New York: Macmillan, 1986.

Hiers, John T. "Robert Frost's Quarrel with Science and Technology." *Georgia Review* 25 (summer 1971): 182–205.

"History of Manufacturing." In *The Grolier Encyclopedia.* New York: Grolier Electronic Publishing, 1993. CD-ROM.

Hoeller, Hildegard. "Evolution and Metaphor in Robert Frost's Poetry." In *South Carolina Review* 23 (spring 1990): 127–34.

Hofstadter, Richard. *Social Darwinism in American Thought.* Boston: Beacon, 1955.

Holland, Norman. *The Brain of Robert Frost.* New York: Routledge, 1988.

Howe, Irving. "Robert Frost: A Momentary Stay." *New Republic* 148 (March 1963): 23–28.

Hudson, W. H. *Far Away and Long Ago.* New York: Dutton, 1918.

Hull, David L. *Darwin and His Critics: The Reception of Darwin's Theory of Evolution by the Scientific Community.* Cambridge: Harvard University Press, 1973.

Hulme, T. E. *The Collected Writings of T. E. Hulme.* Edited by Karen Csengeri. Oxford: Clarendon, 1994.

Huxley, Julian. *Evolution: The Modern Synthesis.* New York: Harper & Brothers, 1943.

Huxley, Thomas Henry. *Collected Essays.* Vol. 1. New York: Appleton, 1910.

———. *Evolution and Ethics.* London: Macmillan, 1894.

James, William. *Collected Essays and Reviews.* Edited by Ralph Barton Perry. New York: Russell & Russell, 1969.

———. "Familiar Letters of William James III." *Atlantic Monthly* 126, no. 3 (1920): 305–17.

———. *The Meaning of Truth.* Cambridge: Harvard University Press, 1975.

———. *A Pluralistic Universe: Hibbert Lectures at Manchester College on the Present Situation in Philosophy.* New York: Longmans, Green, 1912.

———. *Pragmatism and Four Essays from "The Meaning of Truth."* Edited by Ralph Barton Perry. New York: World, 1955.

———. *The Will to Believe.* New York: Dover, 1956.

Jarrell, Randall. "To the Laodiceans." In *Poetry and the Age,* 34–62. New York: Vintage, 1955.

Jeans, James. *The Mysterious Universe.* Cambridge: Cambridge University Press, 1931.

Jones, Howard Mumford. "The Cosmic Loneliness of Robert Frost." In *Belief and Disbelief in American Literature*, 116–42. Chicago: University of Chicago Press, 1967.

Kearns, Katherine. *Robert Frost and a Poetics of Appetite*. Cambridge: Cambridge University Press, 1994.

Kern, Stephen. *The Culture of Time and Space, 1880–1918*. Cambridge: Harvard University Press, 1983.

Kuhn, Thomas. *The Structure of Scientific Revolutions*. Chicago: University of Chicago Press, 1962.

"Labor Union." In *The Grolier Encyclopedia*. New York: Grolier Electronic Publishing, 1993. CD-ROM.

Lathem, Edward Connery. *Interviews with Robert Frost*. New York: Holt, Rinehart & Winston, 1966.

Lears, Jackson. *No Place of Grace: Antimodernism and the Transformation of American Culture, 1880–1920*. New York: Pantheon, 1981.

Lentricchia, Frank. *Modernist Quartet*. Cambridge: Cambridge University Press, 1994.

———. "Robert Frost and Modern Literary Theory." In *Frost: Centennial Essays*, edited by Jac L. Tharpe, 315–32. Jackson: University Press of Mississippi, 1974.

———. *Robert Frost: Modern Poetics and the Landscapes of Self*. Durham, N.C.: Duke University Press, 1974.

Logan, William. "The Other Other Frost." In *The New Criterion* 13 (June 1995): 21–33.

Lurie, Edward. *Louis Agassiz: A Life in Science*. Chicago: University of Chicago Press, 1960.

———. "Louis Agassiz and the Idea of Evolution." *Victorian Studies* 3 (1959): 87–108.

Lynen, John. *The Pastoral Art of Robert Frost*. New Haven: Yale University Press, 1960.

Mandelbaum, Maurice. *History, Man, and Reason: A Study in Nineteenth-Century Thought*. Baltimore: Johns Hopkins University Press, 1971.

Martin, Jay. *Harvest of Change: American Literature, 1865–1914*. Englewood Cliffs, N.J.: Prentice Hall, 1967.

Martin, Ronald E. *American Literature and the Destruction of Knowledge: Innovative Writing in the Age of Epistemology*. Durham, N.C.: Duke University Press, 1991.

———. *American Literature and the Universe of Force*. Durham, N.C.: Duke University Press, 1981.

May, Henry. *The End of American Innocence: A Study of the First Years of Our Own Time, 1912–1917*. New York: Knopf, 1959.

Mertins, Louis. *Robert Frost: Life and Talks-Walking*. Norman: University of Oklahoma Press, 1965.

Meyers, Jeffrey. *Robert Frost: A Life*. New York: Houghton Mifflin, 1996.

Mill, John Stuart. "Nature." In *The Collected Works of John Stuart Mill*, edited by J. M. Robson, 10:373–402. Toronto: University of Toronto Press, 1969.

Miller, Perry, ed. *American Thought: Civil War to World War I*. New York: Holt, Rinehart & Winston, 1954.

Moore, Marianne. "Poetry" (1921 version). In *Heritage of American Literature,* vol. 2, edited by James E. Miller Jr., 942–43. New York: Harcourt Brace Jovanovich, 1991.

Neil, J. Meredith. *Toward a National Taste: America's Quest for Aesthetic Independence.* Honolulu: University Press of Hawaii, 1975.

Nietzsche, Friedrich. *The Genealogy of Morals.* Translated by F. Golffing. Garden City, N.Y.: Doubleday, 1956.

———. *Philosophy and Truth: Selections from Nietzsche's Notebooks of the Early 1870's.* Edited and translated by Daniel Breazeale. Atlantic Highlands, N.J.: Humanities, 1979.

———. *The Will to Power.* Translated by Walter Kaufmann and R. J. Hollingdale. New York: Vintage, 1968.

Oster, Judith. *Toward Robert Frost: The Reader and the Poet.* Athens: University of Georgia Press, 1991.

Pascal, Blaise. *Pensées.* Translated by W. F. Trotter. New York: Dutton, 1958.

Peacock, Thomas Love. *The Works of Thomas Love Peacock.* Edited by H. F. B. Brett-Smith and C. E. Jones. Vol. 8. London: Constable, 1934.

Pearce, Roy Harvey. *The Continuity of American Poetry.* Princeton: Princeton University Press, 1961.

Pfeifer, Edward J. "United States." In *The Comparative Reception of Darwinism,* edited by Thomas F. Glick, 197–200. Chicago: University of Chicago Press, 1988.

Planck, Max. *Where Is Science Going?* Woodbridge, N.J.: Ox Bow, 1981.

Poe, Edgar Allan. *The Complete Works of Edgar Allan Poe.* Edited by James A. Harrison. 17 vols. New York: Sproul, 1902.

Poirier, Richard. *Poetry and Pragmatism.* Cambridge: Harvard University Press, 1992.

———. *Robert Frost: The Work of Knowing.* New York: Oxford University Press 1977.

Pound, Ezra. *Collected Shorter Poems of Ezra Pound.* London: Faber & Faber, 1968.

———. *Ezra Pound: Selected Prose, 1909–1965.* Edited by William Cookson. New York: New Directions, 1973.

———. *Literary Essays of Ezra Pound.* Edited with an introduction by T. S. Eliot. Westport, Conn.: Greenwood, 1954.

———. "This Hulme Business." *Townsman* 2, no. 5 (1939): 15.

Pritchard, William. *Lives of the Modern Poets.* New York: Oxford University Press, 1980.

———. *Robert Frost: A Literary Life Reconsidered.* Amherst: University of Massachusetts Press, 1984.

Proctor, Richard Anthony. *Our Place among Infinities.* New York: Longmans, Green, 1876.

Putnam, Hilary. *Meaning and the Moral Sciences.* New York: Routledge, 1978.

Quirk, Tom. *Bergson and American Culture: The Worlds of Willa Cather and Wallace Stevens.* Chapel Hill: University of North Carolina Press, 1990.

Richards, I. A. *Science and Poetry.* London: Kegan Paul, Trench, Trubner, 1926.

Richardson, Mark. *The Ordeal of Robert Frost.* Urbana: University of Illinois Press, 1997.

Rodman, Selden. "Robert Frost." In *Tongues of Fallen Angels.* New York: New Directions, 1974.

Roosevelt, Theodore. *The Strenuous Life: Essays and Addresses.* 1902. Reprint, St. Clair Shores, Mich.: Scholarly Press, 1970.

Rotella, Guy. "Comparing Conceptions: Frost and Eddington, Heisenberg, and Bohr." *American Literature* 59, no. 2 (1987): 167–89.

Rotundo, Anthony E. *American Manhood: Transformations in Masculinity from the Revolution to the Modern Era.* New York: Basic Books, 1993.

Royce, Josiah. "The Problem of Christianity." In *Josiah Royce: Selected Writings,* edited by John Smith and William Kluback, 219–319. New York: Paulist, 1988.

———. *The Religious Aspect of Philosophy: A Critique of the Bases of Conduct and of Faith.* New York: Houghton Mifflin, 1885.

Russell, Bertrand. "The Free Man's Worship" (1903). In *Russell on Religion: Selections from the Writings of Bertrand Russell,* edited by Louis Greenspan and Stefan Andersson. New York: Routledge, 1999.

Russett, Cynthia Eagle. *Darwin in America: The Intellectual Response, 1865–1912.* San Francisco: Freeman, 1976.

Santayana, George. *Interpretations of Poetry and Religion.* 1900. Reprint, New York: Harper Torchbooks, 1957.

———. *Winds of Doctrine: Studies in Contemporary Opinion.* New York: Scribner's, 1913.

Schiller, Friedrich. *Aesthetical and Philosophical Essays.* Edited by Nathan Haskell Dole. Boston: Wyman Fogg, 1902.

Schopenhauer, Arthur. *The World as Will and Idea.* Translated by R. B. Haldane and J. Kemp. 3 vols. London: Kegan Paul, 1883–86.

Schwartz, Sanford. "Henri Bergson." In *European Writers: The Twentieth Century,* edited by George Stade, 9:45–66. New York: Scribner's, 1989.

———. *The Matrix of Modernism.* Princeton: Princeton University Press, 1985.

Sergeant, Elizabeth. *Robert Frost: The Trial by Existence.* New York: Holt, Rinehart & Winston, 1960.

Serway, Raymond. *Physics for Scientists and Engineers.* Philadelphia: Saunders, 1983.

Shaler, Nathaniel Southgate. *The Autobiography of Nathaniel Southgate Shaler.* New York: Houghton Mifflin, 1904.

Sheehy, Donald. "Measure for Measure: The Frostian Classicism of Timothy Steele." *Robert Frost Review,* fall 1995, 73–97.

———. "(Re)figuring Love: Robert Frost in Crisis, 1938–1942." *New England Quarterly* 63, no. 2 (1990): 179–81.

Shelley, Percy Bysshe. *The Poetical Works of Shelley.* Edited by Newell F. Ford. Boston: Houghton Mifflin, 1975.

Sidney, Sir Phillip. *Defence of Poetry.* London: Macmillan, 1963.

Smith, John E. "Josiah Royce," In *Encyclopedia of Philosophy,* edited by Paul Edwards, 6:225–29. New York: Macmillan, 1967.

Snow, C. P. *The Two Cultures.* Cambridge: Cambridge University Press, 1965.

Snyder, Carl. *The World Machine.* New York: Longmans, Green, 1907.

Sokol, B. J. "Bergson, Instinct, and Frost's 'The White-Tailed Hornet.'" *American Literature* 62, no. 1 (1990): 44–55.

Spencer, Herbert. *First Principles.* New York: Appleton, 1893.

———. *The Study of Sociology.* New York: Appleton, 1874.

Sprat, Thomas. *History of the Royal Society.* Edited by Jackson Cope and Harold Whitmore Jones. 1667. Facsimile reprint. Washington University Studies. Saint Louis: [Washington University], 1958.

Stearns, Harold, ed. *Civilization in the United States: An Inquiry by Thirty Americans.* New York: Harcourt, Brace, 1922.

Steinman, Lisa. *Made in America: Science, Technology, and American Modernist Poets.* New Haven: Yale University Press, 1987.

Stevens, Wallace. *Wallace Stevens: The Collected Poems.* New York: Vintage, 1982.

———. *Wallace Stevens: Collected Poetry and Prose.* Edited by Frank Kermode and John Richardson. New York: Library of America, 1997.

Taton, Rene, ed. *Science in the Nineteenth Century.* Translated by A. J. Pomerans. New York: Basic Books, 1965.

Thompson, Lawrance. *Fire and Ice.* New York: Holt, Rinehart & Winston, 1942.

———. *Robert Frost: The Early Years, 1874–1915.* New York: Holt, Rinehart & Winston, 1966.

———. *Robert Frost: The Years of Triumph, 1915–1938.* New York: Holt, Rinehart & Winston, 1970.

Thompson, Lawrance, and R. H. Winnick. *Robert Frost: The Later Years, 1938–1963.* New York: Holt, Rinehart & Winston, 1976.

Thoreau, Henry David. *Walden.* Edited with introductions and annotations by Bill McKibben. Boston: Beacon, 1997.

Tichi, Cecelia. *Shifting Gears: Technology, Literature, Culture in Modernist America.* Chapel Hill: University of North Carolina Press, 1987.

Trilling, Lionel. "A Speech on Robert Frost: A Cultural Episode." *Partisan Review* 26 (summer 1959): 445–52.

Tyndall, John. *Fragments of Science.* 2 vols. New York: Appleton, 1892.

Waggoner, Hyatt. "Robert Frost: The Strategic Retreat." In *The Heel of Elohim: Science and Values in Modern American Poetry,* 41–60. Norman: University of Oklahoma Press, 1950.

Walsh, John Evangelist. *Into My Own: The English Years of Robert Frost, 1912–1915.* New York: Grove, 1988.

Whitman, Walt. *Leaves of Grass, and Selected Prose.* Edited by Sculley Bradley. New York: Holt, Rinehart & Winston, 1962.

———. "Passage to India." In *The Portable Walt Whitman,* edited by Mark Van Doren, 275–84. New York: Viking, 1973.

Williams, William Carlos. *Paterson.* New York: New Directions, 1963.

Winters, Yvor. "Robert Frost: Or, The Spiritual Drifter as Poet." *Sewanee Review* 56 (1948): 564–96.

Wordsworth, William. "The Tables Turned." In *The Norton Anthology of English Literature,* edited by M. H. Abrams and Stephen Greenblatt et al., vol. 2. 7th ed. New York: W. W. Norton, 2000.

Wyllie, Irvin G. "Social Darwinism and the Businessman." *Proceedings of the American Philosophical Society* 103 (October 1959): 629–35.

Index

214 Index

Under the Sign of Nature: Explorations in Ecocriticism